HANG ON TIGHT

The Revd. Richard Coles

In gratitude for "Saturday Live"

from one ~~Christian~~ Christian to another.

Sue Davies-Jenkins.

Cardiff.

26th January 2015.

HANG ON TIGHT

Christ's Hospital: from Girlhood to Governor

by

SUE DAVIES-JENKINS

The Memoir Club

© Sue Davies-Jenkins 2010

First published in 2010 by
The Memoir Club
Arya House
Langley Park
Durham
DH7 9XE
Tel: 0191 373 5660
Email: memoirclub@msn.com

British Library Cataloguing in
Publication Data.
A catalogue record for this book
is available from the
British Library

ISBN: 978-1-84104-499-6

Typeset by TW Typesetting, Plymouth, Devon
Printed by J.F. Print, Yeovil, Somerset

Dedication

This volume is dedicated in gratitude to my two favourite English mistresses at Christ's Hospital, Hertford, the late Mrs Kathleen Betterton, née Baron (CH Hertford 1924–31) and Mrs Judith Hepper, née Heaven, for the delight which they nurtured in me in English language and literature – a lifelong legacy. Kathleen, as a Hertford 'Old Blue' (former pupil of Christ's Hospital, girl or boy), was gentle and kind to us as pupils. She and I kept in touch right up until her death, and I still treasure her letters. A further tribute to her can be found in the chapter 'Work'.

At Kathleen's memorial service on 30 March 2001 at her parish church in Linton near Ross-on-Wye I renewed my friendship with Judith, whose head of department Kathleen had been at Hertford. Judith has kindly given me hospitality and accompanied me to Speech Day at Christ's Hospital, Horsham, in my rôle as a Donation Governor in recent years, and I'm enormously grateful to her in particular for her patience and enthusiasm, especially in the difficult early stages of getting started, in helping me to compile this, my first ever book.

Sue Davies-Jenkins
Cardiff
March 2007

Contents

Part IV: Married Life

Part V: The Changing Years

Part VI: Later Writings

List of Illustrations

Foreword

This is a lovingly written book by someone who lives lovingly. Sue Davies-Jenkins is a natural writer, although she has carefully schooled herself in creative writing. She writes with flair and poise, choosing her words with joyful precision, and the result is a kind and generous book, flowing out of her deep affection for Christ's Hospital.

Sue has written her own story but she reaches out to the stories of others with remarkable feats of memory. Her story demonstrates how the ordinary becomes extraordinary when it's lived reflectively and thoughtfully. It tells of a life touched both by huge delight and deep, permanent loss; we feel the present absence of Mike throughout, but we are constantly gladdened by her unaffected pleasure in family, faith and that wonderful, formative experience of school.

Anyone who cares to listen to others finds in every person a wealth of fascinating experience. Every life is deep in detail and needs only to be released to be enjoyed. Sue's life story gives us flashes of that detail, observed with tenderness and truthfulness. She seems to want, in any way possible, to pass on her enthusiasm for life, for lasting values, and for relationships that can be cherished. She passes on to the receptive reader a treasure trove of wisdom, grown out of life's inevitable contrasts and complexities.

Sue and I are now related through the marriage of our children and the shared delight of being grandparents. Until I read this text, however, I had not realised how sensitively Sue reflects on experience or how beautifully she can express emotion or capture a rich moment before it hurtles past. She pleases both eye and heart, holding back very little, so that we might be bold enough to investigate our own thoughts and feelings, and the memories that lie asleep in the back bedroom of our mind.

It's a book that has two heroes – the beloved Mike and Sue's own Christ's Hospital, which in its stability, common sense and imagination has released upon the world women and men of character, courage and compassion. Sue Davies-Jenkins is one such. Her book is a kindly, grateful tribute to an old friend.

John Pritchard
Bishop of Oxford

Acknowledgements

So many people have helped me get this book together over the years that it's hard to know where to begin.

As far as **photographs** are concerned, I'm particularly grateful to Old Blue friends Wendy Stone (née Lee) for her help with pictures and to Stephanie Orford (née Etches) for nearly all the photographs of Christ's Hospital, Hertford and Anne-Marie Braun (née Kelly) for several precious family photographs.

My thanks to Patricia Aithie for two photographs of Katie and Jack's wedding (No. 69 and No. 70), and for the one of Akosikya and his unknown grandmother (No. 68) and to Arvid Parry Jones (the *Cambrian News*) for the photograph of Ben Davies-Jenkins with the Bishop of Llandaff (No. 30). I am also grateful to the members of the Christ's Hospital Band for allowing me to photograph them (No. 74). My thanks, too, to the parents of my Presentees, Dominic Parker and Charity Griffiths, for allowing me to use their school photographs and to Hertford Old Blue Rosemary Whiting (née Esch) and her sister-in-law Jane Neville for helping me to find the photograph from Sir Winston Churchill's funeral. Lastly, my thanks to John Fox for the photograph of his parents' wedding and to Rosemary Knapp for kindly copying for me my photograph of her late husband John with their son Edward (No. 29).

All reasonable steps have been made to locate the owners of the copyright material. Acknowledgements will be given in reprints if the copyright owner comes forward.

As far as the **writing** is concerned, I am grateful particularly to Judith Hepper (née Heaven), Robin Case and Dominic Parker for their prose contributions, and to John Pritchard, a successful writer himself, as well as a hard-working bishop, for taking the time and trouble to write the Foreword to this book.

For general help and encouragement, and advice with checking facts I am grateful to:

Christ's Hospital staff including John Franklin, Nicola Mitra, Anne

Sartain, Vicky Haigh, Margaret Wadman, Tony Hogarth-Smith and Carol Blackwell.

From Shrewsbury School: various staff including Ted Maidment, Richard Hudson, Gary Dobbie (formerly Christ's Hospital chaplain), the late Michael Charlesworth and former Shrewsbury pupil, the late Michael Hodges.

Howell's School, Denbigh staff for a prospectus and photographs to jog my memory.

From the Cathedral School, Llandaff: Tony Phillips, former master and editor of 'The Llandavian' magazine.

From Llandaff Cathedral: Organist and Master of the Choristers Richard Moorhouse for a copy of the current 'Making-up' ceremony for cathedral choristers.

From Plascrug School, Aberystwyth: Rhiannon Steeds.

From St Catwg's Church, Pentyrch: John Gough.

From the Royal Welch Fusiliers: Morgan Llewellyn, Charles Hince and John (JL) Evans.

Crystal Davies, editor at the time of the 'Welsh Churchman', where my article about the Right Hand Trust appeared.

Creative writing tutors Helen Dunmore and Susan Morgan, for their inspiration and encouragement.

Kind words and advice from many other friends including Mike James, Wendy Pritchard, Patrick Holden, Jennifer Holden, John Sutherell, Eric Burke, Veronica Baker, Dilys Lloyd, Gentian Hodges and Roz Capper.

Hertford Old Blue friends not already mentioned, especially Kerren Simmonds, Katheen Duncan (née Dale), Chrissy Williams (née Barnett), Susan Savva (née Cottingham) and Diana Gould (née Robinson).

Lynn Davidson, Jennifer Soutter and the staff at The Memoir Club for all their patience and technical help in getting this book into print.

My wonderful mother for unselfishly sending me to Christ's Hospital, recognising all the benefits that it would give me in adult life.

My long-suffering friends at St Mark's Church, Gabalfa, particularly those in my 'A' Saints homegroup, who have given me the will to persevere with *Hang on Tight* 'until it be thoroughly finished'.

Finally, my children, Katie, Ben and Will who continue to bring me great joy and remind me of their beloved father.

I have checked all names, places and facts as well as I possibly can, but beg forgiveness in advance for any errors or omissions in the text.

Sue Davies-Jenkins.
Cardiff
August 2010

How but in custom and in ceremony
Are innocence and beauty born?

'Prayer for my Daughter'
W.B. Yeats
June 1919

Author's Preface

The following piece is the inspiration for the title of the book:

Letter to myself when a child (with the benefit of hindsight)

You could be anything when you grow up. Forty-nine per cent really isn't the end of the world. If Caroline Scott wants to play with someone else, so what? There is life beyond the Lower Fourth.

Even School Needlework will seem funny one day – not the desperate, worrying unpicking that it seems now. Not the irritable comments about your left-handedness and what a nuisance for Miss Richards when she starts you off. One day sewing will actually be useful, soothing even, as you take a welcome breather sitting down to sew on nametapes. Even darning your sons' socks will seem a pleasure after struggling over the hated wrinkly pink-beige lisle stockings over Silent Mending in Lent. Life will be fun and you will be loved, my darling. Hang on tight.

What is it that worries you most now? Miss M with her crooked centre-parting and kirby-grips and her flat, metallic voice and her cruel jibes? I know she's foul as a housemistress, but one day you will feel sad for her with her dying mother and her Sunday frocks and her one good brooch that Lady Somebody gave her. *You* have so much more to look forward to.

Savour the good moments now – the English essay that got read out in class, the surging Magnificat with the whole school on hot summer afternoons in the delicious cool of Chapel. Think of Mudgie and her five wriggling pups, sweet and gooey from Farex feeds. Think of the warmth and peace and privacy of HOME.

But treasure your school friends too. One day you will laugh and cry with them through birth and death and divorce. Being forty will be better than the Lower Fourth.

Written in 1991, this is the first piece I ever produced for Orange Prize winner Helen Dunmore at her Community Writing Workshop at what is now the University of Glamorgan, but was then the Polytechnic of Wales in Pontypridd.

We were given about twenty minutes in class to complete this exercise.

The reader should be reassured that Christ's Hospital Horsham today has a rather more relaxed atmosphere than the Hertford school of my youth. Perhaps it is something to do with the girls now being educated alongside the boys at Horsham, and perhaps because Christ's Hospital has kept abreast of educational changes over the second half of the twentieth century and now well into the twenty-first. Probably most Old Blues would assert, 'We had it tougher in our day!' It is the future that matters now.

Note: Where names, etc have been omitted in, for example, the diary extracts, I have added these in italics and brackets. I have also added footnotes where relevant.

Introduction

Have we not all been there, and wouldn't we rather forget those awkward *angst* years poised uncertainly on the verge of adulthood? The writer in *me* chose to record them honestly in writing, however, as will be seen in the earlier part of the book.

One of the points of this whole venture is to show the development both intellectually and emotionally of a very little Christ's Hospital schoolgirl – and the discovery this year of a five-year diary started at the age of ten has been a particular joy – through to the widow, mother-of-three and grandmother more than half a century later, as grown up now as she is ever likely to get. The book is not just a memoir of school days, but rather aims to show how the Christ's Hospital experience has shaped all aspects of her adult life.

Spelling and grammatical errors in the earlier work have deliberately gone uncorrected, and the only editing of the writing that has been inserted later is in the interests of clarity for the reader, bearing in mind that not everyone who picks up this book may necessarily be an Old Blue or otherwise connected to the school and therefore initiated into its unique language.

I hope that you will be as amused and interested, and at times saddened, reading it, as I have been in writing it over the last fifty or so years, and in bringing the whole work together in the last few months. For me it is an affirmation of comradeship, love, joy and Christian faith so tenderly nurtured at school, and a celebration of more than sixty years of full and exciting living. I am profoundly grateful to Christ's Hospital for the education and shelter provided, for the standards of integrity set, and for the lasting friendships forged there, sometimes in adversity.

On a practical note, you will find Christ's Hospital Girls' School, Hertford often referred to as 'Hertford', and Christ's Hospital as 'CH'. We usually called the boys' school at Horsham 'Housey', and of course since the merger in 1985, all Christ's Hospital children, boys and girls, have been educated on the beautiful 1200-acre site at Horsham.

Claiming proudly to be the original Bluecoat School, Christ's Hospital has always educated boys and girls under the auspices of one charitable foundation, and the first child ever to be admitted to CH in the City of London in 1552, as our wonderful headmistress,[1] the late Miss D.R. West, would delight in reminding us in her famous Founder's Day annual address at Hertford, was a girl.

It is a huge privilege for me, who was 'presented' by Donation Governor Mr John Harrison, back in 1957, to have been elected as a Donation Governor myself, and to have helped to choose and watch grow up happily through the school, both a boy and a girl from Wales, where I have lived for over thirty years.

Like many Christ's Hospital pupils I came from a single, or lone parent family, as they would call it now. My parents had met while serving in the army in India during the Second World War, and my father, John Wilson, returned there when my mother was expecting me, their first child, only two years into the marriage. He died in Kenya when I was eighteen, never having been in touch again with my mother, or with me as I grew up.

My mother was profoundly grateful to Christ's Hospital for giving me a good education. She told me that I would even have been supported through to university level if she had died before I graduated (the Foundation is extraordinarily generous in its help for needy families), and it was thanks to a small legacy from her in 1996 that I was enabled to make the initial contribution to sponsor a child in my turn. I felt that it was the most fitting tribute that I could pay to my brave little mother's memory.

All parents of Christ's Hospital children make financial contributions only according to their means. What we as Donation Governors give towards a 'Presentee's' schooling nothing like covers the full seven years of his or her school career (admission is usually at the age of eleven although there is a limited sixth form entry), and the Foundation makes up the shortfall. Hence, even after extremely generous continuing support from the Corporation of the City of London, and the City Livery Companies, since the school's foundation in the sixteenth century, the need always to raise funds, especially in these difficult economic times. This is to ensure that all the 800 plus pupils continue to enjoy a first-class academic, boarding or day education along with a huge range of extra-curricular activities like sports, CCF (Combined Cadet Force), dance, drama and art. Music is very strong, and conductor Sir Colin Davis is just one of many distinguished Old Blues. Virtually every instrument is taught, and lent to pupils where necessary, there is a magnificent Chapel Choir of over 100 pupils, and the renowned Christ's Hospital marching band is often seen at Lord's, Twickenham, the Lord Mayor's Show in London, or on overseas tours, like the recent one in the United States, as well as at Beating Retreat and on daily Band Parade at Housey when the whole school marches into the vast dining hall for lunch.

At CH there is the chance for each pupil to develop his or her potential to the full in every aspect of school life, regardless of home circumstances. If this volume can do a little to raise awareness as well as some funds for our wonderful, traditional yet up-to-date, extra-ordinary Christ's Hospital Foundation, I shall feel that all the effort of the dedicated staff in educating me there, as well as that of my friends and mentors as well as myself in producing this work, has not been in vain.

May God bless the religious, royal and ancient foundation of Christ's Hospital, may they prosper who love her, and may God increase her number. (The Housey Toast).

Sue Davies-Jenkins
Cardiff,
25 February 2007

Notes

1. All our teachers at Christ's Hospital in my time were female (apart from the Chaplain, who hardly counted!) and were always referred to as 'mistresses'.

PART I

Schooldays

CHAPTER 1

Christ's Hospital: Background

POVERTY IS WHAT UNITED US all proudly as children of Christ's Hospital, which has been described as the only socialist public school to be run on capitalist money.

In 1552 the boy king Edward VI was so moved by a sermon in Westminster Abbey given by Bishop Ridley, then Bishop of London, about the poor and homeless children, that he sent for the bishop afterwards to see what could be done. Ridley suggested that young Edward should enlist the help of the Lord Mayor of London, Sir Richard Dobbs, who persuaded City companies and other benefactors to give generously. Edward VI gave the former Greyfriars site off Newgate Street in the City of London and signed the Royal Charter. Five hundred children were admitted initially, and Christ's Hospital has undertaken to feed and house and educate needy and deserving children, boys and girls, ever since.

It could hardly have been called a co-educational school in the early days, however, the girls being moved to Hertford and the boys kept on the original Newgate Street site. Even when the 'weak' and younger boys were moved to Hertford they were segregated from the girls, we were told, by a high, wooden fence, and then in 1902 the boys were sent to the new site at Horsham, some sixty miles from their Hertford sisters. Being a Sussex girl, I particularly envied the boys their huge green site, but I grew to love Hertford and wept openly when the schools merged, the Hertford site was sold, and all the girls moved to join the boys. I managed the penultimate Old Girls' Day at Hertford, crying all the way through the familiar Psalms. 'I will lift up mine eyes unto the hills' and 'Pray for the peace of Jerusalem'. I knew that I just couldn't bear that final Hertford service.

If poverty was what united us, I certainly didn't feel deprived.

Date of writing unknown.

CHAPTER 2

New Girl's Breaking In

IT WAS ONLY ON THE evening of the second day that it first hit me. Sitting there in the dayroom of our junior house (we called them 'wards' until 1964) on a hard wooden bench, eating an orange, I felt suddenly a huge, unbearable constriction in the throat, and salt tears trickling embarrassingly down my face. 'I want my Mummy,' I wailed inwardly. Already I sensed that there were some things one didn't do, and some things one didn't say out loud.

Suddenly our wardmistress, Miss Robertson, appeared. 'Never mind, Susan, come and try your coatfrock on now.' She was firm, but not unkind. She had tight, snowy curls and wore immaculately cut tweed suits, and the way she carried herself would not have disgraced the Brigade of Guards. She was strict, but with a twinkle in her bright eyes, and I felt safe with her.

I felt less safe with the coatfrock. Stored in the Wardrobe Room, a mass of gleaming wooden cupboards, the coatfrock was our winter Sunday best. Made of navy blue serge, it had poppers at the cuffs and a front panel and belt piped each side in a thin yellow stripe, so that the whole effect viewed from the front was of a cross. And it had a creamy-white collar. How I came to hate that collar. Before the days of synthetics, it was made of tussore, a kind of silk, and shrank every time in the wash. Yellowing with age, it had to be changed every few weeks and sewn on again each time laboriously by the wearer. In some wards it was accepted that as the collar shrank it could not be possible to meet in the middle, but we had no such luck: we had to pin the two ends so that the collar met in a perfect 'V', and then 'ease' the neck somehow. Some girls managed it brilliantly without puckering, but easing was a skill that I never quite acquired.

The other first memory of my coatfrock was that like all our school uniform it felt alien and stank of mothballs. All our Sunday uniform, huge, black felt hats, with blazers and panamas for the summer, was stored neatly in the Wardrobe Room cupboards in numerical order (I was in Ward One and my number was 35, so I was always known as 1.35) and had to be brushed before being put away on a Sunday night, and then inspected for cleanliness by a 'Wardrobe Girl' on a Monday morning, and brushed again if she found fault. Wardrobe Girls were selected by the housemistress and always considered by the rest of us as her favourites, and therefore treated with suspicion.

My first morning at school had started badly. Woken by the clanging of the rising bell at 7 a.m., we had to strip our beds completely, and be washed, dressed and downstairs for prayers by 7.20. Unselfconsciously, in my haste I had pulled off my stiff school issue white calico nightie before putting on my vest. Shock, horror when I exposed my little girl's totally flat chest in front of about seventeen other little girls. Had I no modesty? By day two I had learnt to squeeze on the vest under my nightie in the regulation fashion, glad of a few seconds' privacy and warmth.

Then there was breakfast. Each ward marched to meals in the Dining Hall, ward by ward, two by two, with any particularly naughty girl at the time made by the ward monitresses to march in front. Once into the Crush Hall, we somehow had to get off our thick, dark woollen, belted overcoats and fold them over our arms, still on the move, before rushing up the beautiful spiral staircase – harder if you were on the inside where the steps were narrower – and enter the Dining Hall in orderly fashion. As we approached our own ward's long, thin refectory table, covered in white damask cloths, we split into single file and had our shoes inspected by one of the two stony-eyed monitresses before taking our place in strict seniority order before a wooden bench. Suddenly a gavel sounded from somewhere in the middle of the hall, and a very senior girl intoned the Grace before Meat from a lectern.

At one split second somehow in the ritual, we had to fold our coat in the approved fashion into a huge, bulky heap, and then sit on it, having clambered over the bench. It seemed incredibly difficult at first to synchronise with everyone else, but being so very small, I was glad of the extra height to help me reach the table.

Then for twenty minutes flat, all hell seemed to break loose: the voices of 288 schoolgirls reverberated round the magnificent panelled, high-ceilinged hall with huge oil paintings on every wall. The portrait of the beautiful eighteenth century CH girl Susannah in blue dress, green apron and white pleated cap was the one that we

Hertford girls will remember for the rest our lives. At my first breakfast, I was confronted by cereal, and a pale lard-like pat of margarine and doubtful-looking marmalade on the plate. Somehow, the combination of marmalade and herrings or kippers made the fish hard to stomach, and I found that being the most junior in the ward, and therefore at the bottom of the table, had its uses: as soon as the signal came to clear away I could make a desperate dash for the pig bucket and get rid of the dreaded bony mess undetected. To leave any food was considered a sin, and my fervent hope as I grew more senior was to have a neighbour who would rapidly devour my fish which I had passed surreptitiously when the wardmistress wasn't looking.

The only other hope with fish was to wash it down with school tea, weak and very hot. This was another initiation – learning to drink it from a huge, white bowl which was heavy when full. Innocently on the first day I took two hands to it, hooking the forefingers over the brim of the bowl as I had seen the other girls do. This was met with howls of derision and indignation: 'You're not allowed to use both hands,' cried the righteous ones, senior to me by only a month or two and one term's survival at CH. 'Right,' I thought grimly, trying my left hand, which was the dominant one for me, my finger burning in the hot liquid. Wrong again. 'You have to use your *right* one, silly.' In went the right forefinger, stinging like its left-hand counterpart, the bowl wobbling towards my lips. Golly, it was heavy. And what humiliation.

After a few mealtimes I had almost mastered the tea bowl and felt brave enough one teatime in the ward to go and fetch myself some more tea from the urn. I can still see the wooden Dayroom floor, polished to a rich shine by years of elbow grease from the ward maids – one of the few things we didn't have to polish ourselves every day. I filled my bowl gingerly and then turned the key of the urn clockwise like an ordinary tap, trying to tighten it shut. To my horror, the scalding tea kept pouring out, overflowing the bowl and making a huge, wet stain on the floor. The more I turned the key in my panic, the more the tea seemed to come. Eventually someone rescued me, it was explained as to an imbecile where the off position was on the tap, and I was sent for a mop, polish and rags to restore the damage to the floor. It never put me off school tea, but I'll never forget the shame of feeling different, which every girl comes to dread.

Gradually I learned to fit in, work in class seemed to go well, and my 'schoolmother', the mentor to whom each new girl was assigned, provided some comfort in the ward.

What I missed more than anything from home was the warmth and the privacy – cuddled up with my pet dachshund Mudge and all my cuddly toys. I could dream and dream at home, whereas at school, in that hard, narrow bed with toes sticking into the sides-to-middled bottom sheet, there was little comfort or warmth, and you had to rub your toes rhythmically at night to work up a fug. We each had a cubicle, but our thick golden yellow cotton curtains in my ward were folded regimentally over the iron rail in one corner, Miss Robertson preferring to be able to keep an eye on us all with one flick of the curtain on the little window which opened into Lower Dorm from her adjoining bedroom. If she saw or heard any trouble she would fling open the window and reprove us.

Then there were the torchlight patrols, probing each bedspace, checking up on each girl. There was one assistant wardmistress whom we disliked particularly (it was said that she used to remove her shoes and creep up the stairs to catch us unawares) and when upset I quickly learned to hide my head under the meagre bedclothes and sob silently. I can honestly say that it was only in my final year at school in the Upper Sixth, that I actually looked forward to going back to school. Every time up until then I hated leaving home, and would cry myself to sleep the first night of term (although once through that ritual I would settle down). Yet there was a sense of safety in numbers, of camaraderie in the dorm, which was not unpleasant. I have experienced it since as a patient in hospital, and welcomed the torchlight patrol of the night sister, the feeling that I could switch off and let someone else take responsibility for a time. Whatever else we missed at CH, I always felt safe there, an immense comfort to any child away from home, especially at night.

CHAPTER 3

Extracts from a School Five-Year Diary

For notes, see end of chapter, p. 26.

1958

2 January

I went to see 'Mother Goose' with Mrs Cladon and it was wonderful with Douglas Bing as Mother Goose. The staff went to see 'Cinderella on Ice'. Big Susan[1] was very cheerful. I was very cold.

3 January

Big Susan gave me my longed-for Birthday present, *Are Findings Keepings?* I washed my hair, and stayed up too late.

4 January

Big Susan got up for breakfast, but was very shaky afterwards. It was fine.

5 January

Horrible gale, 'specially when I went down the village for the ice-cream. Big Susan was very snappy with me and had a row with Mummy about the panto. I broke a pane of the veranda door.

6 January

I went to stay at Paddy's, (*my godmother Paddy Fox*) and it was a lowsy train journey as it rained a lot.

7 January

I saw 'Peter Pan' at the Scala and it couldn't have been lovelier, when we had eventually found a place to park Lulu. I saw 'Emergency Ward Ten' on I.T.V. (See today's *Daily Sketch*).

8 January

I came home, and Mummy met me at the station. It was a much nicer journey. I felt sick in the car, but decided it was only 'the town air'.

9 January

I bought Jenny a ballet book, and had it wrapped in the only paper they could find – 'Smiths'. I bought my new house-shoes (13 and a half) and met a CH girl.

10 January

I sorted out my CH clothes, and unpacked. I was delighted to hear that the 'Greenwoods' have got a month-old girl. It was terribley galey, and pouring with rain.

11 January

I went to Kate's (*Greenwood*) for the day. It poured with rain while we were roller skating, and Kate fell over in the mud. At one time we thought it was snowing, 'though there was a rainbow.

12 January

I did a bit of roller skating, and enjoyed taking Mr Piner's logs back on them. It was a sunny afternoon.

13 January

I roller skated again. I rode on my bike, and cleaned it up. I oiled my roller skates. I felt a bit mizzy this evening. I finished! writing my thank-you letters.

14 January

Back to school?

29 March

I rang Inga (*Schalburg?*) to say I was home. She told me to go over there tomorrow.

30 March

I went to Children's Church, and decided I liked the Vicar, but not the Church.

31 March

I went with Big Susan to get Mudge mated. We heard that Pat[2] (*Stannard*) had passed exam.

1 April

Mummy's half-day. We went to Worthing and bought model house. Bought dog for Big Susan.

2 April

I went to Red House (*School*). Mrs Eakerman leaving, worse luck. 3 new children came (*to Beach Court?*).

4 April

Good Friday. I went for about 15 minutes of the 3 Hour Service. Peter (kitchen) and his brother came.

5 April

Oxford v Cambridge Boat Race. Cambridge won worse luck, by two and a half lengths. Trotsky's[3] Birthday. Went to Heene. Swimming.

7 April

Big Susan and I went to see 'The Baby and the Battleship', and 'Private's Progress'. They were both super.

8 April

Went to Farnham (*to my grandparents*) for the day. Heard Nerni (*Miss Earnshaw, our one-time cook*) is coming for a week.

The diary then resumes at end of my Lower Sixth year, 1964:

24 July

Friday. Went to Germany. Panic because I couldn't find ticket man (*Cook's courier*). Very hot. Mummy got me an ice at the last minute, so the parting was too quick to be miserable. Managed to get a berth on boat. Shared cabin with a girl from (*illegible*). Went to sleep after midnight.

25 July

Got up about 6, and dressed quickly. Nearly lost landing ticket. Got on Lorelei Express which didn't stop at Worms.[4] Unbearably hot on train.

18 August[5]

Came back to school with Lucy (*Lissant?*). It rained, but had lovely hectic day with Big Susan buying nightie material, etc. Got mons'[6] badges after tea. Really quite glad to be back.

19 August

Showed new parents round most of the school. Lovely to be able to cheer them up a bit. Went for a short walk with Kelly before tea. Good natter.

20 August

Swimming lesson and school baths in the afternoon. Swimming lesson short because of weighing and measuring. I weigh 8 stone, & am 5ft 4 and three quarters inches tall. Did prep in ward. Very convenient although the light's not really adequate.

21 August

Lovely day, fine but cold. Pat (*Stannard*) sent me £2. Lot baths, nice lessons. Struggled with giving out carrots. Shakespeare programme on wireless. Enjoyed everything.

22 August

Saw Miss West about university. She said I could take 'A' in the summer.[7] Lovely art lesson, & art club in the evening. Miss Esch is a poppet, with a great sense of humour. Pinned on pattern in the evening, & Anna (*Anne-Marie Kelly*) came in. Played a little tennis with Stella (*Sulston*) – both very rusty. Lovely, happy day.

23 August

Sunday. Wrote letters all day. Lovely day. Sat in art school garden after lunch with Suzannah (*Long?*) and Janet (*Porter*). Had a talk about boys in the evening. Didn't attend in services – very ashamed as Mr. Walker had found nice prayers.

24 August

Monday. Squished up lemon curd tart. Was on school block duty. Talked about Chaucer in English. Began *Hernani* in French lesson. I read with more confidence. It was great. Bought Les Swingles and Françoise Hardy fun records with token. Letter from Mummy at Blodwin's (*Mrs Blodwen James*).[8]

25 August

Tuesday. Tension all day because 'O' level results had come, but weren't distributed. Fine & warm. Played tennis, & got a bit better. Cricket in the evening. Didn't bat very well, but *determined* to get in cricket team. Made my time tables. Post card from Liz[9] (*Drucquer?*) from Dorset. Talked about Becket in English and took notes on Jane Austen. Argued with Janet about poetry. Nice day.

26 August

'Cello lesson. Mrs. Lynch quite strict. Felt a worm. 'O' level results still not here, perhaps not even in school yet. Feel I wasted time in prep. Not brave enough to tackle Gerard Manley Hopkins criticism. Janet scoffed at poem in the evening. Listened to Françoise Hardy record with Mrs. Drake. Very hot – 86 degrees F in shade? Tried to play cricket at Ashbourne. Felt quite light-headed. Argued with Janet (*Porter*) about love & marriage. We both wouldn't concede an inch.

27 August

Got 'O' level results. Poor old Mary only got four, so had to stay down.

Thursday. Swimming lesson – lovely – and school baths. Tried to learn new breast stroke. Letter from Mummy. Sounded a bit exhausted because of coping at Blodwyn's. Very hot again here. Practised quite hard and really thought my tone was improving. Ghastly double-stopping study which I grappled with not very bravely.

28 August

Very happy, full day. Mary moved down to lower (*form?*) and is still feeling miserable. Stella a bit hard, perhaps rather hurt. Judith also unsympathetic. Orchestra great fun. Pam (*Henson*) tried with her oboe for the first time – sound stunning in its volume. Net practice after music practice. Quite fun. Battled in the evening with *Schimmelreiter* vocab. It got dark v. early. Pitch dark by 8.45.

29 August

Played tennis all afternoon. Exhausted but exhilarated as I felt I'd improved. Lovely art lesson in the morning. Miss Esh (*Esch*) showed us how to use the wheel.

30 August

Went to Communion. It was windy and sunny all day, and I went for a walk with Jo (*Joanna Yates*) after lunch. Lovely. Saw Miss West about VSO, and spent ages waiting in the ante-room. (*Susan*) Flood told me I was in tennis team.

31 August

Practised tennis at break and before lunch. Cricket in all-out time. Batted last, and knew I wouldn't be in the team. However, got a couple of runs off Josephine (*Sutton?*)!

1 September

Felt rotten all day and went up t'inf (*the Infirmary*) before tea with sore throat and temp. Was going to play tennis match with Stella (*Sulston*) against 8's, but postponed it.

2 September

In bed all day. Gargling only treatment. Felt groggy and had temp in evening. Slept badly on a couple of aspirin. Read and slept all day.

3 September

Much the same as yesterday. Letter from Mummy and from Big Susan. Card from Devon from Rosalind (*Emberson*). Big Susan has started her job – obviously still exhausted from the Jeacocks. Mummy told me about her interview.

4 September

Felt much better in myself today, but my temp up again in the evening. Infuriating! Started on penicillin, so I expect dramatic results tomorrow!

5 September

Fathers' cricket today. Very exciting – 102 all out. Jo Sutton got 25 runs. Kerren's (*Simmonds*) dad hit a six. Flood (*Susan Flood*) bowled well.

6 September

Pleasant morning. Jill (*Gillian*) Clarke and Linda joined me in the annexe. *Got up* after rest. Met Flos[10] in the kitchen. She seemed very pleased to see me.

7 September

Monday. Catarrh – sinusy headache. Jill (*Gill?*) Clarke came into the annexe. Got up after rest. Jolly good play about mistaken identity of an M.P. Wrote to Mummy about Long Sat. Had beplex pill and pink 'bombs'.

8 September.

Tuesday. Sister in foul mood at first this morning, but got better later. Played cards with Jill (*Gill*) Clarke all day. Great fun, we had hysterics. Inhalation. Jill went down this p.m. Nattered to Sarah Snellgrove. Lovely.

9 September

Lovely day nattering to Sarah Snellgrove. Cleaned fish-knives – played cards, etc. Walked across field after rest. Came back to ward after tea. Lovely to be back, although a bit strange. Saw Anna (*Anne-Marie Kelly*).

10 September

Thursday. Three German lessons. Haven't missed too much. Took notes on Keats in English. Mrs Hepper mad on him. Talked rapturously about his house in Hampstead. I felt a bit mizzy with my cold and found it difficult to concentrate. Did garden, practised. Got VSO Form. Terrifying, but Janet explained everything.

11 September

Felt a bit lousy with my cold, a bit worried that I wouldn't be better for Mummy tomorrow. First aid lecture in the afternoon. Funny old girl – Red Cross with squeaky voice. Lecture very elementary and rather boring.

12 September

Mr Poole died?
   Long Sat. *Lovely* day with Mummy and Big Susan. B.S. looking tired. Mudgy much bigger and redder. Had picnic in field near Hadham and sunbathed and nattered and saw my photos. Nice ones of ?Cabourn. Lovely one of Josephine. Bought hockey boots (30/-!). Really happy. Wonderful day.

13 September

Went to Wendy's (*Wendy Stone née Lee?*) party in the evening. Lovely grub. Great fun.

14 September

Flos deliberately kept me off games, but feeling fine.

19 September

Old Girls' day. Judy (*Douglas or Bennett?*) and Pat came down. Both very sophisticated. Joan and Hilary (*Greatrex?*) too, both straight from work camp in Norwich, which they loved. Jill Kesseler came too. She seemed very lonely.

21 September

St Matthew's Day. Lovely sunny morning. Service in St Sepulchre's. Crummy sermon, but lovely otherwise. Tremendous fun marching through the City. Saw Armorel Drew – v. happy at Sussex.
    Dead scared when getting money.[11] Nice sandwiches etc. for lunch. 5 quite nice boys. Talked about Housey. Great fun. Felt awful coming back to cold, empty house. Did prep all evening.

22 September

Hockey trials at Ashbourne. Played Left Wing. Tripped over new hockey boots when running, and got a dreadful stitch. Hadn't realised I was quite so out of training! V. hot. Played without tunics.

23 September

Nice music lesson. Went up late to Ashbourne, but balls hadn't been brought up, so we lay on grass and sunbathed. Only a few minutes' hockey. Tried to do prep, but Caroline came and we nattered about VSO.

24 September

Lovely letter from Big Susan. Hertford Trade Fair. Great fun. 'Top of the Form' competition v. Hertford and Ware Grammar. Hertford beat us 62–54 – very exciting. Trade Fair jolly interesting. Saw a teleprinter in action. We phoned Denmark. Felt miserable in the evening because had an argument with Janet about poetry etc. and wasted prep. time.

25 September

Most encouraged in German – Alpha– for Diktart and Beta+ for prose. (Also Beta+ for long essay on education). Cleared up 'her' and 'him' muddle. Lovely poetry by Keller. Saw I was in 2nd XI (probably not for long!). First Aid lecture by Doctor. V. amusing and interesting. Finished Scripture essay!!!

26 September

Finished ghastly Use of English paper. Nearly made a lovely pot in art but squished it at the vital moment. Away match against Hitchin. We drew 2-all. I got the first goal, thrilled. Nice tea, but I wasn't very hungry. Concert in the evening with bass (funny-man) and very good pianist. Bass not very funny, but serious stuff lovely.

28 September

Saw an episode of *Antigone* on general television. Very moving, but picture kept flickering. I thought Greek tragedy would be even more formal, instead very real and colloquial.

   Netball trials. Played shoot. Quite reasonable. Tried to practise. Not very inspired. Lovely 'Barchester Towers' reading after prep. Got on with (*making*) nightie. Quite excited about it. Nice letter from Mummy. She has started her diploma course and needlework classes. She said Ray's mum was very ill. Also old lady next door.

29 September

Netball trials again. Shot very badly. I shouldn't think I've a hope for the team. Finished German prose and French one. Started German essay on housing problem. Read Keats 'Lamia' this morning. Mrs. Hepper obviously thrilled, although she hates one bit. Frankly, I was a bit bored. *The Eve of St Agnes* far more powerful. Happy day. Exhausted.

30 September

Finished German essay and French prose. Heard from VSO that I've got an interview for next Tuesday. Very thrilled. Saw Miss West about it this evening. She was a poppet. Gave me all my instructions. Asked her if I could start Spanish course on the radio. She took it like a lamb. Flos highly amused.

1 October

Thursday. Missed Netball trials to go up to Old Folks' Home at Hertford Heath. Old girls thrilled to see Christine (*Barnett*) and me. We started making cushion covers – great fun. Place quite bright and well-decorated. Georgian silver teaspoon with our cuppa. Cut out, tacked and began machining. Bus arrived 25 minutes late, so we were late for lessons. Met Haileybury music master. First Spanish lesson this evening. Easy to follow. Beta + for Scripture essay.

2 October

Got Alpha– for English criticism from Oxford Entrance paper. Thrilled. Sent a P.O. for Spanish booklet. In dilemma over *Murder in the Cathedral*, whether to go home or not. Very amusing first aid lecture by doctor. Arranged for medical. Read up stuff about hormones. Kathleen (*Dale?*) told me I was to play in netball team.

3 October

Subbed in netball match at Poles. Quite fun, but we didn't get any tea and we had to get back for special Evensong for West Gift people. Lecture on modern music by professor from the Guildhall. V. interesting.

4 October

Sunday. Went to Communion. Nice walk. Quite reasonable sermon. Harvest decorations lovely – gorgeous smell. Compiled list of clothes for Stratford and lots of instructions from Mummy. Wrote to Kay (*Jeacock?*). Nice Bible Study meeting in geography room. Asked everyone to pray for?

Doreen (*Buvyer*) and I saw Miss West about Stratford. Television hopeless for general lesson – couldn't see or hear a thing. Miss West told us we were going home on Saturday morning because of the bug. We're all thrilled, and naturally it's marvellous about my birthday being at home. Thick fog this morning, but sultry later.

6 October

Went up to Hertford Heath. Had a go on electric machine and washed up teas. Old people thrilled to see us. Went up t'inf in evening with swollen glands. Mizzy.

10 October

Bought anerak – lovely.

11 October

Went to Mattins. Lovely service. No-one I knew was there.

12 October

My (*seventeenth*) birthday. First driving lesson. Quite fun. Went up to London after lunch. Passport photos done 12.30. Mummy came home for lunch. She didn't like my French roll. Lovely bus ride from Victoria to Holborn. Met Anne-Marie (*Kelly*) etc. at St Sepulchre's. *Murder in the Cathedral* disappointing but knights were good. Walked through City with Kelly. Spent night at Doreen's.

28 October

Worked on 'Southerton Essay.' Went to library to find maps of Stratford. Filled in questionnaire about Public Schools. Found myself very pro. Saw Miss West about university. She gave me UCCA form and suggested Sussex, York, Reading, Durham, Nottingham and Exeter. Very torn between them. Can't decide what order to put them in.

29 October

H.T.P. (*hockey team practice?*) at Ashbourne. Very wild and great fun. Mrs Hepper read us extracts from ? translated from German. V. naughty and extremely funny. Broadcast of revolution in German. A bit boring. Interesting Spanish programme. Thought the curse had started, but not sure yet. Foggy and cold out.

30 October

Practical First Aid lecture. Bandaging. Very funny. Wrote German essay on old age and prepared proses. Looked up Sussex prospectus. Had letter from Hilary (*Greatrex*) at Reading. She's obviously loving it.

31 October

Hallow'een. Pam (*Henson*) organised party – skull, masks, bob-apples, buns, sausage rolls, drinks, etc. Quite fun. Rosalind (*Emberson*) came for the day. Lovely. She seems very happy, although Lord Mayor Treloar Hospital sounds horribly like school! Miss West gave university prospectuses, and said I was definitely leaving in the summer. I've just *got* to get good grades for 'a' levels!

1 November

Went to Communion and collected. Walk with Janet (*Porter*). Argument about Mummy's office being pinched. Ghastly. She has interview at Royal Free tomorrow. Perhaps she's het up. Filled in UCCA form in the evening. Miss West perfectly sweet. Curse started in evening.

2 November

Mon. N.T.P. (*netball team practice?*) Not bad, but a bit cold. Read about Japan in German magazine and *Paris Match*. Very amusing bit of *Barchester Towers* in Sixth Form Reading. Lovely T.V. programme on Leonardo da Vinci with very wild, strident (*?harpsichord?*)

3 November

Tuesday. Miss West took me up to Hertford Heath. Old people pleased to see me. Helped with teas and started ruffles for curtain pelmets.

4 November

Wed. Southerton essay. I **finished** it. Took me all morning and I did it very badly. Played netball. Shot quite well. Hilarious music lesson. Coffee with Mrs Drake. Lovely.

5 November

Got Southerton essay back. Beta +. Interesting discussion on characters. H.T.P. Mary a bit tactless about my not being in the team. My pride was hurt, which is stupid, because Mary never realises until too late that she's being tactless. Barbarina rehearsal in evening, but I did prep. Anna came back from grandmother's funeral, obviously very shaken. We talked for about an hour.

6 November

Tried to write essay in German on 'Frankreiten in der modernen Welt'. Couldn't find word for anti-biotics anywhere. Very annoying. Talked to Sixth Form (just Steph (*Etches*) and Kerren (*Simmonds*) still healthy) and Upper Fifth about behaviour in Ward. Terribly amusing First Aid lecture by Dr Jory. Last.

7 November

Concert. Mummy, Maggie (*Margaret Hulmes*) and Big Susan came. Lovely lunch together in 'the Salisbury'. Mummy obviously a bit nostalgic about my leaving, very mixed feelings. Kathleen's (*Dale*) organ solo very good and 'Barbarina' quite fun, although all the soloists dead nervous.

8 November

We were in isolation all day but saw (*?Balneil?*) and Dr Jory in funny hat at Remembrance Day parade. He looked rather sheepish. Had rest after lunch. Wrote to VSO and Barbara Müller.

9 November

N.T.P. I shot quite well. B.B.C. French – Louis XIV. Quite good.

10 November

Went to Old People's Home with Chris. Great fun making frills and washing up. Nice tea and cake.

11 November

Lovely music lesson. Finished 'Schimmelreiter' summary. Got on frantically with 'Mansfield Park' summary. Practised netball shooting. Gave people 200 lines for talking in dining hall. Had to sit with them. Exhausting.

12 November

Lovely German B.B.C. on Keller. H.T.P. at Ashbourne. Miss Westhorpe (*Westhorp?*) showed us diagrams on tactics. Very frivolous.

13 November

Upper Sixth went to play at Haileybury, 'The Insect' by ? brothers. Amusing, propaganda against Nazism. Very powerful. The tramp was the only human. Couldn't believe people sank as low as insects. Finally killed.

14 November

Struggled with needlework. Created nothing again in art.

15 November

Got up at 8.15. Felt very lazy. Wrote to Mrs Harrison (my Governor's widow) and Mummy. Nice walk with Jo (*Yates?*). Tried to find out why she's so shy. Mrs. Hepper came to coffee. Talked about our ideals, war and peace, having children, etc. It really was lovely.

16 November

Went for a walk with Pam (*Henson*), Janet Rothwell, Ruth (*Rantzau?*) and Barbara (*Kempston?*) around All Saints' graveyard, as matches were scratched. 'Read round' and got good vocab. from 'Le Figaro'. Talked to Miss West with whole UV1 about visiting rules. She listened vaguely. Discussion about Mary.

17 November

Went up to Old People's Home. Made a bed, washed up, and practically finished frills. Had great fun with Miss West and leaking hot water pipe. Finally got it fixed, or cloakroom pipes might have disintegrated.

18 November

Wednesday. Lovely music lesson. Mrs. Lynch signed my Duke of Ed. book. Tried to revise 'Cinna'. Did needlework in evening. Anna, Wendy (*Lee*) and Linda (*Smith?*) went home. Jo (*Yates?*) very excited about preparing for trip to Greece.

28 November

My French translation exam. Had to go at the last minute to Herts and Essex to play hockey. We lost 4–2, but I got a goal.

29 October

Spent all day finishing nightie. Wrote letter in bed. Janet discovered at the last minute that she'd done her buttonholes wrong.

30 November

Bronwen (*Sly?*) finished needlework at 8.45! Netball match against 7's. Most exciting. We won 10–9 and I got a goal in the last few seconds which clinched it. Got German results. 68 for average (Doreen (*Buvyer*) 69). Very pleased.

1 December

Got French results. 63%. A bit disappointed. Very short letter from Mrs. Harrison. Went to Old People's home. Nearly finished frills for curtains. Started brass-rubbing notes.

1965

21 January

Came up to the flat. Very thrilled about it.

30 January[12]

Stayed the night in Miss Esch's flat. Slept on camp bed in Miss Cordery's sleeping bag. Very comfortable. Sir Winston Churchill's

funeral. Got up at 3.30. Breakfast. Out of house by 4.45, arrived at
Ludgate Hill at 5. Saw whole procession. Quite thrilling.

31 January

Trouble with Miss Richards in flat. Had Rosemary and Jo up here
for a few minutes. Tremendous fun, but in walked Miss Richards.
She reported us to Miss Blench. Dreadful stink.

2 February

Phoned Mummy and told her not to come on Saturday as miserably
behind with preps. Converted curtains into screens at old people's
home. Miss Richards causes stink again.

3 February

Wed. Went up to London in Miss West's car with Kate (*Dale*), Ruth
(*Rantzau?*) Elizabeth (*Stillman?*) and Susan (*Templar*). Saw a bit of
'The Wooden Horse' at film theatre at Waterloo. Gorgeous dinner
in Festival Hall restaurant. Brahms concert conducted by Klemperer.
Heavenly.

4 February

Thursday. Felt pretty dead.

5 February

Saw Miss Esch and she said come to coffee any night. I said I thought
it a bit dodgy, so she saw Miss West, who said O.K. provided
housemistress knows where we are.

6 February

Nice pottery art lesson. Rosemary very helpful. Tried to do
Mansfield Park essay. In the evening, Pam (*Henson?*) came to the flat,
and we played lovely records and made toast and tea.

7 February

A bit groggy as we didn't get to sleep till midnight on Sat., but got
up for communion. Went to Methodist Church. Missed beauty and

dignity of C.of E. Service. Had Miss Cordery and Miss Tavernor (*Taverner*) to coffee.

25 April

Came back to school – Sunday. Everyone thrilled about VSO. I felt a bit miserable but a bit better in the flat.

26 April

Utterly miserable, having sent letter to Hugh (*Starkey*). Wondering what his reaction would be. Couldn't settle. Felt how petty everything was. Terrified Hugh wouldn't write . . . Saw a film of 'Murder in the Cathedral'.

27 April

Tuesday. Letter from Hugh. Very nice, very heartening.

28 April

Had sweet letter from Hugh, mostly in French. It cheered me tremendously.

29 April

Played tennis all afternoon. Used tape-recorder to practise for French oral.

30 April

French oral. Mrs Bearman very sweet, and most complimentary. Quite a nice dictation. I didn't read passage very fluently, but she said I had a good accent.

1 May

Heard I'd failed Use of English. Pretty miserable. Saw Lawrence of Arabia. Very good.

2 May

Sun. Wrote long epistle to Hugh and Jean Toft. Also letter to Mr. Lees[13] and to Mummy.

9 June

Cricket match against 5's. We won 31 all out to 37 for 6. I got 13 not out. Very pleased.

10 June

Cricket finals against 1's. We lost 61–54. Very exciting. I was out for a duck.

Notes

1. After I was born my mother teamed up with Louisa May 'Susan' Dipper ARRC, another QA (Queen Alexandra's Imperial Military Nursing Service), and fellow London Hospital nurse and midwife some sixteen years her senior. Together they ran a children's home called Beach Court in Lancing, Sussex, for the first fourteen plus years of my life. There were twenty-six children, many of mixed race, and Susan Dipper was loved and known by them all as 'Big Susan'. When they decided to give up Beach Court because of her age and angina, she and my mother could have gone their separate ways, but I was heartbroken at the thought of life without Big Susan, so they bought a house in Worthing, my mother eventually nursing her until her death at their last home in Anglesey at the age of eighty-three. Like my mother's, Big Susan's memory is still very precious to me.

2. Pat Stannard had worked at Beach Court, as I remember, helping to look after the children before doing her nurse training. Throughout my time at school she would send me beautiful fine art post cards, which I used as page markers in my Bible, and still treasure.

3. 'Trotsky' (Mrs Trott), originally from the Forest of Dean, was our charwoman and general factotum at Beach Court. She could find anything, so was also nicknamed 'St Antony'. There was considerable banter between her and 'Cookie' (Mr Cook), a salt of the earth ex-Queen's Regiment NCO, who helped my mother in the kitchen, cleaned twenty-six little pairs of shoes for the children every day in the back kitchen, fended off any difficult visitors at the front door looking as stately as any butler, and generally made us all feel safe. I adored them both, and Trotsky in particular was very generous to me, giving me a solid silver napkin ring engraved with my initials which I've treasured all my adult life. She was desperately hard up, her husband often out of work, and listening to the football results late on a winter Saturday afternoon on the huge curved Bakelite wireless in the Beach Court kitchen was a ritual while she and my mother checked their pools coupons, Vernons or Littlewoods, Trotsky convinced that one day she would win her fortune, my mother probably a little more realistic about the odds. Big Susan would have a modest flutter on the Grand National, Cookie being sent, I think, to place the

bet for her, entering a bookie's shop not being considered ladylike. She never studied form, but always chose a horse because she liked the name, backing both ways and sometimes with surprising success, giving away her winnings on presents almost before she had the cash in her hand.

One day Cookie asked my mother in the kitchen if he could sit down, an unprecedented request so she knew that he must be ill. Shortly afterwards I visited him one Good Friday at his bungalow in North Lancing, clutching a bunch of violets. 'Mr Cook is very ill,' his wife told me, which I could see. It was cancer. It was the first death 'in the family' that I can recall and I just couldn't believe that he had gone, he had been so much part of my young life. Trotsky, on the other hand, lived to a good old age, and my mother had a sad letter in Anglesey from one of her daughters, Jean or Joyce, to say that the old lady's heart 'just wore out.'

For a few years at Beach Court we also had 'Nearnie' (Miss Earnshaw), a magnificent cook and staunch Congregationalist who left us when her dream cooking job came up at Westminster College, Cambridge, which trained Congregational Church ministers. She kindly had me to stay in her little semi-basement flat opposite the Fitzwilliam Museum and I was very touched years later to be informed of her death in a letter enclosing a picture of me as a child which she'd always kept.

4. Worms was where I was supposed to get off the train. Because of a postal strike, my letter to the *Waisenfamilienheim* (orphanage) where I was to work giving the arrival date and ETA hadn't reached them. I therefore had to find a telephone box in a strange German town and announce myself: '*Ich bin Susan.*' '*Ah! Tante Susanna!*' came the astonished reply. It didn't get much better after that: the rations (mainly *Schwarzbrot* and lard and out of date US army rations of hard biscuits, peanut butter and jello) were meagre, the tiny outdoor swimming pool was slimy green, and I was put to work gardening in the midday sun. The only light relief was taking a sheep called Schwendli and a little girl called Maria for a daily walk with strict instructions that I should supervise Maria's violin practice while Schwendli munched calmly away at the parched grass, undeterred by Maria's screeching. Still, I learned some German, although the *Süddeutsch* spoken by the children bore little resemblance to Miss Nutto von Stetten's careful enunciation in class. I was sixteen.

5. Miss West had pioneered the four-term year, which is why we were at school in August, but then had a fortnight's holiday in October. It was difficult for parents who were teachers, but on the whole, I think the experiment was a great success, with staff and pupils alike getting less tired, especially in the otherwise very long autumn term. Miss West, indomitable lady that she was, took some girls off to France one October break, and there are hilarious stories of her pacing the corridors on the train fending off foreign soldiers and sailors from her precious girls.

6. 'Mons', or monitresses, were like house captains, and two were appointed for each House, while Miss West had her own headmistress's monitresses. The badges were solid silver, with the head of our founder, King Edward VI, in profile polished so lovingly as to be almost unrecognisable. All the way up the school I had coveted one of those badges, and when I was eventually made a monitress, new badges were issued with a horrid grey patina that didn't need cleaning. I was disappointed beyond words. By my last year I was also a school prefect, only a handful of whom were chosen from the mons each year, and we wore an enamelled full colour school badge. Duties included ringing the bell in the school hall, dead on time, and watching every girl in the school file past into Chapel, and picking up any sloppiness in dress like an undone button, which proved excellent training for the army!

One of the embarrassments of going for university interviews in those days was that we had to wear school uniform, competing with mini-skirted girls in mufti who flaunted their make-up (disallowed at CH) as well as their legs in front of male lecturers. The ultimate humiliation for me was not being allowed to wear my mon's badge or prefect's badge, the only thing that distinguished me in school uniform, I felt, 'in case you lose them on the journey, dear,' as Flos explained. It didn't stop me getting some university offers, however (and it was tough getting in *anywhere* in those days), and I remember with particular gratitude a golden evening train journey travelling back from York, enjoying a full British Rail dinner thanks to the kindness of our headmistress, Miss West, who had pressed some cash into my hand especially so that I could have a good meal on the way home. I had already fallen in love with York Minster, and been bowled over by the sheer beauty of the mediaeval building, King's Manor, where kindly mediaevalist Elizabeth Salter had made encouraging noises about my Chaucer essay, and I absolutely *knew* that York was my destiny.

7. I had applied for a year in advance, and was offered a waiting list place. In fact, I got a B rather than an A for English, and when on my VSO gap year in Malawi received an unconditional offer from York for 'language' (main) and 'education' (subsidiary). I hadn't a clue what 'language' meant, but accepted anyway, and then found myself stuck on a very dry preliminary course for two whole terms getting to grips with phonetics and phonemics, often incarcerated for hours on end in a lonely little brown soundproof booth, before the Language Department would release me to major in English Literature as I'd always wanted to do. This meant that I had missed the whole of the preliminary course in English, and effectively had to complete my English degree in seven terms flat. I felt at a huge disadvantage because of that, but was still grateful and triumphant to have achieved my place in York's English Department, and have valued that time to read every since.

8. Mrs Blodwen James was the housemother in one of the thirteen children's homes in Brighton for which my mother was Homes Supervisor. When the houseparents went on holiday, my mother often stepped into the breach to look after the children, taking them to Butlin's in a caravan, where I helped her look after them, or to an outdoor pursuits centre at Burwash, abseiling alongside them. One of the girls in care used to sing to her 'Mrs Wilson's got a lovely daughter' with a wonderful glottal stop on 'daughter'.

9. Liz Drucquer was a Guide friend from Worthing with whom I used to go to camp. Tragically, her mother died while she was still at school, and I found expressing my condolences hard at that age, I was so shocked at the time. She was a very good Christian, and I think that her faith really helped her through.

10. Flos or Flossie was Mrs Winstone, the wardmistress in Twos, my senior ward (house) a red-headed, basically kind lady who used occasionally to fly into rages, not surprising as she had terrible headaches said to be from a brain tumour. How she went on working, putting up with 36 noisy teenage girls night and day, I'll never know. Unlike houseparents, housemasters or housemistresses today in boarding schools who usually have teaching as well as pastoral duties, our wardmistresses, latterly housemistresses, were the descendants of the CH matrons. I felt that they did not have the kudos or respect of the academic staff, and since the accommodation was so basic, only a sitting room and bedroom with no en-suite facilities, it was suitable only for women on their own for whatever reason, who didn't always seem the happiest of people.

11. By tradition, monitresses were each given a guinea by the Lord Mayor of London at the Mansion House. Grecians (Upper Sixth boys) from Housey were presumably given the same.

12. I can hear her now: Mrs Winstone, our housemistress, popped her head found the Dayroom door. We looked up. There was something different about her. 'Girls,' she announced quietly, 'Sir Winston Churchill has died.' I was stunned. Rather like King George VI, at whose death I had wept as a small child, Churchill was just part of life, the hero to our parents who had steered the Nation through the darkest days of the War. Now he, too, was gone.

The next thing I remember was being called into Flos's room. Miss Esch, our Old Blue art mistress, had offered to take the school prefects (six of us that year, I think) up to London for the funeral. Flos was clearly disapproving, saying how the Funeral March sent shivers down her spine, but I was thrilled: a trip up to London witnessing history live sounded wonderful. It got better: Rosemary Esch put us all up in her Earls Court flat – the height of sophistication to me – the night before, and her brother Vivian, a dashing young former cavalry officer, was there at supper. They were both immensely kind and great fun, and I think it was then that 'call me Rosemary' was introduced, a daring concept in itself to me at the time, when relations between CH pupils and staff were still pretty formal. We played Tom Lehrer records, very naughty to us innocent schoolgirls, and I suddenly felt aware of being on the threshold of womanhood, entering an exciting, and slightly dangerous adult world.

The next morning we must have breakfasted very early after our 0330 hours reveille, as the diary records, and I remember vividly passing Westminster Hall, the pale yellow light, I imagined from the candles round the coffin, clearly visible through the huge window set in the ancient stonework. There was Churchill lying in state for the final few hours through the emerging grey London dawn, and we were part of it.

We found an excellent spot on Ludgate Hill on the same side as St Paul's, very close to the cathedral, and stood waiting – for hours, it seemed – in the bleak January air. It was very cold. The parade when it finally passed us was stunning, however, in its hugeness and its colour, the reassuring crunch of British boots, highly bulled, in perfect time with the beautiful, sombre funeral music. Then came the reason for the whole occasion, the gun carriage, remarkably simple in itself, and the sailors with reversed arms, I think. We had a clear view of all the dignitaries arriving at St Paul's, a military policewoman in scarlet forage cap and white gloves throwing up an immaculate salute to General de Gaulle as she opened his limousine door. I felt hugely proud to be British, and a Londoner, in the heart of the City, our school badge bearing the City of London coat of arms, and I probably finally decided subconsciously there and then that one day I too would join the British Army and fight for freedom as our parents had done before us. (Written from memory 18 May 2007.)

13. Mr Lawrence Lees, headmaster of Malosa Secondary School, Malawi, where I was to serve for a year on VSO.

CHAPTER 4

Miss West – an early infirmary memory

S HORTLY AFTER ARRIVAL AT CH, I found myself marched up to the infirmary with a sore throat and a temperature.

The Sister in charge, Great Ormond Street-trained, was assisted by a young London Hospital (LH) nurse, called, as I remember, Pat Archer, who was a delight. I think she was an Old Blue, great fun and very kind. She wore a simple mauve outfit with her distinctive LH badge. Sister, by contrast, looked positively ancient to me, resplendent in her belted silver-buckled navy dress, white cuffs, huge white starched apron and frilly cap perching on tight grey curls. She always looked exactly the same. One Hertford girl in my time had gone for interview at GOS. She described it glumly as 'a starchified edition of CH', and decided to do her sick children's training elsewhere. Sister Summers was certainly starchy, not a bit like the hands-on, cuddly, soft-overalled figures of my mother and Big Susan nursing sometimes pretty sick children at Beach Court, and although CH girls said that if you were really ill, Sister could be very kind, I never quite discovered her gentler side.

Luckily, however, in the next bed to mine when I was so little with my sore throat was a very senior girl, Jane Olds, who would read me *Diary of a Provincial Lady* in an actressy voice and tell me stories of daring senior girls accidentally singeing their 'blues', our thick issue elasticated dark blue outer knickers, by draping them over their bedside lights so that they could read undetected after lights out. She would keep me howling with laughter in rest after lunch in the infirmary, when we were supposed to be sleeping. Suddenly, one afternoon, clonking down the corridor with her distinctive dot-and-carry-one gait came Sister, and even Jane froze. At CH, you didn't mess with authority however senior you were, unless you wanted a very rough ride.

Sister on this occasion did start making a fuss of me, and then I *knew* I wasn't very well. The one advantage was that I qualified for her famous home-made lemonade, still slightly warm from infusion.

It was wonderful. They even gave me a large glass bottle of Lucozade, fearfully expensive at the time, with its pretty, golden crackly cellophane wrapper, and told me to drink all I could. Much to their astonishment, I demolished the contents within minutes. I was never offered another!

One afternoon I was wrapped in a blanket and carried downstairs to Long Ward, presumably for ease of nursing, by the steward, Mr Robinson, an imposing-looking man with huge eyebrows, to whom I once had to report, complete with pieces as evidence, when I broke a blue patterned Christ's Hospital china plate. He solemnly charged me 6d for the offence, and gave me the statutory rocket. In the infirmary, however, he was kind, and Dr Jory on his morning round prescribed oral penicillin — still pretty unusual in those days. It tasted of the smell of the syringes that my mother used to boil up on the gas stove in the children's home, the same whiff that I was to get from our own children's bottles of Amoxil years later — nasty and bitter — but it must have worked, and gradually my temperature started to come down.

Meanwhile, my mother had been informed by Miss West in a letter that 'Susan was not at all well' — I found out much later that it had been pneumonia — and there was no question of her being encouraged to visit me, so my poor, worried, generous little Mum sent me some flowers. Sister regarded this as a gross extravagance, and somehow seemed to hold me personally responsible. Still recovering from the mortification, and pretty shaky from the fever, I spilt a mug of tea all over my bed during Miss West's daily visit to the infirmary. I let out a horrified yell: 'What will *Sister* say?'

Mercifully for me, Sister must have been off duty at the time. Without a word, our revered headmistress gathered me to her ample bosom — she was surprisingly cuddly — placed me gently in an adjacent bed, re-made my own with clean sheets and blankets, carried me back, and tucked me in. 'There, Susan,' she said in her matter-of-fact way, 'now Sister need never know.'

30 July 2007

CHAPTER 5

School Needlework

F OR SOME OF US MORE neatly challenged girls, school needlework could be a fearful experience. I think I had more nightmares about it than any other aspect of life at CH. The only thing I ever did right for Miss Richards, our nervy ex-ATS wartime junior commander, was to be able to work the Singer treadle sewing machine first time without needing instruction. What she didn't know was that I had had plenty of practice with the treadle at home, helping my mother and Big Susan mend sheets and children's clothes at Beach Court.

Once we graduated to no lessons, we had to make a garment each term, to be put on and inspected by Miss West and Miss Richards for the needlework show. If the hand sewing on the hem was too visible, or the garment didn't hang right, heaven help you! There was a desperate fight for the iron on deadline morning, followed by a clumsy sewing-on of a white paper name label, which had to be attached in cross stitch at all four corners. With Chapel looming (and one couldn't possibly be late on parade) I was so terrified by then, that I would prick my finger. Horrors!

What I dreaded most was a 'below standard', which was not only considered a personal disgrace, but worse, lost house points. Somehow, I always just avoided such humiliation, and even won a commendation – in my very last term.

I wrote the following for Miss Pizzey in English, I think in the upper fourth, while struggling with the tablecloth featured in the poem, which I found recently amongst my late mother's things. Miss Pizzey was an Oxford graduate with a bun, quite the archetypal bluestocking, as intellectual women used to be called, and she could look rather severe. However, as she began to read this twenty-minute 'prep' of mine to the class, saying that she couldn't possibly comment on the ending, I thought I detected a hint of a smile.

The poem is as accurate as I can recall it after some forty-four years!

Needlework Lesson

When I open my eyes on a Tuesday
A sudden thought leaps to my head:
We've a needlework lesson this morning!
And the very thought fills me with dread.

I am filled with remorse when I think of
The times when I played with a friend
   When I should have got on with my sewing.
    Will the yet-to-be-sewn ever end?

Three yards of pulled threads there before me,
Crying out to be neatly hemstitched,
The bright yellow threads staring at me,
I feel helpless, then strangely bewitched.

Bewitched by a power I know not,
Arousing new hope from despair:
She may not be terribly angry.
If she is, do I honestly care?

Susan Wilson. (*Upper IVA2?*)

The shriek of laughter from the class at the end still feels sweet to my ears after all these years. How wonderful to provide some comedy for others to enjoy!

CHAPTER 6

Work

ALTHOUGH THERE WERE MANY sorts of work at CH, the word was usually referred to in the context of academic work, which was strictly forbidden on a Sunday, a rule inevitably flouted by senior girls anxious about impending public examinations.

When I arrived as a little nine-year-old, our school work was dominated by the First and Second Form mistress, Miss King. Tall and upright, she cut an imposing figure, and apparently had been teaching at CH forever. She marked all our work meticulously with a red ink pen, and every wrongly spelt word had to be copied out three times correctly. Not for her any reticence common when I was trying to teach English much later about pointing out mistakes, the fashionable theory by then being that too much correcting would discourage a pupil, and the odd timorous comment in pencil would be kinder: for Miss King, if it was wrong, it was wrong, and the red ink was never spared. And in English, the odd spelling mistake and lack of 'tidiness' could pull down your mark, however much you might have put your heart into a piece of writing, as I found to my cost.

Nevertheless, it was an excellent grounding in what I suppose equated to the top two years of a junior school education, although at CH, of course, I felt at the bottom of something very much bigger and more important. Scripture, history, geography, arithmetic and English were all covered thoroughly. We would have to learn a poem by heart every week and recite it in class, and I still remember declaiming with gusto the deeds of brave Horatius from Macaulay's 'Lays of Ancient Rome'. Miss King was extremely keen on the Roman Army, which she clearly admired for its discipline as well as its clever tactics, and in describing the subsequent fall of the Roman Empire would attribute its decline to a general idleness and lack of moral fibre, deftly linking this with the likely fate awaiting *us* **if we didn't kneel up straighter in Chapel**. She was a vicar's daughter of the old school, and I once incurred her shocked disapproval by remarking innocently that in Brownies at home in Lancing we went for Church Parade to the Methodist church because Brown Owl said they sang better than the C of E.

Having flourished on the whole under Miss King's direction, I found the Third Form a horrid shock, joined as we were by LCC scholarship girls who had all been told by their primary schools that they were brilliant (as some undoubtedly were) and had no respect for those of us who had already 'done our time' for two years in the school. By definition, if they were brilliant, we Presentation girls must be thick, so they said. It was galling. A new form mistress coupled with a new wardmistress and all these little upstarts with whom to contend made for an unsettled year, and Miss West in one of those agonising regular rituals of 'the Interview' had clearly picked up on this. At the end of each term she would sweep into the ward at evening prep time and settle in the wardmistress's armchair in her sitting room, while the wardmistress would be banished to the Dayroom to supervise prep. We would have to line up on the bench outside the sitting room, and one by one face the Headmistress for an end-of-term appraisal on our school work and our behaviour in the ward. Not ever invited to sit, I remember standing awkwardly, trying not to wriggle, unsure of what to do with my hands, wondering wretchedly what criticism I would have to take on the chin this time.

'Do you like Miss M., Susan?' I was stunned by the directness of this question referring to our new, and much disliked wardmistress, but sensing that this was a delicate issue, and knowing that all staff appeared to be solidly on the side of Authority, I answered cautiously, 'Well, not as much as Miss Robertson, Miss West.' She just cocked her head and gave me a half smile.

Of course if you were unhappy in the ward, your school work tended to suffer, and for the first and only time in my school career I was given a dreaded 'classroom', by our otherwise rather nice and earnest new form mistress Miss Nolan, for a particularly scruffy maths prep (my left-handed writing was even more wobbly than usual and the ink had smudged badly). 'You are having a bad patch,' was the bald comment. A 'classroom', considered a disgrace, was a particularly cruel punishment involving having to do the prep again at the beginning of Long Saturday, when on one precious weekend out of only three termly parental visits we were let off Saturday morning lessons and allowed out mid-morning instead of at lunchtime. I smarted for my mother over what I saw as the injustice of her having got up extremely early to arrive in time by public transport from Sussex only to be made to wait while I was incarcerated in the classroom block miserably re-doing the prep. It was humiliating, and I don't think I ever really liked or understood maths again, although there was a certain satisfaction in the logic of algebra, taught later by the long-suffering Miss Holmes, an Old Blue and former head girl.

I think it was in the Third Form that I even failed one or two exams, and when I was feeling at my lowest one day outside the swimming pool, a kindly word from Miss Park made all the difference. Auntie Park, about as ancient as Miss King, I reckoned, was the senior games mistress, and she taught us games, gym and swimming. I loved it all. It was a little respite from the difficulties of school work and life on the ward, and I thought Miss Park was wonderful. Wiry, with straightish iron grey hair and neat divided skirts, she was passionate about gymnastics and hockey, and she with Miss King seemed to personify CH, Hertford. She and Daphne King were great friends, and when the girl on chapel duty, Lavinia Minett I think it was, had put out, apparently wrongly, for it was not a Red Letter Day, red colours in Chapel for St Valentine's Day, one was reputed to have whispered delightedly to the other, 'I think Lavinia must be in love!' That any of our spinster staff could understand the concept of romantic love seemed to me at the time to be astonishing.

The Third Form was overall a miserable year for me, and doing badly then could, I knew, have dire consequences for a girl's academic future: I could be relegated to the B form in the Lower Fourth, thereby missing out on Latin, then considered essential for many professions including law or medicine which I already thought I might want to do. I was desperate to get into the A form. As it happened, we were thought to be a particularly bright year, and they created two A forms for the Lower Fourth, I scraping into the A2 form and thus qualifying for Latin and my first encounter with the classics mistress, Miss Blench.

'Queenie', as she was universally known, was a legend. An Oxford classicist, she had a dry, donnish wit, and was one of the cleverest women I've ever met. She would joke that Blench was probably a corruption of Blanch(e), and her ancestors had come over with the Normans as washerwomen. As I listened to her beautifully modulated

Oxford voice, this seemed to me an unlikely lineage, which of course was the joke. She could inspire fear, especially if you dropped more than half a mark out of ten in the weekly test, and when exasperated would drawl, 'Child, why don't you jump out of the window?' No-one ever dared take her at her word, although one of my feistier contemporaries, Chrissy Williams (then Christine Barnett), was so incensed by the suggestion that she apparently stormed down to the Headmistress's study immediately to complain to Miss West herself. The Headmistress's reaction at the time is not recorded, but when years later Chrissy told her that she too had achieved a headship, Miss West could only manage a gasped, 'Oh, my dear!' Perhaps she remembered that early indignant outburst!

For some reason, Queenie liked me, perhaps because I caught her fascination with words, and I shall be eternally grateful to her for everything she taught me through Latin about English, its derivation and even spelling. As Christmas approached she would make us learn and sing '*Adeste Fideles*' which always sounded to me so much more exotic than 'O come all ye Faithful', even without any Italianate 'Church Latin' pronunciation, and a pretty close translation. Good Protestant girls that we mostly were, we had to learn the '*Pater Noster*' by heart and recite it together, and of course Queenie was our resident expert on the 'Carmen', our school song, which we all had to know word perfect in the first few weeks of our school career. She would explain gleefully that the verse, written apparently by a man especially for the girls' school in honour of our beautiful new gym, beginning, '*Artes palaestrae floreant*', should most accurately be translated as 'May the arts of the wrestling ring flourish'.

To my sadness, our three children all turned their backs determinedly on Latin, despite their teachers' efforts. Our chorister sons, of course, would sing sublime whole Latin masses in Llandaff Cathedral, Sunday by Sunday, Mozart or Haydn or Schubert amongst the most beautiful settings, I thought. But ploughing glumly through Latin prep in the few precious minutes allowed at home for tea on a Wednesday or Sunday, Ben would admit, when pressed, that *Agnus Dei* meant Lamb of God, yet refuse to accept *dei* as a useful example of the genitive case. 'I just perform it,' he declared, with all the haughty dismissiveness of a pre-pubescent boy. Will, faced with a Latin or French prep at home, was even less interested, as I tried to make sense of the vocabulary and grammar for him. 'Don't explain it to me, Mum, just *do* it,' he would urge wearily, as the home time ticked away. I'm sure that in Queenie Blench even *he* would have met his match!

Queenie taught us sheltered schoolgirls about Life, too, describing exciting foreign holidays like one to Egypt and riding a camel, which she said stank abominably. And lest we should be harbouring any secret ambitions of a glamorous career as BOAC or BEA cabin crew – becoming a pilot seemed pretty unattainable for a girl at the time despite the heroic wartime exploits of W.E. Johns' Worralls of the WAAF (although I believe that one Hertford Old Blue from my generation did achieve her Private Pilot's Licence) – Queenie dismissed air hostesses as 'glorified waitresses, mopping up vomit.' She was, you might say, mistress of the one-liner, long before the phrase came into common parlance.

I nearly opted for Latin at A level because of her brilliant teaching, and certainly found German from scratch instead of Latin in the Sixth Form a tough choice. So although in the end Queenie didn't teach me in my last two years, as our Sixth Form mistress, where she was in her element preparing girls for university, she was surprisingly kind and encouraging to me, and really helped me to blossom at the top of the school. As senior mistress, she was also, I suspect, an excellent administrator, running the school when Miss West went off to America for a term's sabbatical, it seemed to me with very little fuss. Old classics pupils kept in touch with her, and on an enquiry from one of my friends into her father's health is reputed to have sighed, 'Oh, Anne-Marie, I fear he is immortal!' That was typical of her sense of humour.

Sadly, Queenie wasn't immortal herself, and like so many of 'our' generation of Hertford mistresses, has died in recent years. They were a bunch of enormously dedicated, sometimes quirky women, with whom many of us corresponded happily for the rest of their lives, touched by their continuing interest in us as individuals, our careers and our families, and visiting them or even having them to stay, as happened with our darling senior English mistress, Kathleen Betterton, the slightly embarrassed author of *Teach Yourself to Write*, who even squelched through the muddy car park with me at the Polytechnic of Wales one dark, miserable winter's afternoon in

Pontypridd to sit in on a community writers' workshop led by Helen Dunmore. I remember lending Kathleen D.R. West's autobiography *Half to Remember* which she ploughed through resolutely in our guest bedroom with her poor failing eyes, I regretting very much that a large print edition had not been available. We were both struck by Miss West's unquestioning certainty from an early age that she was destined for a headship. I suppose that as a Cambridge Blue, and with her family background and an early teaching post at Roedean she undoubtedly was, and she was appointed as head of CH, Hertford at the then extraordinarily young age of twenty-nine. It was fascinating to get Kathleen's take on her as a headmistress from a staff perspective. She was unhesitatingly loyal: 'Miss West was always very kind to me,' she said.

Being a Hertford Old Blue herself, Kathleen was particularly understanding and kind. She had won a scholarship to CH, and with not a thought, she told me later, for her poor mother, then in service, bounced off excitedly to Hertford, full of stories by Angela Brazil of jolly boarding school life. Doubtless the reality of CH life presented a harsh contrast to the fiction, but being immensely clever, she went on to Oxford, a typical example, I think, of the horizons that a CH education at Horsham or Hertford could open up for a bright child from however poor a home. She could seem delightfully vague, appearing sometimes not to be sure which room she was supposed to be teaching us in, although I'm sure she was not nearly so dippy as she made out: her teaching was spot on and she brought Chaucer alive for me in a brilliant way. I still treasure the postcard she sent me when I eventually got into the English Department at York, she, as I discovered much later, having had a similar tussle at university, in her case to change from Oxford classics to English. When I was struggling under the marking workload in my probationary teaching year, she passed on the best piece of advice from a head of department under whom she'd served: 'Make a forget of setting homework sometimes.' Her apparent insouciance of school rules, enforced so rigidly by others, came as a welcome relief. She could make a forget of English essay deadlines, too, when I was struggling desperately with German prose, and of course I always came up with the goods in the end, and always with her careful, encouraging feedback.

Tiny from my earliest memories of her, Kathleen seemed to shrink even more with age, and on what we knew instinctively would be our last visit to her at her fascinating Herefordshire cottage, with treasured pieces of Hertford memorabilia, on a day when she'd 'had a little fall', Anne-Marie and I were able to lift her together gently from sofa to chair and share our microwaved culinary offerings together, the old lady chatty and concerned for us and charming as ever, despite her frailty. It is a poignant memory.

I was slightly saddened to read in Norman Longmate's foreword to Audrey Griggs' excellent autobiography about her wartime experience of CH Hertford *Away from the Bombs and the Boys*:

> Whatever is written about it, CH Hertford can now never achieve the eminence of CH London or CH Horsham. There can be no *Fortunate Bluecoat Girl* to rival *The Fortunate Bluecoat Boy* of 1789, no Hertford-educated Foreign Secretary or Lord Mayor, no Hertford Golden Generation like that produced around the end of the eighteenth century by Newgate Street which established the school's reputation for nourishing literary talent and for turning the sons of country clerics and City clerks into famous writers.

Longmate is right in that Hertford has not produced an Old Blue female equivalent of Lamb or Coleridge, but for a school where the first girls in 1552 were mostly allowed only to read the Bible and do the sewing for the Foundation, boys and girls – although singing, reading, writing and figuring appear to have featured on the curriculum from the school's beginning in 1552 – we have come a long way. Headmistresses Miss Robertson and then Miss Craig and Miss West pioneered university education for Hertford Old Blues, in some cases, I believe, making it possible financially for them to achieve, as indeed still happens in cases of need through the Benevolent Society of Blues. From CH, Hertford we can boast the Principals of two Oxford colleges, and should be particularly proud, I think, of two girls with whom I overlapped at school, Ruth Fraenkel, now Baroness Ruth Deech, who described CH, Hertford on the radio as 'my rather tough boarding school,' if I heard her aright, and Kathleen Duncan OBE, (Kathleen Dale at school) who served on the CH governing body, the Council of Almoners, vastly outnumbered by the men, but I'm sure well able to hold her own very graciously.

1. *Army nursing sister mother: Eileen Lane, QAIMNS, World War II*

2. *Chindit father: John Wilson, World War II*

3. London Hospital nurse, Miss Louisa May 'Susan' Dipper QAIMNS assistant matron, World War II when she won the ARRC. Later christened 'Big Susan' by the children at Beach Court, Lancing

4. Christ's Hospital, Hertford old school fronting on to Fore Street

5. Detail of Christ's Hospital girl from one of the statues at the front. Sketch by CH, Hertford art mistress Miss Hilda Keppel-Barrett

6. Christ's Hospital, Hertford. Reference Library with classroom block to the left

7. *Christ's Hospital, Hertford. House study party, Twos. The author standing (L) with birthday girl Stephanie Etches (R). Seated L-R: Joanna Yates; Kerren Simmonds; Susan Flood*

8. *Christ's Hospital, Hertford. Daily brass polishing in Ward 2*

9. Christ's Hospital, Hertford. Steward's house with the flat at the top

10. Christ's Hospital, Hertford. View from Fore Street: the front entrance with the School Hall beyond

11. Confirmation Day: 19 March 1963. In the coatfrock with Confirmation veil

CHRISTMAS GREETINGS • CHRIST'S HOSPITAL. HERTFORD

12. Christ's Hospital, Hertford Chapel. School Christmas card by Wendy Lee 1962

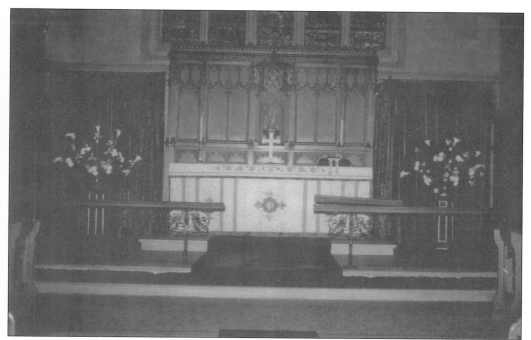

13. Christ's Hospital, Hertford. The altar in the Chapel donated by Miss West to Alfriston Parish Church

14. Katie, Ben and Will Davies-Jenkins discover their mother's first home: Beach Court, 16 Brighton Road, Lancing, Sussex, 1992

15. Beach Court from Lancing Beach. Nostalgic return, 1992

16. Bedside locker treasure at school: my mother, Mrs Eileen Wilson with dachshund Mudge

Generations of Hertford girls have enjoyed distinguished careers (and I certainly wouldn't count myself amongst the distinguished ones) in many fields including law, medicine, the Church, education or the arts, or in public or voluntary service, while successfully holding marriages together and raising their families. We were all expected to train for a profession, and most of us have earned our living somehow throughout our married lives, which I think was rarer for our generation than for girls today, with all the benefits of maternity leave unknown to us then. And what strikes me at every Hertford reunion, now held down at Housey, is the thoughtfulness of the women with whom I reminisce. These were friendships forged often in adversity, and all the more precious for that, and they have lasted ever since school days. Loyalty, kindness and integrity are what count, I believe, in the end.

CH, Hertford did not actively encourage us to pursue worldly success like wealth or fame – in fact it would probably be considered by Miss West as rather suspect unless properly earned – but what our 'Old Girls' like Kathleen Betterton achieved was incalculable, and just as valuable, I would contend, as the career of any Lord Mayor, politician or famous writer: she passed on her human values and her scholarship learnt at Hertford unselfishly to future generations; she was a star.

CHAPTER 7

Childhood Experiences of Non-Fiction

NON-FICTION SOUNDS SUCH A dull title, I suppose, but I've always enjoyed facts, and growing up in the fifties and sixties long before the internet was heard of, with its access to apparently accurate information, we had to rely on books. We also relied on newspapers, and people bought their 'daily' to find out the news. Before there was twenty-four hour television news coverage and cinema treats with the plummy Pathé news reports were rare, we looked to newspapers for facts.

Christ's Hospital, Hertford was quite enlightened in that the senior pupils could read *The Daily Telegraph* at breakfast, and the rest of the House could see it during the remainder of the day. And what could be more respectable than *The Daily Telegraph*?! Even that could have pages torn out by our housemistress before she handed it over, so that we were forced to run round to friends in more liberal Houses to find out what news we had missed. Usually, it was a report of a particularly nasty murder or sexual attack, we discovered. 'Flossy', our sad, red-headed lady was only trying to protect us. This was strange, really, because we were encouraged to read the Bible with its vivid accounts of many atrocities. Of course, it is debatable how much of the Bible is truly non-fiction, but much of it is an apparently accurate historical account, and we impressionable girls might read it as such. I could not quite believe that a woman could ask for the head of John the Baptist on a platter, or understand the savagery of Old Testament fratricide or Christ's crucifixion. Such barbarity seemed incomprehensible then, as it does now.

CH was a charity school, or course, and most of us came from very hard-up families who had to provide very few items for us except for a fountain pen and a Bible. I still have my school Bible, with my name written in ink in large, wobbly, nine-year-old's joined-up writing, smudged as usual. Given to me by Big Susan, it is brown leatherette, dense text riddled with footnotes, and the occasional full colour illustration. Other girls with real leather volumes printed on fine India paper derided my copy, but I adored it. Of course it is the King James' authorised version, which was also read daily in the school chapel. The beautiful cadences have lived with me ever since, and I still find I can quote whole texts verbatim.

My mother gave me a *Bible Reader's Encyclopaedia and Concordance* for my Confirmation in 1963. The leather still has that delicious aroma, and the maps give an authenticity to many of the Bible stories, and at school managed to bring to life otherwise rather dull lessons on Church history. It is also a thoroughly scholarly work, with references easy to cross-check, and never a misprint to be found.

I suppose it is accuracy that one most respects in a work of non-fiction. It simply has to be correct, whether it is a dictionary, an encyclopaedia or any other reference book. For a child it also has to be readable and fun. I well remember the joy of Arthur Mee's *Children's Encyclopaedia*, and begging my mother for the materials to make a chemical garden, instructions for which I found there. There was the thrill of watching the crystals 'grow'. There, sadly, my interest in chemistry ended, science books seeming to me to be particularly obscure, and chemical equations quite impossible to balance. The names of the elements were another matter. They were interesting because they were **words**: Pb for instance, easy to remember for lead because of 'plumber'.

The other reference book which delighted me as a child was the *Oxford Junior Encyclopaedia*. My mother started buying the volumes for me as presents for birthday or Christmas, and I longed to own the whole set. I think there were twelve in all, and I have never parted with them, even though one or two spines are puppy-chewed. There are titles like *Natural History*, *Mankind* and *Law and Order*. I loved *Law and Order* the best. I remember cuddling it happily in bed in the few precious minutes before lights out in the dormitory, a perfect end to my birthday. The housemistress of my junior House, whom I loathed, peered over my shoulder. 'What an extraordinary book,' she remarked coldly. It made me love it, and hate her, all the more. It was full of battleships and tanks, judges and courtrooms (I cherished ambitions of being a barrister at the time) and the history of the Bow Street Runners. There was a picture of Stalin, Churchill and Roosevelt, I think at the Yalta Conference. The tiny black and white photographs were all we had at the time, but the images were so sharp, that one could imagine the characters behind the faces. Perhaps those early encounters with black and white pictures were what led me into press photography many years later, and writing the human stories to explain the images. As for the q.v. references, they would send me for hours on happy chases, only thwarted frustratingly sometimes when I hadn't yet acquired the volume to which they referred.

Later additions to my own little reference library were Roget's *Thesaurus* and the *Oxford Dictionary of English Literature*, both of which I cherish as rare prizes with the school badge embossed in gold. The *Thesaurus* in hardback is rather cumbersome to take around, but the dictionary is ideal for travelling, and has proved a wonderfully compact way of storing plots of plays and books, descriptions of characters, and biographies of authors and poets with lists of their works. I was allowed as a sixth former to work in our school reference library, where of course I found the much larger *Oxford Companion to Literature*, as well as huge French and German dictionaries, much needed by me, and several volumes of *Grove's Dictionary of Music*. One could have looked things up for ever.

The reference library, a single storey brick building, was beautifully designed in an octagonal shape, so that natural light flooded in onto each solid, light oak reading desk. There was a rule of absolute silence, respected by all, and to me it was bliss to find somewhere quiet to work. There was a long table, reserved for only the most senior girls, and a tantalising array of broadsheets and periodicals, which I rarely had time to read, so stretched was I studying German from scratch for A level. Over the library entrance was carved the motto 'Light and Life', and we peeped in longingly from the playground as juniors. Perhaps because it was regarded as such a privilege, we valued our learning in the Sixth Form all the more, especially in the library where we could get used to working on our own, in preparation for university.

There is one other publication which I remember with delight from my teenage years, a modest magazine called the *Elizabethan*. Dull and tame by today's standards, with only limited colours on the A4 cover and the odd black and white picture inside, it had some excellent articles. One was by an ex-Cadet (school leaver) VSO volunteer, then at university, describing his year in the Gilbert and

Ellice Islands. Clearly, every word of his enthusiastic report was true, and when I read the graphic account of his delivering a baby in the back of a Land Rover, I decided that VSO was definitely for me. So at sweet seventeen, I found myself nervously perched on a chair in a smart London office in Hanover Street facing a kindly selection panel including a Lady Somebody who pretended not to notice as the sugar lumps on my precariously balanced teacup and saucer slid to the floor. VSO broke the rules for me about being under eighteen, and that September found me boarding a rickety old Dakota for Malawi for a year – a whole life-changing and totally wonderful experience. So I have much for which to thank that article in the *Elizabethan*, and learning, thanks to my early experiences of non-fiction, is still fun.

8 March 2005

Written for the 'Creative Writing at the Museum' course, Cardiff.

CHAPTER 8

School Chapel

C HAPEL WAS COMPULSORY FOR EVERY girl at Hertford, whatever her religious persuasion, or lack of it, every weekday before lessons, plus Mattins and Evensong every Sunday. The only voluntary service was Holy Communion on Sunday mornings at 8 o' clock, and most of us who had been confirmed, when we were encouraged to make a rule of life, went at least once a fortnight. This required a huge effort of will, as it meant sacrificing the only possible lie-in of the week. As we all confessed our sins, I would glance wonderingly at Miss West kneeling humbly amongst us, yet on her own: what could she possibly have to confess? She was so *good*. Miss West did occasionally take Roman Catholic girls to their own church in Hertford, which must have been quite hard for her Protestant soul, and it was said that they were given a missal instead of a Bible when they left school. There were two distinguished RC head girls in my time, as it happens, Catherine and then Claire Roper Power.

When I started at Hertford in 1957, the chaplain was 'Daddy' Walker, a local parish priest from Great Amwell, I think, who was succeeded by his son. They managed to squeeze in a prayer for the souls of the faithful departed at the very end of Evensong, before making a quick getaway. It was said that Miss West, not being from such a high church Anglican tradition, disapproved.

To a little girl of nine, the Sunday services seemed interminable, especially the sermons, but I grew to love the Anglican liturgy, especially the singing, and the short daily service before lessons was a haven of calm before exams in particular. We learned all the old favourites from *Ancient and Modern* (revised), chanted Psalms regularly from battered navy blue psalters, and belted out wonderful traditional settings of the *Te Deum* or *Magnificat* and *Nunc Dimittis*, the whole school joining in, and one of the thrills of Hertford Old Blues' reunions, beautifully organised by Kerren Simmonds, has been the chance to sing the familiar settings again as a 'scratch' choir (no audition required!) thanks to the efforts of Susan Howell-Evans, a brilliant practising musician.

To reach such a high standard at Hertford, however, the whole school had to endure so-called choir practice once a week, a rather joyless session when Miss Weaver, the organist, would make us all get to grips with the pointing in the Psalms, as she urged us to read ahead, while we all knew that only the élite got into the chapel choir. Twice I auditioned; twice I failed. It nearly broke my heart.

Then there were the eight Organ Girls, who got free organ lessons and learned to accompany services and play voluntaries magnificently, but you had to be good at the piano for that, so I was a non-starter. The nearest I got was to sit at the organ while a friend, Stephanie Etches, I think it was, practised. I was fascinated by the names of all the stops, and awed by the sort of mind which could read the music at a glance, and co-ordinate hands and feet with apparent ease. What a talent, and what a magnificent sound.

The other job I really coveted was as a chapel reader. These were chosen by Miss West, and perhaps she thought I didn't quite have the confidence. I was chosen once to read from the large-print leather Bible in my last year, I think it was, thanks to our Sixth Form mistress, Queenie Blench, and it was a huge thrill. There was no microphone, so you really had to project your voice well, and I have read happily in parish churches ever since.

Despite never getting the plum jobs, I grew to love our chapel. It was red brick, with a very green copper spire, not that imposing from the outside, but after a longing glance to the right at the bright lights of the County Cinema opposite, I found inside that it had a special atmosphere of intimacy, and I especially enjoyed the St Francis window, the sun streaming through it behind the organ and the pulpit, showing up the bright colours of the animals and birds.

Of course we behaved – with our housemistresses sitting in the back pews, the teaching staff at the front behind the choirstalls, and senior girls scattered all around, any misdemeanour could be minutely observed. When a wasp landed on my bare arm once and I let out a little squeak, I was in terrible trouble afterwards with Miss King!

Occasionally we would have a visiting preacher, sometimes a girl's father – many Christ's Hospital children came from clergy families – and I remember Margot Phelps' father, a Methodist minister,

questioning from the pulpit what was sacrosanct about the organ. I
could feel Miss Weaver positively quivering with indignation at this
heresy! I confess I was a little shocked myself. Clearly, Methodists
were not quite like us.

What *we* were like really, I'm still not sure. I suppose the
churchmanship would be thought of as middle-of-the road Anglican-
ism. We were certainly nowhere near the Roman Catholics, who
were said to have tried to get rid of Christ's Hospital in Queen
Mary's reign, and whilst it would have been shockingly Papist
perhaps, to have a statue of the Virgin Mary in chapel, and there was
never a whiff of incense, I absolutely loved the wooden carved figure
of Jesus behind the altar, his head bathed in a golden glow, I guess
from a hidden light bulb. It was a wonderful gesture on Miss West's
part to buy the figure and its carved surround and the altar and have
it all transported to her parish church in Alfriston when our chapel
was tragically demolished to make way for a Tesco car park after the
merger with Housey in 1985. This was when the girls moved to
Horsham. Every single day of my school career, except for one term's
sabbatical, there she had been in her simple, no-nonsense dark felty
hat (did she ever have more than one?) sitting in her Headmistress's
pew by the door, a symbol of solidity and continuity, as we filed past
her on our way out. Now that she has died, it is good to know that
something tangible remains of the Hertford chapel which she loved.

Clearly, many girls have not kept their faith after school, but I'm
still grateful for the grounding which school chapel gave me, have
never lost my Christian beliefs, and remain a lifelong Anglican,
grateful for the breadth and relative tolerance of our tradition. At
school, I loved the two simple candles on the altar at Evensong, and
the blessing which included 'those whom you love', particularly
poignant on a Sunday evening, when homesickness often reached its
peak. Sunday was still thought of very much in those days as a family
day, with no Sunday opening of shops, and a national tradition of
family Sunday lunch, and here we were, separated from our loved
ones at home. Somehow, the break in routine, the tiny bit of free
time on a Sunday, gave us time to brood.

Having time to brood, or at least to reflect, however, is one of the
great benefits of going to church, I believe. It is so important
sometimes to be still. I was fortunate in that however long a weekend

I had worked in the TA or the Army Cadets, I could nearly always make the evening service back home on a Sunday. When desperately busy in one teaching job, and I was tempted to skip church because I had so much marking and preparation to do, I knew that the job was just too much for me. I stuck resolutely to making time for worship, and have never regretted it. I really think it has helped to keep me sane. To be surrounded by sensitive, loving fellow Christians, especially since I have been widowed, and since I discovered St Mark's Gabalfa, where worship is both joyful and thoughtful, has become the most important influence on my life. Our music group, where we singers are often outnumbered by instrumentalists, ranging from highly competent flautists or string players to drummers, is a far cry from the formality of the services in our chapel at Hertford, but it is still a thrill to 'make melody unto the Lord', and that love of worship was nurtured in me at Christ's Hospital. In retrospect, I'm even grateful to Miss Weaver.

CHAPTER 9

Guiding at School

BEING A GIRL GUIDE AT HERTFORD for me represented extraordinary freedom through its outdoor activities. I can still remember the delicious whiff of woodsmoke by the cricket nets on a cloudless summer's evening, and the joy of making dampers – basically a conical wedge of flour mixed with water and stuck on the point of a dampened stick, then cooked over an open fire. With a dab of margarine added, for a hungry CH girl they were a feast.

We learned to gather wood and make an open fire, coaxing the flame into life and cupping our hands to shelter it from any wind because only two matches were allowed: if the fire went out you could fail your skills badge, or worse still, have nothing to eat after all your efforts.

I loved camping, and my friends in the local Guide company in Worthing were kind enough to invite me along. There was a huge feeling of contentment as we sat round the communal camp fire in the evening singing innocent Guide songs, the dew wetting our wellies as we made for our tents. We would sing the traditional Taps with the comforting 'All is well . . . God is nigh.' I also picked up from somewhere Canadian Taps, and tried to teach it to the others:

Softly, at the close of day
As the camp fire dies away.
Silently each Girl Guide asks
Have I done my daily tasks?
Have I kept my honour bright?
Can I guiltless sleep tonight?
Have I done, and have I dared
Everything to Be Prepared?

There was an embarrassed silence from the Guiders which puzzled me at the time. Later I found out why: Canadian Taps was set to the tune of the Red Flag!

I was allowed one year to go to the English Schools' Camp at Foxlease, the Guiding centre in the New Forest. It had a most beautiful outdoor swimming pool, the clear, clear blue of the water complementing the deep blue of the summer evening sky, where I swam length after length of breaststroke. It was bliss. A Guide from another school even admired my style, which was a huge surprise to me as it had taken me years at CH to eradicate a 'screw kick' and Auntie Park awarded me the coveted orange 'stripe' for style at 'Passing', a misnomer in my case as for me it was nearly always 'failing'.

How I admired the CH girls who finally achieved their 'box' by passing at lifesaving as well as breaststroke, front crawl and back crawl, as we called it then. (It was years after I left school before I discovered what a box was in cricket. Girls talking proudly about getting their 'box' might have caused some confusion or amusement to sporty brothers or fathers if the cricket box had been invented by then!). For years, you were not allowed in the deep end at school until you'd achieved your orange stripe for breaststroke, until they introduced an unimposing white stripe, a mean little piece of white tape for those whose style wasn't good enough but who were eventually considered safe enough to enter the deep end, beyond the springy coir 'jumping in' bridge which separated the deep and shallow ends.

Apart from the lovely swimming pool, Foxlease provided a good opportunity for girls from boarding schools from a wide geographical area to come together. We also honed many of our camping skills. Gadget-making was taken frightfully seriously and I can remember perching precariously over a bowl behind some musty-smelling canvas screening. The bowl rested on three sticks that we had lashed together with string, and we were on our honour to carry out the daily all-over wash.

Fearsome senior Guiders would dangle a plumb line to test that the central pole in the bell tent was absolutely vertical, but after CH inspections of all sorts I found Foxlease a piece of cake and even won some sort of Best Camper award again.

More challenging was an Easter camp I volunteered for with a friend from Worthing to help her qualify for her Queen's Guide badge. It was bitterly cold and wet and as we huddled over our camp fire with what damp sticks we'd managed to gather locally, she pronounced cheerfully, 'I suppose this is fun, but oh what soggy fun!' The white kapok sleeping bag my hard-up mother had given me felt woefully thin, but the local Commissioner doing the assessing, a hearty, well-built woman, told us bracingly to put newspaper (which in our case we had not got, to misquote that wonderful poem 'Naming of Parts' by World War II poet, Henry Reed) under us against the cold. When I peeped into her tent and beheld the luxury of a camp bed suspended well above the ground I sensed all the indignation a soldier can feel if a senior officer has warmer or more waterproof uniform or equipment than he or she has been issued with, and I later came to appreciate our officer training which taught us to suffer, and be seen to suffer, with our men – or women – by wearing the same kit. Despite, or because of the cold, I enjoyed it in some funny way and felt proud to have stuck out that Easter weekend camp. I can still remember the joy of the early morning Communion service with my Guide friends in the beautiful old Sussex church, the sun streaming in through the window above the altar.

Guiding in England was unquestioningly Christian in those days as we promised 'on our honour to do our best to do our duty to God and the Queen'. On Remembrance Sunday, we paraded proudly at the Cenotaph in Hertford, and after all our marching practice at school and in our navy regulation woollen school coats, we felt infinitely smarter than the town Guides and other youth organisations and even than the TA and army cadets. I remember the solemnity of 'O God our help in ages past' in the biting November morning air, and in the two minute silence wishing fervently that my father had died a hero in the war, although as a 1947 baby I would have been just too young for that. In fact, I found out only recently that he had served as a Chindit in Burma as very young man, nearly dying at the time from the tropical diseases he'd picked up in the jungle and from which he never fully recovered, so he'd certainly done his bit in the war and suffered for it.

God, Queen and Country – I knew I was hooked. I believed in them all, and still do, although perhaps not quite in the unquestioning way that I did as a child. I was immensely proud of my mother who, of course, had served in the war in the British Army as a nursing sister, and as a small child playing soldiers in her battledress had coveted her pips and her medal ribbons and promised myself even then, I think, that I would carry on the family military tradition.

In many ways, Guiding, like CH, was a good preparation for the army, although rather kinder than the military to its junior members.

You had to press your Guide uniform, and fold your tie, which doubled as a triangular bandage, in the prescribed manner, and polish your belt and shoes and cap badge. Getting ready for inspection, and following our 'Be Prepared' motto, we would stuff the statutory notebook and pencil and four old pennies for a telephone call and other goodies into our breast pockets, despite some giggling about the extra shape it gave already buxom girls. Guide captains in bulky Civil Defence-type serge jackets urged us to give hot sweet tea to our first aid 'victims' and in that post-war era and before the days of nil-by-mouth teaching in first aid, it all seemed perfectly sensible and logical to me: black and white photographs of cheerful W.V.S. ladies dispensing tea to dazed young soldiers rescued from Dunkirk still felt very real.

A particular joy of becoming a patrol leader at CH was being invited to our Guide captain's home in Hertford for a 'patrol leaders' meeting'. A kindly lady, and not on the school staff, she made this an excuse for giving us a magnificent afternoon tea, untold luxury for us hungry boarders used to simple CH rations.

Being in the Guides gave us many legitimate excuses for getting off the school site, and I'll always be grateful for the experience. However, the crunch for me came one afternoon in the Upper Fifth, I think it was, at an enrolment ceremony, a solemn affair held in the gym. As the Colours were marched on, they got stuck in some ropes hooked up to the wall, and to my shame, I got the giggles. I suddenly realised that I was growing out of Guides and decided to opt instead for the Duke of Edinburgh's Award, something I never regretted, as again, it involved all sorts of outdoor expeditions, but organised by ourselves.

A group of us had a memorable trip to Stratford to see all Shakespeare's history plays at the RSC, and I seem to remember the young Ian Holm as a brilliantly evil Richard III. We stayed at the youth hostel and technically we hadn't hiked quite far enough, I think, to qualify for the expedition section of the award, but Miss West, having clearly agonised about it, signed our books as we had written such good reports. I was totally bowled over by the experience of live theatre, and it has been a thrill to celebrate our fiftieth and sixtieth birthdays with fellow Hertford Old Blues back at the RSC.

Another delight of our Gold Award was working on my Aunt Jean and Uncle Johnny's farm in Suffolk with three other sixth formers. We went for a week, and loved Old Church Farm so much that we asked to stay an extra week. With three small children by then, Jeannie had two of us helping in the house, while the other two worked on the farm. She had to write reports on us, and Miss West had asked me in all seriousness beforehand, 'Is your aunt an honest woman, Susan?' When I relayed this at the farmhouse lunch table, there were shrieks of laughter from Jeannie, but it was years before I realised the other meaning of 'an honest woman'! How innocent we were.

The 'D. of E.' syllabus was very broad even then, and the scheme was good in so many ways and helped us to grow up; yet I shall always treasure those early memories of Guiding. And Be Prepared is still a pretty good motto for life.

CHAPTER 10

The Flat

ONE SUNNY JANUARY MORNING in my Upper Sixth year Miss West stopped me on the Square. Would I like to move to the flat? I was overjoyed. Living there was a recent innovation, reserved for Senior Sixth girls and a handful in their A level year, and I couldn't believe my luck. Situated next to the school hall, our flat was at the very top of the steward's house, a beautiful old building, full of character. We had three double bedrooms in my time, one occupied by Kathleen Dale, our popular and much respected head girl. There was a sitting room and a minute kitchen where, oh bliss, we could make a snack at any hour of the day or night. Standing by the little gas ring, the sun streaming in through the window under the eaves, I felt a delicious sense of independence, and anticipated the delights of student life to come. Perhaps best of all, our flat had *two* bathrooms; showers were non-existent in those days. Suddenly, after years of being restricted to a weekly hair wash, or fortnightly if we had a cold, as juniors in the communal washbasins in the House cloakroom, in the flat we could wash our hair every day, luxuriating in the bath for a few precious minutes longer than in House, where baths were limited to three nights a week, and always a rushed affair followed by a quick scrub with Gumption as the other girls queued up. The difference to morale of having both a little privacy and constantly clean, shiny hair was indescribable.

The only downside to the flat was that Miss Richards occupied the one below, and she would come storming up if she thought that we were making too much noise or were a fraction late in returning from a coffee party – and it was impossible to creep up the ancient winding stairs in our clodhopping school issue outdoor shoes unheard. The coffee party, always with one or two of our Sixth Form mistresses, in their own quarters on site, was an innocuous enough affair, although one girl, I remember, now a consultant surgeon, found the whole business of small talk such agony that she would carefully construct a list of 'safe' topics of conversation before each event! I loved it myself, getting to know these intelligent women and appreciating their humanity, but it can only be imagined what trouble the 'offending' members of staff might have found themselves in the next day for keeping us flat-dwellers out even a minute or two late.

Despite Miss Richards' complaints, however, and her clearly feeling *in loco parentis* – irksome to us senior girls at the time – and despite our still having house monitresses' and school prefects' duties, Chapel and games every day, and of course A level or S level exams looming, the flat represented unimagined freedom after life in House, and because of it, my last two terms at school were immensely happy. Even the dreaded school needlework garment felt less painful to sew in bed as we nattered into the night. At last we began to feel a little grown up – and to be treated as such most of the time. University began to feel like a real possibility. Life was good.

Leaving Hertford

IT WAS JULY 1965. My last few days at Hertford were both exciting and harrowing. My grandmother, on seeing the teaching staff floating around in their hoods and gowns had exclaimed delightedly to my mother at prize giving, 'O, my dear, *pure* Joyce Grenfell,' but I think that we girls took the staff pretty seriously at the time – we *had* to – and academic dress certainly appealed to me as a symbol of success after school.

At my final prize giving, I had the thrill of receiving my Duke of Edinburgh's Gold Award badge from Sir John Hunt, and also the Robertson Gift for service to the school, nicknamed 'The Good Girl Prize'. It is a crumb of comfort now, having lost our beautiful hall at Hertford, to find my name, amongst many other girls', on one of the honours boards preserved in the Counting House, the administrative centre at Housey, an evocative piece of Hertford history.

The Charge

I charge you never to forget the great benefits you have received in this place, and in time to come, according to your means, to do all that you can to enable others to enjoy the same advantage, and remember that you carry with you, wherever you go, the good name of Christ's Hospital. May God Almighty bless you in your ways and keep you in the knowledge of His love, now and for ever.

On top of prize giving came the Leaving Service in Chapel. All through the school I had longed for that moment of collecting my Bible from the headmistress, and leaving the school with honour, having 'done my time', but when it actually came, I wished myself back in the First Form again so as not to have to go through the ordeal for another nine years. Miss West read 'The Charge' with great solemnity, and suddenly the enormity of leaving the shelter of Christ's Hospital hit me and I dissolved into tears, like many other girls before me, in front of the whole school and all the staff. Being a monitress, I was also given a Book of Common Prayer. Both it and my Bible, in beautiful black leather, pages edged in gold, again with the school badge in gold, remain almost untouched but treasured in their original maroon boxes. To me they are too precious to use on a daily basis, but I was impressed to see former head girl, and in my time maths mistress Miss Joy Holmes, who, rather radically, was allowed to lead us keen sixth formers in voluntary Bible Study sessions in the geography room, using her Leaver's Bible all the time, saying simply, as I remember, 'What else is it for?'

The leaving girls at Hertford were at least spared the emotion which followed the Leaving Service for our Housey brothers in a final 'Beating Retreat' by the band, but there were many similarities in the service itself, and it is a great credit to Miss Jean Taverner, our inspired organist in my final days at Hertford, that her 'Hertford Grace' has been incorporated now into the Housey Leaving Service, which of course is for all leaving pupils, boys and girls. We used to sing the Bach setting of 'May the Grace of Christ our Saviour' as a winter vesper, two simple candles on the altar, which was such a comfort and delight to me that I chose it for our wedding and for my husband Michael's Memorial Service in Llandaff Cathedral, but now I have grown to love the Taverner setting too. To me the last two lines, 'And possess in sweet communion/Joys which earth cannot afford' were special. I don't think I really understood the meaning of 'afford' in the sense of 'provide', we schoolgirls all being so hard up that I read it in the financial sense, but I think now that perhaps it can be meant either way.

After the Leaving Service, we went round to say goodbye and thank you to all the staff. I shall never forget Mrs Johnson, the physics mistress, who had noticed my distress in Chapel, and comforted me by telling me simply, 'Well, Susan, remember that it's those who feel the most pain who also experience the greatest joy.' She is dead now, but I've always held on to those words through the darkest times. As for The Charge, it is probably partly the reason that so many Old Blues go on, like me, to become Donation Governors, wanting to give another child a chance, however limited the family's means, of a Christ's Hospital education.

Ten of us Hertford leavers had one last rite of passage: CH, Hertford had been one of the first girls' schools to run the Duke of

Edinburgh's Award, thanks to Miss West, and ten of us in our year were invited with our parents to Buckingham Palace to receive our certificates. My mother had made me a pretty bright pink dress and coat, the cotton satin floral lining of the coat matching the dress, and I found a huge straw hat to match the coat. Prince Philip made a beeline for my hat, and spoke to me. We explained that all ten of us were from CH, and he was clearly impressed. Then one of the twins, Gill or Jack Clarke, ruined the effect by saying that getting our Gold Award had been easy. For me it had been a real struggle, fitting in all the syllabus on top of three time-demanding A level subjects. We had been taught first aid and home nursing – useful to this day. I had worked once a week in an old people's home as well as on the farm for a fortnight. Then there was playing my cello, brass rubbing, producing a 'Design for Living' scrapbook, and of course that wonderful week discovering the RSC at Stratford. The Award syllabus for the girls was not nearly as physical as for the boys in those days, but as my mother said, to fulfil the requirements in all sections certainly demonstrated 'stickability', a quality that I've certainly needed throughout my life.

PART II

Gap Year and University

CHAPTER 12

Malawi

AFTER THE PALACE I HAD a few weeks to prepare for my year in Malawi. Miss West had given me a grant of £25, I think it was, a fortune to me at the time, to get myself kitted out, and when I thanked her, she replied, 'Well, I heard that the boys (from Horsham) were getting it when they went on VSO, and I thought you should have it too.' I was in fact the first CH girl to go on VSO as a school leaver, and it was fun being something of a trailblazer. At last my needlework skills felt useful as I ran up cotton slips and dresses, guided by my mother and Big Susan who had both served in the Tropics in the war.

Departure day arrived. We VSOs met at Victoria, and a Yorkshire lad sat on his suitcase and declared glumly, 'I don't know why I bloody well volunteered.' (It sounded less rude with a northern accent!). I, on the other hand, couldn't wait to be off. I hugged my mother happily at Gatwick, and she admitted only when I was safely home a year later, that seeing me through the departure doors had felt just like the crematorium. I never realised how important my aerogrammes home must have been to her until our elder son Ben took off for Uganda in his gap year, and we had to rely largely on his airmail letters for news. He and his excited fellow Right Hand Trust volunteer missioners left from Heathrow one bleak New Year's Day, and I can still remember the sense of desolation after he'd gone.

We VSOs back in 1965 had a stop at Khartoum, where the searing night heat and silent Arabs poised menacingly on every corner with small arms made me very glad to take off for Salisbury, as it was then. Here those of us for Malawi changed to a tiny Beaver, and it was quite thrilling watching the landscape below as we lurched through pockets of turbulence. We landed at Blantyre to be met by members of the British High Commission and British Council, my grey linen striped dress looking sadly crumpled in the official group photograph. The last lap was by pickup truck to Malosa, about twenty miles north of Zomba. There were four of us new VSOs bound for the school, Martin Hollins, a graduate with a first from Birmingham, Diana

Leach, a trained teacher, and Margaret (*MacPherson?*), a fellow school leaver, or 'Cadet Volunteer', as we were called.

I wrote the following piece for Helen Dunmore in her creative writing class at Pontypridd in about 1992:

Malawi Mission Home 1965–1966

Barely twelve by nine feet square of whitewashed bungalow with a thatched roof that cools in the sun and leaks in the rains. Plastic bowl sits on top of battered wardrobe to catch drips.

Two scratched iron beds with mosquito nets much mended which keep me from room-mate in a peaceful, private cocoon. A gently spluttering hurricane lamp between us with pinky-golden light brings comfort through the smoky tapered glass.

Basic sink with cold tap. Water spurts out reddish-brown sometimes. Sometimes doesn't come out at all.

A few cotton clothes, a few books, precious photographs and writing materials. All I need for a whole year. Bliss.

Margaret and I were to share the little bedroom described above, plus adjoining sitting room, occupied previously by boys, and our first job on arrival was to cobble together the areas of mosquito nets where we found gaping holes. She still got malaria pretty badly despite our sewing efforts and regular prophylactic tablets, Paludrine and Daraprim, and I certainly had the odd nasty unexplained fever. We couldn't have been more different in background and temperament, Margaret having been to a co-educational Edinburgh day school, and much more worldly-wise than I, but we co-existed easily enough.

We lived at the top of the hill, near the girls' dormitories, and were ruled over by Miss Evelyn Orford, former headmistress of The Tiffin Girls' School, who had come out, like fellow Brit Lawrence Lees as a USPG (United Society for the Propagation of the Gospel) missionary, he as headmaster, and she as his deputy. She instantly put me in charge of distribution of 'chim' (lavatory) paper to the girls, and would check up if I had remembered this task by asking me at supper in front of everyone else in the Mess, much to my embarrassment. She clearly didn't realise how conscientious we CH girls had been trained to be. She was very much in the mould of some of our more senior mistresses at Hertford, however, and you knew exactly where you were with her, and her air of slight aloofness hid,

I think, a kind lady. Mr Lees, in comparison, had an easier manner. He had been in the British Army, and served as a missionary in Pakistan before coming to Malosa, and I found him extremely kind and a delight to work for.

The Mess was housed in the same building as our quarters, and we had a tremendous welcome at our first meal, especially from Maurice Carver, a delightful retired head from a school in Rhodesia, who was about to marry Mary, niece of Sir Humphrey Gibb, the Governor General there. I loved them both dearly. Then we had three Peace Corps Volunteers (PCVs), and Jeff Schiffmeyer, our American school chaplain in his grey cassock. I tried on one occasion, when not quite so new, to introduce them to our CH 'Grace before Meat', and just about got to the end despite snorts from the astonished PCVs, but when I started on 'Blessed Lord' at the end, we were all reduced to helpless laughter by what they saw as the anachronistic language, which we as schoolgirls had taken as just part of normal life, although I hadn't always felt entirely grateful for the charitable benevolence after 'toenail slush' (apple pie) or boiled cod.

Grace before Meat:

> Give us thankful hearts, O Lord God, for the table which thou hast spread for us; bless Thy good creatures to our use and us to Thy service, for Jesus Christ His sake.

Grace after Meat:

> Blessed Lord, we yield Thee hearty praise and thanksgiving for our Founder and Benefactors, by whose charitable benevolence Thou has refreshed our bodies at this time. So season and refresh our souls with Thy Heavenly Spirit that we may live to Thy honour and glory. Protect Thy Church, the Queen and all the Royal Family and preserve us in peace and truth through Christ our Saviour.

The Mess was also used for Compline, the late evening service, always quiet and dignified, which we often said together round the table by the light of a single oil lamp, and the traditional language made me feel peaceful and safe. Where we lived at the top of the hill was close to the parish church, too, and I could follow the liturgy, if not the language, with Fr Rashidi, I think it was, presiding, and my enduring memory is of the mixed aroma of incense and wood smoke and all the mothers sitting on the floor breastfeeding their babies as they sang.

I loved Malosa. I suppose by modern standards we enjoyed quite a colonial lifestyle, with a houseboy to wash and iron our clothes and a chef to produce every meal. 'Mr Willie', as he liked to be called, had cooked, it was said, for the Officers' Mess of the King's African Rifles, which became the Malawi Rifles. He could do wonders with a charcoal oven. He was a big, burly Malawian, and I always kept out of his way and blocked my ears when the chickens that I had brought from Zomba Market squawking in the back of the ancient Peugeot pickup were about to be dispatched by him with a huge knife in preparation for our supper, which was always excellent, with plenty of fresh tropical fruit. The only direct effect on food for us of UDI in nearby Southern Rhodesia, as Zimbabwe was then known, was a lack of icing sugar – a great frustration to him. I can still remember his delight when I managed to find some icing sugar for him again and he produced a huge cake proudly decorated with the words 'Mr Willie's Cake'.

It was a simple life, and I enjoyed equally the brilliant sunshine and the rainy season, sloshing though the mud in flip-flops and a nylon mac. Our luggage allowance had been only 55lbs for the aeroplane, so we could pack very few clothes, and fashion really wasn't a consideration, although I always envied the Peace Corps girls their superior fabrics which didn't seem to crease. We VSOs had been told to bring a pair of nylons for our evening at the British High Commission, and that was probably the highlight of our social calendar in the whole year.

We did, however, have a good social life, living and working with decent, kindly people on Likwenu Mission where Malosa was based. The mission included an ecumenical lay training centre, hospital and a leprosarium, as well as the school, and the Bishop of Malawi, Donald Arden, was based there. We young women could be summoned by Jane Arden, a formidable lady, to her sewing bees, very much a royal command, which, with my good CH training I took as perfectly natural. John Leake, an Anglican priest, and Richard Baxter, a Presbyterian minister, ran the lay training centre, and I remember a very helpful 'Preparation for Marriage' course where even sex was covered – certainly not on the CH curriculum in my day – and a beautiful outdoor service there when at the point of receiving the bread and wine we had to break off, as inter-Communion was not yet allowed. It was extremely painful.

Since it was a USPG mission, which had grown out of the UMCA (Universities' Mission to Central Africa) tradition, it was quite high Anglican, and we even observed the angelus in school every day, with a simple ringing of a bell, which I found curiously comforting, to pause and be quiet even for a few seconds at noon. The school chapel was a long, simple, thatched building, said to be riddled with ants which would literally be its downfall, but it certainly survived my year there, and I can remember kneeling on my own there to give thanks when I heard through one of the precious aerogrammes from home of my university place at York.

There was no keyboard of any sort, and we sang all the good old C of E hymns unaccompanied with huge spirit, the pupils, 100 boys and 100 girls sounding wonderful to me, as they broke into spontaneous harmony. They were not all children by any means, as a whole village would sometimes save up to pay the £20-a-year school fees to send a student to Malosa, and we certainly had in our classes some very mature-looking young men.

I was asked to teach French and English (as a foreign language) and to run all the girls' games, as well as working in the school office. Education was considered to be a privilege, and although the pupils played up sometimes, compared with British secondary classes that I sometimes had to face later as a qualified teacher, the Malosa pupils were a delight.

It was not all work. There were play readings among the staff, and 'aeroplane tray' meals on Mr Lees' verandah, and he would march us up Zomba Mountain and treat us to a fish meal at the top. The fish from Lake Malawi was delicious, and lager and lime was a special treat after the exertion of the climb.

I also climbed the 10,000ft Mount Mlanje with a mixed group of Brits and Americans, just in tennis shoes, shorts and top. We were led by a confident Englishman who strode on ahead, not guiding us less experienced climbers at all. I found it fairly terrifying in places where the vegetation which had been struck by lightning came off in my hands as we scrambled, or there were gaps of several feet in the rocks where the only thing to do was to leap across. A PCV called

Craig Gjerde kindly stuck with me at the rear and told me when we finally got back safely that I'd 'hung on real good.' Out of this a sweet friendship developed, and I was thrilled by his music system, very advanced to me, where I could listen to Peter, Paul and Mary (great stars at the time) in stereo through his headphones. The friendship fizzled out when I left Malawi. Craig, already a graduate, told me firmly, 'You must go back home to school, little girl', school of course meaning college in his language, and he was right. University was the goal I'd set myself, and I had to go through with it, however homesick for Malawi I might be at first.

CHAPTER 13

Coming Home

Gatwick

'Beneath you, ladies and gentlemen
On your right
You can see the lights of Paris.'
Paris – Europe – excitement of civilization
Piercing through the dim mistiness
Of the night. I press my nose eagerly
Against the obdurate glass,
Tense with excitement, waiting, waiting.
Suddenly more lights, and then a murky greyness:
The sea! The channel, the English Channel.
I can almost smell the strong salt smell
So strong, so manly, after the soft feminine sweetness of tropical lake.

More lights, and then we are losing height
circling, circling.
Can this myriad of multicoloured light
Really be Gatwick, and am I home?
Tense seconds as we touch the strip of tarmac
And slowly come to rest.

Shakily I go down the ladder
Drift through endless fluorescent halls
Dazed, and curiously happy, exultant,
But chiefly I am grateful. I am home.

I walk through the huge booming entrance hall
And see a policeman – the first English one for a year.
There are tears in my eyes.

I creep outside savouring with ecstasy
The stiff freshness of an English morning
And the grey promise of an English dawn
And the green green of the grass
Unbelievably green after the dull muddy colourlessness

Of an African country.
I am unutterably thrilled.
   I am home.

3 September 1967

Also returned from VSO was Hugh, who had served in Chad. We had written across the Sahara all year, and before he got a serious girlfriend we had a happy few weeks meeting in London, where his father was the chaplain at Mill Hill, doing Proms together. What a thrill to stand in steamy silence breathlessly listening for the next note, jammed in with so many other young music enthusiasts, almost, it felt, on top of the orchestra. Afterwards, we would run hand in hand through the streets for me to get the last train back to Worthing, and I can remember my first real kiss on Victoria Station as the train was about to pull out. Inevitably, I suppose, we drifted apart when he went up to Oxford and I to York, but I shall always be grateful for that first love. Miss West had also been surprisingly trusting, allowing me to go out alone with Hugh in Hertford, after we had met on our VSO orientation course the Easter before we left school. For those days at CH, Hertford, it was certainly pretty enlightened.

Chapter 14

University

THE NIGHT BEFORE I STARTED at York I had a sudden crisis of confidence. Was I really clever enough for university? My mother had driven us up, and she, Big Susan and I stayed in a little B&B in the shadow of the Minster. I had not actually seen the Heslington campus before and I was surprised to find myself in Langwith College in a three-bedded room – an architectural mistake, apparently. While Isabel from Northallerton, away from home for the first time, sat on her bed and howled after her family had left, our more sophisticated roommate from a smart north London girls' day school showed her disdain for us by carefully locking her expensive china coffee set in a cupboard so no-one else could use it. It was not set to be a happy threesome, particularly when the coffee set girl quickly acquired a boyfriend whom we would come back in the evening to find in bed with her. It was disconcerting to clean my teeth, being observed, I felt, by him. She also resented the intrusion, as she saw it, and so erected a newspaper screen across her third of the room. Eventually she started behaving so oddly that even the college staff noticed, and she was moved out to a single room where she could entertain her lover for the statutory fine of 50p a night, which she – and he – could well afford.

After that came Claire Powell, and a much more harmonious time followed, she converting Isabel to active Christianity though the Christian Union. Claire was a sweet girl, although I went through a slightly bolshie phase when I would come back from acting in the chorus in a Greek tragedy to find Claire, Isabel and other CU friends in our room, engrossed in an earnest Bible study, which I found rather disconcerting at the time.

I had also joined the Officers' Training Corps (OTC), where friends were certainly less overtly holy than in the CU, and training inevitably took me away from York at weekends. People ask me why I joined, and it was through the Societies Fair, with a bewildering array of activities on offer. Each appeared to cost 50p to join (serious money to me at the time) whereas the OTC paid about 75p a day in new money (worth much more then, of course) to wear the Queen's uniform as an officer cadet, with a big pay rise if you got commissioned. There was little contest! We students at York and Bradford, being new universities, had to join the well established Leeds University OTC, and a York undergraduate and fellow VSO called Barry drove us potential recruits to a party there in the Mess the next night. He had got his PSV licence through the army, which impressed me in itself, and as I had already been thinking of the army as a career, discovering the OTC felt like manna from heaven. The officers were very welcoming, and there was a sense of order and courtesy in the Mess rather different from the Junior Common Room, which appealed.

I couldn't believe my luck: here I was, being driven in the back of draughty old Land Rovers or 4-tonners into the spectacular countryside of the north-east, to wild, open sites in Otterburn or Warcop, scattered with sheep and daffodils, fed *free* filling food either in mess tins in the field, surprisingly hot straight out of a haybox, or back in camp, and even being paid. It was a huge adventure. Even the barrack rooms in Nissen huts or 'spiders' were fun, if nippy, we girls all in our late teens trying to coax the old coke stove into giving off a little heat, and laughing at the silliness as we saw it of parades and bull. It was so cold that I remember one girl, another Sue, going to bed in full combat kit, which she had carefully embroidered on the collar with pink flowers. She had emerged warm but crumpled in the morning, and we waited with stifled giggles for the RSM's (*Jack Warren, the Regimental Sergeant Major*) wrath to descend. To our disappointment he barely seemed to react, and simply told her, 'Unofficial embellishments will *not* be worn, Miss . . .' (*McWhinney?*)

Yet gradually it dawned on me that it wasn't *all* silly, and if I wanted to be an officer I would need to start working hard, make a real effort with my kit and start taking some responsibility. I went on a commissioning course at the Women's Royal Army Corps College at Camberley, and managed somehow to impress the senior Ma'ams enough to pass, despite an ultra feminine but terrifying five-foot nothing blonde colonel who tore our teaching practices apart, one by one. The day I went for my Selection Board at Imphal Barracks in York, 21 January 1968 and was awarded a TAVR (Territorial Army

17. *Wartime romance: Major George Philip 'Joe' Fox RAMC marries my godmother, Sister Evelyn Mary 'Paddy' Lloyd QAIMNS. Both trained at the London Hospital*

18. *Army friends: The marriage of Captain Richard Seton-Browne and Miss Elisabeth Simpson. Edinburgh, 1954*

19. At my Aunt Jean's wedding in Eltham, aged 4, with fellow bridesmaid Ann Walker. 5 July 1952

20. Mike D-J with his parents Gerald and Sybil. Aberystwyth late 1960s

21. *Arriving at Bishop Gundulph Church with my grandfather Brigadier Charles 'Tug' Wilson, late Glosters and Royal Army Educational Corps. Chattenden 14 April 1973*

22. *Bridesmaids L-R: chief bridesmaid Kate Greenwood; cousin Helen Johnson; Ellen Hodgson; Sarah Hodgson (later Ben D-J's godmother)*

23. *Family group: L-R Stephen Jones, Nicholas Jones, Auntie Nell (Jones), my mother, Mrs Eileen Wilson, Michael and Sue Davies-Jenkins, Grandpa and Granny Wilson, Auntie Win (Jones), Michael's cousin Mrs Barbara Jones ('Bardy') with husband Eric and AuntieVi (Jones)*

24. Sir Winston Churchill's funeral 30 January 1965. In the crowd (in school uniform, bottom left) on Ludgate Hill awaiting the arrival of the funeral procession © The Times and 1 February 1965/nisyndication.com

25. Marriage of Hertford Old Blue and art mistress Rosemary Esch to Douglas Whiting, Director of VSO. Wedding dress in peau de soie made by Rosemary's sister-in-law Jane

26. Family sadness: wafer box given to St Botolph's Church, Cambridge in memory of our firstborn son (stillborn). Box made by David Kindersleys Workshop, Cambridge

27. Family joy: father Mike Davies-Jenkins in Anglesey with baby Alexandra Katherine 'Katie' Davies-Jenkins, born 19 July 1976 at Cambridge Maternity Hospital

28. More family joy: Katie shows grandfather Gerald her little brother Benedict Morgan Davies-Jenkins (born 11 February 1978 at St David's Hospital, Bangor, Gwynedd)

29. Headmaster of the Cathedral School, Llandaff, Mr John Knapp, with his cathedral chorister son Edward

30. *Former vicar of Holy Trinity, Aberystwyth, later Bishop of Llandaff, the Rt Revd Roy Davies with Holy Trinity choirboy Benedict Davies-Jenkins (8) who had just won a choral scholarship to Llandaff. Pictured at Holy Trinity's Centenary, 1986*

31. *All in the family: another former Holy Trinity choirboy, Ben's brother Will (11) newly promoted to Dean's Scholar in Llandaff Cathedral Choir, pictured by the Garden of Remembrance where their father's ashes were to be buried on 10 April 1999*

Volunteer Reserve) commission was really the turning point in my happiness as an undergraduate – I suddenly had a sense of self-worth again.

This letter written at the beginning of my second term at York, which presumably I didn't then have the courage to send, probably marks my lowest ebb as an undergraduate. It seems to have been written on 4 January 1967, when I was just nineteen.

Mummy darling,

I feel I must apologise to you both for having been so moody this holiday. I feel I must have appeared so cocky, so unbearably arrogant, and every time I argue with you I hate myself for it, because honestly, I *do* care what you say.

The thing is, I'm still clinging to an illusion – at least most people would call it that. I believe in the ideal of youth – the ultimate state of civilization where everyone will be happy. I know that it won't happen in my lifetime, but I believe we must live in the hope of it. People tell me that as I grow older I'll grow wiser. I'm terrified they really mean cynical. I can't bear cynicism. We *must* believe in the value of goodness and beauty.

Now I know that you and Big Susan share these beliefs and you are both achieving more in your lives than I ever will probably, but when you talk about the good old days, I just have to defend my generation as you defend yours. This loyalty to my contemporaries is, I know, quite irrational. For instance, what earthly reason prompted me to spring to the defence of Marion Tinsall, a girl whom I've never even met? Simply that we, as young people, have in common the longing for responsibility, and at the same time lack the confidence in ourselves. I know we appear to be bursting with confidence, longing to impress, but naturally we are basically unsure. We feel we are being judged by our elders, and they are convinced that our standards aren't as high. This is why I feel so impractical under your experienced eyes. I anticipate criticism and resent guidance – and loathe myself for my stubbornness.

Then there is the question of the student's position in society. At university we are taught to question everything – this is our job – but the moment we criticise things we have the fact that we're dependent hurled at us. I wish I could be earning my living, so that I could face the challenge of making ends meet and making a home, but since I have the unique opportunity of studying something I love, I feel I would bitterly regret having wasted it. I also feel that you think I despise people doing a routine job. I don't in the least, I admire them, but it still does upset me very much to see people unhappy in their work. I am appalled at the thought of being a slave to money. When you said I'd join the N.U.T. and strike for money, I was horrified. Because, you see, I've only taught at Malosa where all the staff were there because they wanted to be and were passionately interested in their job and their pupils. We wanted to give our very best. I still want to, and I believe that my generation wants to – if it's given the chance.

I feel that you must think young people today very bolshie and disrespectful. But the fact that we are less inhibited and bolder is surely an indication of our teachers' attitude. They do not want subservience or unthinking respect. And that is why I argue so much – it is the only way I can get things straight in my own mind. I'm sorry you happen to be the guinea-pig. The wisest guinea-pig I've met yet, and I jolly well need you as a guideline.

So, all I can do is to be a responsible student. Please forgive me all my folly and stubbornness and inexperience, and believe that I'd carry the whole weight of the world on my shoulders, if only I were able.

Sue.

I was clearly more cheerful by the time I wrote this next letter to my godmother Paddy and her husband, Dr 'Joe' Fox, who had met in the army in the war. Paddy was my mother's greatest chum from their nurse training at the London Hospital.

18 Feversham Crescent
York
12 November 1967

Dear Paddy and Joe,

I've just realised with horror that I never wrote to thank you for your cheque and birthday card, and for returning my Commission form so promptly. Anyway, it was lovely to hear from you, and the cheque will be more than useful . . .

I was very military today: there was a Remembrance Day parade in Leeds, and for the first time in years the OTC took part. Apparently we were the only lot who could have been taken for Regulars, but then you should have seen the competition! I knew the T.A. could be scruffy, but they were worse than I could possibly have imagined. There were no regular soldiers and we really enjoyed the marching and I felt very proud in front of 'the unwashed thousands' as our RSM calls the spectators. He's a good bloke, and has the most wonderful sense of humour. He'd make anyone do his best.

Well, apart from military activities I'm also busy trying to fit in hockey, philosophy, psychology, Chaucer and French symbolist poetry – oh yes, and housework, to mention only a few activities. My academic work is extraordinarily diverse this term, although switching from mediaeval alliterative poetry to the use of psychology to the teacher can be tricky. This is always the problem of doing a combined course, but I'm very glad I'm doing education. Yet another commitment this term is an attachment to a youth club. At the moment I go every week to coach netball. I hope gradually to get into play reading, as it's a marvellous club for the athletic types but the others tend to get very bored . . .

If ever you're up here, you must come and see our flat, only let us know and we'll try and get tidy. Actually if we weren't always washing it wouldn't be so chaotic. However, it's very much a home and we love it. It's about fifteen minutes' sweaty bike ride from the university and a bit more if I take it easily. Normally I go pretty fast. The nicest thing is coming into the warm at night. We have a coal fire in the kitchen and so we all tend to work in there. The fire heats the water which saves the immersion, but we're awaiting the electricity bill with some trepidation. Still, we've paid the rent for the rest of term, so we should be fine.

I'm hoping to go to Czechoslovakia for about ten days after Christmas so I'm trying to save. It's an exchange with Prague University and we'd spend three days in Prague and the rest ski-ing. Twenty students from York can go so I got my name down quickly. I'm dying to see just how intense Communist suppression is. I've heard stories (I think true) that 'subversive' books which it is illegal to print are written out by hand and passed round furtively amongst students. I wonder what the Czechs will think of York when they come in May. In our university virtually nothing is frowned on officially and of course absolute freedom of speech both verbally and in print is taken for granted. I don't think I approve of this entirely – there's a very narrow gap between tolerance and moral cowardice. Sorry, that looks like a piece of muddled arguing. What I mean is that both in print and in conversation there's a great deal of criticism of 'them', who are normally the university authorities or other students, but very few people have the guts (or is it audacity?) to criticise others to their faces. Everybody is superficially friendly. The trouble is that one is forced in one's work as well as socially to question values which before one held as sacred.

'There are no absolute values' is the cry from my education tutor (a headmaster of a local grammar school, incidentally).

'Then what are we to teach our pupils or our children?' I ask. 'Are we simply to give them no moral guidance and let them make their own mistakes?' That's when he starts hedging. It's very tricky. I've decided that I've just got to have some values and stick to them and just go on respecting my friends for their good qualities.

Draft of letter abandoned here.

As early as May 1968, I was considering joining the Royal Army Educational Corps (RAEC), and the concept of women wearing the RAEC cap badge rather than the WRAC one, was pretty revolutionary at the time. This is a fragment of a letter to an RAEC University Liaison Officer, Major John Chown, I think, which I must have decided not to send, mercifully perhaps. I was prescient, though, in imagining women in the army back in khaki as the ATS (Auxiliary Territorial Service, forerunners of the WRAC) were in the Second World War. I guess that women medical officers had always worn khaki, but they were such a rare breed then that I never came across one during my service. My mother served with one in India who always insisted on walking round alone at night, carrying a revolver, which the QA sisters thought rather odd at the time.

18, Feversham Crescent.
York
24 May 1968

. . . If the girls *do* get integrated into the RAEC, please don't forget, someone, to design a glamorous hat. I bet a slightly more feminine version of your S.D. Caps would be lovely, actually, as could khaki generally be if it were well designed. Your service dress can look fabulous and I should think a suitably modified version would suit the girls. I've decided that feminine girls can look good in military shaped clothes (only, please, not battledress again).

Did you meet anyone interested in the Army at Lancaster? I'm fascinated to hear. Do you find most universities anti-military? You seemed to think that I ought to be scared to be seen talking to an Army Officer in the J.C.R.! I think it's good for students to be forced to realise the presence of unpopular professions. There seems to be a frightening cushioning at York against any disturbing infiltrators into the academic haven. What I would like to prove is that all soldiers are not sadists, and that some can actually be idealistic. 'Only idealistic for what?' the student probes. What I try to do is to pretend to be perfectly normal (i.e. be myself) and then admit that I'm in the Army. It usually causes quite a stir. I think the Education Department thinks it's a great joke, but as many of the staff have done war service, they're not totally unsympathetic.

CHAPTER 15

Central Hall University of York

CENTRAL HALL WAS BUILT JUTTING into the lake at the University of York (some said that even in *my* time all the buildings were sinking into the water!), so that inside I had the impression of being afloat, but static. It was there that our Degree Ceremony was held, an occasion that could have done, I felt, with some fitting ceremonial music to add joy and dignity at what was, after all, a university with a very high standard of music.

Cardiff University does it rather well in St David's Hall, the organist playing at the beginning and end of the proceedings. Was it coincidence, or fate, I wondered, that the organ let out a huge, continuous bellow at my son Will's MSc ceremony last year, just as Lord Kinnock, who had not been brief at the start, was trying to wind up the ceremony some two hours or so later, on a dignified note. The organ outburst gave a whole new meaning to the phrase 'old windbag'.

Bristol and Edinburgh Universities both do the ceremony well, and at Edinburgh the Vice Chancellor even made the new graduates turn round and give their 'supporters' club' a clap on Benedict's big day – particularly poignant for me as his MA in Fine Art and Art History had taken five long years, and his father had died some three years before Ben graduated.

Edinburgh also allowed the University Chaplain, a woman, to read a prayer at the Graduation, having held a special service for graduands and their families in a city church on the ancient Greyfriars' Monastery site on the morning of the ceremony, which for me was a real chance to give thanks. York, on the other hand, in my day was avowedly humanist in its leadership, from the Vice Chancellor, Lord James of Rusholme down to more junior academics, and I suspect that the Revd James Bogle heading the university's Anglican Chaplaincy, which surprisingly was housed on campus, had a difficult path to tread. We Anglicans could use Heslington Parish Church across the road from the campus, or go into the city for services. I was dragged, reluctantly I must admit, to the Revd David Watson's church, then St Cuthbert's, by my Christian Union roommates (by then I was outnumbered in our room, two to one!).

Hearing David Watson preach, before he took over the redundant St Michael-le-Belfry next to the Minster, changed my life – for the better. He was electrifying. St Cuthbert's would be packed to overflowing every Sunday evening, young lads in leathers clutching motor bike helmets, standing spellbound in the aisles. David had also been an army officer, during National Service, and so I as a young, keen territorial officer could relate to him easily. I believe he said he had been in the Royal Horse Artillery, a very smart regiment, and while he had clearly accepted and enjoyed much of army life at the time, he did question in later life why officers had to get their silk underpants made! He became my parish priest for a while, and would start a session in his study with, 'Well, Sue, how is your *soul* today?' – a question which I still feel uncomfortable about answering honestly some forty years on. My asthma would be easier to describe.

I notice that when the General Synod of the Church of England meets nowadays in Central Hall, a huge Christian cross is hung on the famous purple curtains, so perhaps the humanist element on the staff in my day has mellowed or simply died out.

The best experience I had in Central Hall was doing drama workshops as part of our education course, when the building really came alive.

Central Hall, University of York (written in my undergraduate years sometime between 1966 and 1969).

Warm, comfortable, congenial apart from the sickly-rich purple drapes which are like a glut of mediaeval frippery in contrast with the golden, polished cedarwood.

A balcony peeps provocatively from behind the drapes. I long to hide there – wouldn't it be fun.

The high-spined, uncluttered ceiling structure is rather like a well-lit big top, but with none of the precariousness or the smell. Neither dangerous, nor exciting, but vaguely *pleasing*.

Amorphous spurts of white glow superimposed on the reflecting glass in front of the twilight blueness remind me of the excitement of a night sailing. People stand gazing at the water around and beneath but there is no voyage imminent: the tragedy is that we are static – there is no progression.

Mais, ô mon coeur, entends le chant des matelots! If only I could. We are strangely imprisoned on this island of static pleasure.

'All for your delight we are not come
as meaning to content you.'

But of course they are – pleasure on a plate, that's the trouble.

'You must learn navigation,' said Shotover. What *is* the physical struggle here, but to sit still?

'Teach us to care and not to care.
Teach us to sit still.'

CHAPTER 16

Postgraduate Year 1969–70

MY POSTGRADUATE TEACHER TRAINING year left me still uncertain about careers. Being an 'indigenous' York education student, I could spend two terms away from York doing practical work, one on teaching practice, and one perhaps in industry. I managed to persuade my tutors to let me do an attachment to a hospital in London instead. I spent a fascinating fortnight at St Thomas' Psychiatric Day Hospital, looking after autistic children, and discovering the value of furry animals for the children to stroke, and of art, painting when they couldn't really express themselves in words. We also did eurythmy, a Rudolf Steiner-inspired form of movement to music, in our case each child and adult sharing a copper rod, which required coordination and teamwork. I thought it was wonderful – all the children looked so happy doing it. The sister in charge, who wore uniform in those days, was extremely kind to me, and I was allowed to sit in on case conferences with the multidisciplinary team. I loved it, but feeling filthy at the end of the day after travelling on the tube, I decided that London commuting was not for me: I was more of an outdoor girl.

I moved then to the London Hospital, where my mother had trained as a nurse, and where I was born, to spend three months in the Department of Social Work. I had been brought up on stories of the London, and I couldn't quite believe my luck to be walking those historic wards as a member of staff. I was employed voluntarily as a welfare assistant, and also helped out on reception in Casualty, as knifing victims were wheeled in by matter-of-fact Cockney ambulance men. Despite the violent incidents, though, I would pound the streets of Whitechapel and Stepney on my own, visiting patients at home or looking for hostels for them, and never once felt unsafe in those days, even at night.

I had a tiny cubicle for an office in Outpatients, and was shocked, as we all were, by the sudden death from a virus of a young social worker who had the office next to mine, her white coat still visible through the obscured glass partition for weeks afterwards, an unsettling reminder of the fragility of life.

My main job was to try to re-house patients on their discharge from hospital. I remember visiting a Salvation Army hostel where one poor lady with a new colostomy had lost her cubicle while an in-patient, and a male hostel with a large notice at the entrance proclaiming, 'Do not urinate on the walls.' Often our patients were well known to the local hostels for their misbehaviour, and for some of them, even the Sisters of Mercy had run out of mercy, and refused to have them back. It was sad to see once proud men, many of them ex-Service, on their uppers, and almost impossible to find them any permanent accommodation, as they were mostly rolling stones.

I lived in John Harrison House, a tower block behind the hospital for third-year student nurses and staff nurses. The pay-as-you-eat scheme had been introduced, and the girls would rush back to make snacks in their very short breaks to save money, barely having time to cook themselves a scrambled egg before getting back on duty. I loved them. To me they looked so beautiful and professional in their traditional starched, carefully gathered caps, huge white aprons which crossed over at the back, and dresses with leg-of-mutton sleeves, midi length still at the height of the craze for mini-dresses.

Suddenly there came the bombshell: my mother rang from Worthing and told me that they'd found 'another little lump' on her breast. My godmother Paddy's husband Joe Fox was senior consultant anaesthetist at the London at the time. Paddy and Joe had been immensely kind to me, having me for weekends, when not on TA training, and Joe was able to use his influence to get my mother a bed and a surgeon instantly. She was admitted the next day. Out of this came my poem 'Mastectomy' which I wrote for my education tutor at York, but I don't think he really understood the enormity for me of what had happened. My grandmother had written me a stiff letter telling me, 'Now you must look after your little mother,' and I felt that responsibility for the rest of her life. I was so blessed to have an understanding husband who loved her deeply, having lost his own adored mother Sybil to cancer before we'd met. My mother embraced Mike as the son she'd never been able to have, and he never complained if she came for a week and stayed for a month with us, as she became increasingly unwell with cancer and chest problems. He was an absolute gentleman, thank God.

Mastectomy

Midday. By now my mother would be back,
Back on the ward after the operation,
And I must face whatever was the outcome.
The plan had been so clinical, so simple:
If it were cancer they would amputate
The breast; if not, merely remove the growth.

Last time the lump had been benign, and so
Although there'd been a lot of mess and pain,
The fear had gone and we had breathed again.

This time, who knew? Sister Sophia did,
And as the only surviving relative I
Must also know before I faced my mother.

Fumblingly I asked a junior nurse,
Feeling somehow that she would understand.
'Oh', she said, 'Sister will tell you about it.'

And Sister did. 'She had to have it off,'
She said, and went on counting dishes
(How inconvenient to come at dinner time).
I stood, dazed, for a second unbelieving
And then believing all in sudden horror,
And anger. It wasn't Sister's fault –
To her it was just another routine case –
Simple mastectomy, a common-place occurrence.
As a social worker I should know about it
In my white coat, symbol of detachment.

With even voice I said, professional, cool,
'May I see her, or would you rather not?'
'Oh yes, you can if you want, though she's still a bit dopey.'

'Thank you,' I said, and quickly walked away,
Glad to be rid of the dulled efficiency.
And suddenly I was me – Mrs Eileen Wilson's
Only daughter and I must face my mother.

At first it was relief – no blood this time
Just a clean white strictly neutral theatre gown,
And though I felt indecent in the looking

You couldn't see her breast that wasn't there.
But her face, yellow, taut, and a pungent odour –
I supposed of anaesthetic. Did she know?
Eyes closed and breathing deep but strangely fitful.
Had Sister told, *that* woman told my mother?
Instinctively I felt she had, for Mummy
Had a look of disappointment round the mouth
Somehow, and resignation. Yes, for certain
My mother knew. And I knew. Then I left
Swiftly before the other patients could see me cry.
For cry I must. White coats are no protection
When your own mother's life is in the balance.

But professional objectivity *is* a help:
The senior registrar to whom I went
For details of the many implications
Of carcinoma in my mother's case
Was kind but factual: she had a chance,
In fact a two in three chance of complete recovery.
However, for one in three women in her position
There would be a recurrence of the cancer,
Perhaps next time in an inoperable place.
And then there would be no cure. Only waiting.
True, they could give her a bit more radiotherapy
But not much more; an overdose is lethal
And as she'd have to have some after the operation
Already the safety margin would be fine –
In the last bid to stave off the unmentionable.

Curiously, these cool statistics helped.
Mummy herself a nurse would have weighed the odds,
And I could face her knowing that she knew
The exact odds for a favourable prognosis.
The worst I couldn't make myself imagine
Although I knew that we both *could* imagine.

Mummy was brave, cheerful, optimistic.
The scar, they said was healing perfectly.
They even said the scar was beautiful.
But when I dressed her, Mummy was strangely shy.
'Darling,' she said 'You don't have to look
If you don't want to.' But of course I did.

Pink it was, and big, neat, but big.
Appalled I blurted, trying to be calm,
'You're still my mother and I love you just the same.'
Trite, perhaps, but it helped. We were one, together.

As it happened, we were lucky. When the tests
Came back a week later from the path lab they were negative –
The growth was non malignant, cancerous-looking
But definitely benign. Radiotherapy was now
Unnecessary. Cancer was not there
Creeping insidiously round my mother's bloodstream
Threatening at any time to reappear.
The relief was indescribable. I wept
And Mummy wept with joy and gratitude.
The ghastly suspended threat of execution –
For so it seemed when first we'd feared the cancer
Was lifted now and we could live
As if the nightmare never had existed.

Except for the once clear tangible vestige
Of the fear. 'But what's a breast
To lose,' said Mummy brightly 'in comparison with a life?'
Nothing, except that in hugging her for joy
There was a new gentleness, and delicacy
In trying not to hurt her any more.

Sue Wilson
London
January 1970

By May 1970, I was into my last postgraduate term at York. I was a full lieutenant by then serving with the Middlesbrough-based 34 (Northern) Signal Regiment (Volunteers), commanded by a charismatic colonel, Paddy Evans. This piece is dated 10 May 1970.

Regimental Parade, Scarborough

The volunteer band squeaks out cheerfully and in time to the reassuring boom of the bass drum the regiment marches onto the parade ground. Squadron by squadron the regiment assembles, the RSM watchful, tall, in control. The troops look cold but calm, secure, detached.

We officers perambulate slowly, deliberately in step with our partners but trying so hard not to march to the band that we simply feel self-conscious under the gaze of the entire regiment facing us.

Suddenly, as if by instinct, we know that the Adjutant is emerging. The RSM stiffens, his normally substantial chest appears to broaden visibly. He throws up a quivering salute which the Adjutant returns immaculately. One is conscious of sparkling brass, of two soldiers facing each other with pride, their Sam Brownes gleaming, each symbolic of authority, of tradition. The sheen of the leather is not the joke of 'bull' but rather invokes admiration. Suddenly, I am proud of the effort I've made with my own uniform. Simultaneously, however, there is a tautness in the stomach, a maddening quiver behind the knees – the nagging fear of making a mistake myself on parade has taken hold.

'Regiment, Regiment – shun.' A pregnant pause, hushed, chill, then the Adjutant's voice again, full of calm authority: 'Fall in – the Officers.'

We're on! I grit my teeth, making a determined effort to swagger with apparent confidence. The troops are watching (sniggering?) and I concentrate hard to keep in step with the girl next to me. Miraculously, we halt together, two paces in front of the WRAC privates who stare brazenly. A shaky about-turn, but at least I haven't fallen over. I pull myself firmly to attention. 'Get a grip. Stand still.' Suddenly I'm confident again. I'll show them, those cocky girls. I'm rigid, eyes centre front, locking my knees to stop them shaking in the cold of the Scarborough breeze. It's easy. Of course I want to move, to share jokes which present themselves suddenly to my numbed mind – but I don't. This is the discipline for which I've always admired soldiers on parade and I'm proud to do my best, to partake of that shared discipline, so precious in the sharing, in the common suffering.

The commanding officer is reviewing the troops. I brace myself extra hard as he approaches my squadron. As an officer in front I know that my slightest twitch might be noticed by the entire squadron. I won't let them down. I trust that they feel the same about their officers. Mutual pride is the great bond which has united officer and soldier in that unique human relationship which at its finest seems to me to be the ultimate ideal. 'Lord, make me worthy.'

At last, the march past. We swagger delightedly, make the most of the 'eyes left', eyeing the commanding officer fixedly almost to the point of defiance. The regimental march blares out jauntily. It sounds good. For us at this moment 34 Regiment is the finest regiment in the British army. We are proud to belong, and immensely privileged to be serving soldiers. With this regiment I would cheerfully risk my life.

My last long vacation I needed to earn the rent to stay on in York, as I wanted to go on serving with my TA signals regiment. My vicar at the time, Clifford Barker, who was also my TA padre, heard that Miss Snowball, matron of the local geriatric hospital, needed nursing auxiliaries and put me in touch. I nearly funked it at the last moment, terrified of having perhaps to lay out a body for the first time, but Cliff held me to my promise to turn up at the hospital, saying that Miss Snowball was relying on me, and it turned out to be an extraordinarily fulfilling experience, nearly leading me to do my nurse training instead of joining the army.

My poem 'Dream Voices' was the title given us by Helen Dunmore in her Community Creative Writing class in Pontypridd some twenty-three years later. Sadly, I've lost the rest of the poem, but it began 'Mrs Lee wants to pee.' Indeed she did: a huge, cheerful lady with a deep, booming Yorkshire voice, she and her one leg needed to be heaved onto a bedpan. It was day one for me as an auxiliary. This was real life. I suppose I had imagined myself as a mixture of *Sue Barton, Student Nurse* − I adored the books − the beautiful nurses at the London, and the glamorous little blonde on *Emergency Ward Ten*. Instead, as I entered the ward, I was handed a hideous brown gown, and invited to step behind the faded floral curtain to meet my first patient.

The bedpan round finished, we were on to bed making, and I surprised my more experienced partner with my proficiency, especially finding hospital corners so easy. CH training had its uses, as had our Red Cross home nursing instruction where keeping the bottom sheet taut and the pillowcases neat was insisted upon, as well as getting the smoother side of the sheet next to the patient. I was given a white button-through dress and was getting on quite happily until the ward sister realised with dismay that I might be taken for a doctor. Heaven forbid! Instantly, a nasty little paper cap was found, which perched over my bun, and I was told to get white hairgrips.

I had only my black army lace-ups for shoes, highly bulled, and they had long since broken my feet in. After the miles which we must have walked each day up and down the ward, by the time I got back to our postgraduate hall of residence, any intellectual conversation was irrelevant: all I could think about were my feet. Often I would finish a shift at 9 p.m. and then be on duty again at 7.30 the next morning. It felt relentless. One morning, I overslept, and had to run all the way to the hospital, at least a mile, arriving gasping and sweaty on the ward to apologise. The younger ward sister, a beautiful fair-haired mother-of-four was on duty, slim and elegant in her silver-buckled sister's belt. 'We've all done it, nurse,' she said simply. She had called me 'nurse' and I felt humbled. Would I ever deserve the title?

It seemed that the patients would be there until they died. Many of them on that huge, long ward had no visitors at all, and I as a mere auxiliary had no idea what was wrong with most of them, although the beautiful young sister, seeing my interest, would show me how to test urine with a dipstick. Some of the nurses were tougher nuts, and would gossip to me over the patient we were bathing as if the she were invisible. I found this very difficult. Certainly, it was a constant slog feeding, changing and keeping everyone clean, and little jobs like washing their hairbrushes and combs tended to get left. When an old lady had an accident I found to my surprise that I could scrub her slippers in the sluice to get rid of all the brown mess without my stomach turning, just glad to be able to help restore to her a little dignity.

The sluice was where we younger nurses were ordered to hide for the consultant's ward round. First, we had to put out a clean towel and new bar of soap for Sir and scrub his washbasin to Sister's satisfaction – no hardship for me after all the cleaning I'd done at CH – and then we were banished to the sluice so that the great man didn't have to set eyes on us minions. Thus, the consultant in the poem is entirely fictitious, but of course, 'the one in white' is myself, and I couldn't stick it for long, because I was due to join the regular army.

The doctor in this poem is an amalgam in my mind of a consultant I'd met who refused to be called a geriatrician, and an obstetrician with a large ego and a bow tie, both 'very happy with themselves,' as my Granny used to say.

Dream Voices – an extract

'Consultant Physician in Geriatric Medicine'

'Good morning, Sister, how are you today?
(For God's sake don't start telling me. I'm late.
It's my Half Day. I want my round of golf).
The notes all ready? Good. Let's fire away.
Good morning, Mrs Holdsworth, how are we?
That leg still paining you? I'll change your tablets.
Remind me, Sister, would you, later on,
To write her up for different analgesics.'
'Yes, Doctor,' she replies, already finding
The next bed's patient's notes for me to see.
A good old stick this Sister, knows her stuff
And knows her place. Now let's see Number Two.
This catheter still giving trouble, Sister?
Perhaps we need to keep an eye on it.

These deaf old women. Can't think why I ever
Went in for Geriatrics at the time,
Except consultants' posts were plentiful.
Deep down I knew I'd never make the grade
In London where I trained, so full of hope,
And Chiefs were really God, in pinstriped glory
Of lovely tailored suits from Savile Row.
My dreams of Harley Street have long since gone.
At least up here I play the big white chief.
It pays the school fees, keeps the wife in clothes,
And me in golf balls. Hell! Is that the time?

This woman in the end bed bothers me.
She stares at me with old, grey sunken eyes
As if she dares to question my opinion.
I shout at her the usual platitudes
And wonder when she'll have another stroke.
Perhaps I'll get a hole-in-one today
And win some extra kudos with the chaps.

'Elderly Woman Patient'

He swings his stethoscope and struts away
Out of the ward into another world.

Fancies himself in that bow tie of his.
Old Clever Clogs. Playing God with me.
He says he'll give me something for my heart,
Thinks he can heal the hurt with little pills
When still it throbs with loves lost long ago.
He thinks I'm stupid, just like all the rest,
Because I never speak. But I can think
And feel and dream about that other world.
He'd never guess I'd been a beauty once.
The lads, they chased me right across the moors,
My golden curls attracting bright spring warmth,
My waist as slender as these nurses' here.

The one in white, I think she understands.
She washed my comb today, and brushed my hair,
And held my hand 'til she was called away.
She's different from the others, not so perky.
She'll not stick this for long, I'm sure of that,
And I'll be left alone with all my dreams.
I beckon her. She comes. I grab her hand,
Will her to live her dreams while she's still young
And she has golden hair and life and strength.

Perhaps I should have stuck to my instincts and done my nurse
training. The ward sister thought so, Cliff Barker told me later, but
I was still army barmy. Joining up was what I had worked towards
for years, and my teaching practice on the Hessle Road in Hull had
made me realise that sitting in a lonely garret marking books every
night was not for me at that stage. I had already discovered the huge
workload involved in English teaching, because of the detailed
marking required, and the difficulty of trying to decide just how
much or little punctuation or spelling to correct, so as not to
discourage a less able pupil.

PART III

Army Life

CHAPTER 17

The Regular Army

THEY WERE POSITIVELY WOOING YOUNG graduates to join the regular army in those days, and it was only when I finally joined as a regular officer that I realised the full might of the WRAC hierarchy, and their suspicion of us straight from university as uppity young things. It is not surprising that we didn't quite understand the system: as sparky young students we had flourished in mixed units, mostly serving with male senior officers. Suddenly, I realised what wearing the WRAC cap badge meant – we were under the jurisdiction of senior ladies, one or two of whom often seemed difficult to please, however hard I tried. Our regular WRAC officers in my day never wore combat kit and boots – they didn't need to as they never went on exercise. As our corps was non-combatant, they'd probably never be required, like us TA girls, to handle a weapon, and do all the 'warry' things which we accepted as normal.

In fact, I loved our WRAC bottle-green greatcoats with officers' silky scarlet lining, bottle-green peaked forage caps and lovat-green No 2 Dress, said to have been designed by Norman Hartnell, with bottle-green proper ties – the dreadful 'tab' ties were introduced much later – and crisp white Van Heusen shirts with detachable collars, double cuffs and cufflinks – my mother managed to find me some delicate little oval chased gold ones. (However, my once being taken for an air hostess perhaps said something about the overall effect on the average civilian!) The front collar stud would dig uncomfortably into my neck, leaving a red mark every day difficult to hide when in mufti, but the discomfort did serve to remind me that I was on duty, and therefore needing to be on my best behaviour: of course, we had to set an example to our servicewomen at *all* times. And although we were told in the army that the Mess was our home, we had to tread pretty carefully all the time with the senior Ma'ams. As for *on* duty, even quite junior regular officers could be easily shocked, as when my fellow OTC officer and I once chose to wear our combat kit for a helicopter ride on an attachment in Germany, after having been advised to wear our No 2 Dress by a young regular WRAC lieutenant. It seemed ridiculous to us to climb into a helicopter in a short, tight skirt, but clearly we had behaved unwisely in her eyes.

The young regular officer cadets who came straight from school, many of whose fathers were senior army officers, were put on the 'long course', eight months of training, or a year if they were 'back-termed'. They had their own mess in a separate building, sat in seniority order at table (very CH!) we were told, and were frightfully keen. Their Commissioning Ceremony was held indoors rather than on the drill square, a moving culmination to their training, slow marching down the aisle accompanied by the excellent WRAC Staff Band resplendent in bottle-green No 1 Dress, sadly obsolete for the rest of us by then, and band regalia. It was a very quiet affair compared to the Sovereign's Parade at Sandhurst, but of course just as important to our new officers themselves, and to their proud parents. The girls *were* able to joke about the Sash of Honour, awarded to the top cadet on each course, which was displayed between Commissioning Ceremonies at the entrance to their mess. The WRAC colours were bottle green and beech brown, and the coveted award became known as 'the bloody sash,' beech brown looking remarkably like the colour of dried blood.

In contrast, we on the graduate 'short course', lived in the Student Officers' Mess, separated by a thin partition from the Permanent Staff Officers' Mess, so that we had the unnerving feeling of being overheard all the time by our instructors when we were trying to relax. We were expected to have learnt enough to be sent to a unit after only seven and a half weeks, so our training was not so rigorous or thorough as that for the 'long course' officer cadets, and we were likely to consider everything we were told with a more questioning attitude, having spent three or four years at university. I'm sure that we graduates had all started keen as mustard – after all, like the girls straight from school we had chosen voluntarily to make the regular army our career – but I certainly found our course disappointing. I was not sorry, however, to have escaped the flower arranging on the 'long course' syllabus: I'm sure I'd have failed!

Our 'short course' had an unhappy start when an officer cadet, Shelagh (*Sheelagh?*) Arnold, lost her father suddenly and had to go home, although she did return and bravely finished the course. Another girl, teacher-trained, I think, but not a university graduate, had been proposed to by a farmer the night before she joined, and being an officer cadet, was allowed to leave instantly. Another, Erica (*Gunnell?*), a very bright French graduate, quickly decided that the military life was not for her, but since she was already a second lieutenant, a Retirement Board had to meet to consider her case, which meant she was forced to 'soldier on' for most of the course, thoroughly disaffected, which didn't help morale. She was great fun, however, and made up naughty songs which we sang under our breath as we marched, so that the diminutive, very proper woman RSM drilling us could never quite catch the words. The handful of us who were left didn't really settle as a course, and the commissioning lunch with no parade or ceremony was a tame affair, although producing my brigadier grandfather, Charles 'Tug' Wilson, proved a surprising coup, as he turned out to be the most senior guest present.

I longed for the day when women potential officers would be moved to Sandhurst, but now that it has come, I'm quite glad not to have had to go through their training. Although many WRAC officers and servicewomen were very good sportswomen, the Sandhurst training is far more physical than anything we were put through at the WRAC College, the young women students now tested on rigorous assault courses and exercises in the field, and taught weapon training in deadly earnest just like the men, and – horrors! – bayonet drill. However, in these days of equality, the Sandhurst approach would seem to prepare the young women well for their role in war, and of course they can be in just as much danger as the men in theatres like Iraq or Afghanistan, as recent casualties amongst female soldiers have shown. The war training we had been given in the OTC had never seemed real like that, somehow, because as students we knew that we couldn't be called up. 'Target neutralised. Over,' I would report happily on the radio, proud of my voice procedure, little thinking what devastation one live shell from our 25-pounders might have produced, had we been firing in anger. We saw little of the dreadful effects of bombs or shells in current conflicts on television in those days, and by the time I was commissioned in my second year at university, I was absolutely prepared to go to war, believing myself immortal I suppose, like most young people in those days, but of course quite prepared if necessary to die for Queen and Country.

I never anticipated the demise of the WRAC, and I am very proud to have worn the cap badge (a lioness rampant!) which certainly represented high standards of discipline and service. Our motto, 'Gentle in Manner, Resolute in Deed' has served me well: in the WRAC, we were encouraged never to lose our femininity, but survived in the system by courtesy and quiet determination. I also found that the senior ladies could be quite protective of our junior officers, and our postings branch, AG16, would come up very sensibly with a quick posting if a young woman had difficulties in a mixed unit.

My first posting was to Chester, to be the WRAC detachment officer at Saighton Camp. I was to report to my Commanding Officer, Lieutenant Colonel Peter Dryland MC, Royal Welch Fusiliers at the Castle. It all sounded very grand.

Saighton Camp was rather less so, a hutted camp, but comfortable enough.

My Officer Commanding, Phil, left as I arrived, as so often happens in the army, and was replaced by Captain Sue Wing, who was to go on to become a full colonel and then ordained in the Church of England. She tried to initiate me more fully into the ways of the WRAC, and it was good to meet her again at a Corps reunion in Cardiff, where a tiny, extremely smart black woman RSM in khaki No 2 dress (or do they call it Service Dress now, I wonder?) tried to get us old and bold organised on parade with a 'Come on, girls, move your bloody selves,' or some such order. It was very funny. Looking at our average age, 'girls' was not the first word that had come to my mind, and as officers we always used to be addressed as 'Ladies'. How the army has changed!

To my horror at Saighton Camp, I was put in charge of an account, and also had to pay all the servicewomen in cash every week on Pay Parade. This was a harrowing experience, as to be sixpence *up* when I got to the last in the queue would have been a serious as being sixpence *down*, but mercifully I always managed somehow to get it right.

With no mobiles in those days the WRAC girls had one payphone in the Junior Ranks Club which I constantly had to empty, and bank the coins. It was extremely popular, and soon there was so much money in the account that they were able to have a slap-up dinner at the Grosvenor Hotel in Chester, ending with cigars. I was rather relieved not to have been invited, and still wonder how the hotel staff enjoyed the evening!

One Saturday afternoon two rather merry bridesmaids arrived at my quarters inviting me to the wedding reception in the Junior Ranks Club. Since the bride was another of my privates, of course I had to go, and determined to keep sober, stuck smugly, or so I thought, to my usual non-alcoholic tipple of dry ginger, with which I was plied gleefully by an RMP (Royal Military Police) corporal. Unknown to me, he had slipped a vodka into every one. How I walked back to the Mess I'll never know, but suddenly the ceiling of my bedroom was spinning and I felt *very* ill. Meanwhile an Old Blue boyfriend, John, had arrived unannounced from Germany to see me. I was far too embarrassed to see *him*, but calling through the locked door, agreed to meet him at the hotel where he was staying in town (the Queen's), for breakfast the next morning when I had sobered up. Meanwhile, Sue Wing was very understanding, saying that every young officer has to go through some initiation, in her case, I think, being thrown into a swimming pool in full No 2 Dress uniform. I kept the breakfast appointment next morning and John and I were seen coming out of the hotel by one of my WRAC privates, who kept him entertained on the train all the way to London, apparently. From that moment it seemed that my 'street cred' on camp had gone up considerably, people thinking, mistakenly, that at least this woman had got stamina!

One of my happiest memories of Chester was going swimming with the young servicewomen to the Junior Leaders Regiment at Oswestry on beautiful, long summer evenings. The minibus chuntering along the country lanes, they would sing at the tops of their voices to the tune of 'Mademoiselle from Armentières'

It wasn't the Wrens that won the war,
Parlez-vous?
It wasn't the Wrens that won the war,
Parlez-vous?
It wasn't the Wrens that won the war:

The Girls in Green were there before.
Inky pinky parlez-vous?

It wasn't the Wrens that got the men,
Parlez-vous?
It wasn't the Wrens that got the men,
Parlez-vous?
It wasn't the Wrens that got the men:
The Girls in Green were there again!
Inky pinky parlez-vous?

It is left to the reader's conjecture whether or not the writer joined in this musical rendition!

On the wall of our beautiful chapel at the WRAC College hung a large, framed copy of the hymn 'Father, hear the prayer we offer' which asks for 'strength that we may ever/ live our lives courageously'. I think of it as the Battle Hymn of the WRAC. It reminds me of all the loyal, spirited women with whom I served, and I hope that it may be sung at my funeral.

Because so many young officers left on, or shortly after marriage in those days, promotion prospects were good, and I found myself within a year of joining the regular army being promoted to acting captain, and being sent back to the WRAC College – as an instructor, which was slightly tricky as I was then working with a few officers who had been my own instructors. On arrival I was interviewed by the commandant, a rather grand full colonel, who asked me what my father did. When I replied that he was dead, she pursued relentlessly, 'But *when* did he die?' I felt deeply embarrassed, but with my home and CH upbringing I found myself unable to lie, and told her what little I knew of the sorry story, ending lamely, 'But I'm told he was a good soldier, Ma'am.' Perhaps trying to be kind, she said something about the Gurkhas, in which he'd served, being a fine regiment, but I just felt sad for my mother, still recovering at the time from her mastectomy. How she had coped over the years, or what sort of career she might have had, seemed to be of little interest; what my *father* did was apparently all that mattered. And had I been able to say that he was a colonel instead of a humble captain I felt that I might have won a few more Brownie points!

The best part of that posting was being appointed Unit Press Officer, and being sent on a course in London. We visited *The Daily*

Telegraph, still in Fleet Street then, and at the first clatter of the presses and whiff of printer's ink I was hooked. We were taught how to write press releases, and I just longed to get our local boy and girl stories into the papers, as we'd been taught on the course to do. This was not easy in my unit, as there was a certain wariness from on high about the press, but I was allowed to produce a recruiting display, and spent many happy hours with an artistic WRAC corporal in the library captioning PR photographs which I'd chosen at MoD. I little dreamed that one day I would take my own pictures and get them printed in the papers to complement my stories. In fact I was to notch up some twenty years' service, first in the regular army, and later in the Army Cadet Force and with the Reserve Forces, as a press officer/PRO, and I absolutely loved the work.

When I was posted from the WRAC College, I went to say goodbye to the RSM, Miss Jean McIntosh, a tall, imposing woman, who, sadly, died in 2009. 'Haven't you done well here, Ma'am,' she said.

'You're very kind, Miss McIntosh,' I replied, and we both grinned. That sort of encouragement from senior ranks (sergeants through to the RSM) could be very important to a young officer who was still learning the ropes, and we couldn't have done without their experience and advice. The system works through mutual respect, and you certainly have to earn *theirs*.

Shortly after joining the army I'd been sent on the Basic Winter Mountain Leadership course at Glenmore Lodge near Aviemore. It was extremely tough, carrying maximum kit and starting the first day in a whiteout, but I knew that the honour of the WRAC was at stake (the only other woman on the course was a civilian mountain rescue member and PE teacher, very fit, from North Wales). At the bottom of the ski lift (broken, so we had to walk up) there was an advertisement for the army proclaiming 'Join the Professionals', and this spurred me on – I didn't want to be branded by the men as a weak or moaning woman. Moreover, just as I'd loved Zomba Mountain and Mount Mlanje, I was thrilled by the wild Scottish hills, and soon joined the Army Mountaineering Association. This gave me the opportunity to go on AMA courses, mostly in the Highlands or Wester Ross, and then one day in North Wales, Bethesda Drill Hall of all unpromising places, I met the love of my life, Mike

Davies-Jenkins, a major in the Royal Welch Fusiliers. He had very blue eyes, an open face and a lovely smile, and after a week of being roped up together on rock faces, I just knew that I could trust him to be roped up for life. Moreover, he was a bachelor, the greatest love in *his* life at the time being a beautiful, silky-coated, sweet-tempered lolloping Labrador/springer spaniel cross whom the soldiers at the Welsh Depot had christened Sam, I believe, although his master always called him Brown Dog, thus leading to wags like Michael Hodges calling him 'Sam Brown(e) Dog' like the officer's Sam Browne belt. By the time I met him, Mike D-J had decided to leave the army, as he had always wanted to go to university, and that also intrigued me.

I took his sweater back with me to darn, and cried all the way back to Camberley, just longing for his first letter. It came, in the distinctive turquoise ink, as did several others, and within six weeks he had proposed. I then had to wait until the next weekend before I was allowed to share the good news, as he insisted on first asking my mother face-to-face for her permission to marry me. I knew that she would just burst into tears with delight and hug him, which she did, and Big Susan was equally excited. Not having been warned, they had no champagne in, so we celebrated with a cup of tea, which tasted just as good to me.

My former commanding officer, Colonel Peter Dryland, under whom Mike had also served, was delighted at the engagement, telling everyone that two of his officers were getting married. Since the Royal Welch Fusiliers was an all-male regiment, he enjoyed watching people's reaction!

Life was suddenly very sweet. I was posted to Chatham to serve with the Royal Engineers as a staff officer, where I didn't really know what I was doing, and I have to admit that my heart wasn't really in my in tray.

I was agonising about whether or not to continue serving after marriage, and Mike put no unfair pressure on me to leave. For my last few months I commanded a detachment of forty-two service-women, really my happiest job in the regular army, but Mike had by then got into Cambridge, and Chatham was the nearest WRAC posting that was on offer. I would have been stuck in camp on duty every other weekend as well as all through the week, of course, and

I decided that starting married life apart was not a good idea. I've never regretted the decision, although fatherly senior Sapper officers, on hearing that I was marrying a potential undergraduate, were horrified: 'How will you *manage*, my dear?' I knew that I should do my probationary teaching year, and felt confident that somehow we would get by, which indeed we did – just – even if it meant ice on the inside of the windows and trying to do without even a coal fire in winter.

I left the army on Friday 13 April 1973. I wasn't superstitious, but admit I felt a pang of shock and sadness as a male military clerk cut my identity card in half – straight through my face, a particularly pretty photograph, as it happened. The umbilical cord had been severed (as well as my face!), but in that moment I resolved that one day I would be back in uniform, probably as a TA volunteer again. I knew that my soldiering days were not entirely over. I had more to do.

PART IV

Married Life

32. Malawi: Malosa Secondary School pupils returning to school. 1966

33. Malawi: Malosa pupils Odetha Mandoloma and Dinah Midaya making palm crosses. Easter 1966

34. *Malawi: living quarters for a year at Malosa Secondary School. 1965–66*

35. *Malawi: on the road to Zomba with PCV Eileen (L) and VSO Diana Leach (centre)*

36. *Mike D-J's MA graduation day, Cambridge. 1979*

37. *More family joy: Christening party at Arwel for William (born Bronglais Hospital Aberystwyth 29 October 1980). L-R: (standing) my cousin Helen; Granny Eileen Wilson; the author, Will's godfather Patrick Holden holding Ben. Seated: Big Susan with Will; Katie; Dr Jennifer Holden*

38. My Aunt Jean with my Granny, Mrs Avril Wilson at my cousin Helen's wedding at All Saints Church, Thorndon, Eye. 8 August 1987

39. Katie, Ben and Will at my cousin Helen's wedding

40. Ben sightseeing in London. 12 October 1982

41. London bus trip: Mike D-J with Katie and Will. 12 October 1982

42. *Visiting Granny in Menai Bridge: Katie, Ben and Will at St Tysilio's, Church Island where Ben was christened. Early 1980s*

43. *Plascrug School, Aberystwyth. Ben with Mrs Rhiannon Steeds. 1986*

44. *Holy Trinity Choir, Aberystwyth with the vicar, the Revd Bob Capper. Back row, 2nd from left, the author and far right churchwarden Mike D-J. Front row far left: Will and Katie D-J. 1987*

45. *Off to boarding school: Ben to Llandaff as a chorister, and Katie to Howell's, Denbigh.*
With Uncle Malcolm, Llanbadarn Fawr, Aberystwyth September 1986

46. *Dean's Scholars Will Davies-Jenkins and Christopher Spurgeon make a retirement presentation*
to the Dean of Llandaff, the Very Revd Alun Radcliffe Davies. 1993

CHAPTER 18

Early Married Life

T HE WEDDING DAY PASSED IN A haze of excitement, my oldest
school friend from Red House School in Worthing, Kate
Greenwood, doing a brilliant job as chief bridesmaid with my
makeup and hair. 'Don't wear it *up*, Sue. It makes you look so
efficient!' I was particularly thrilled that Clifford Barker came down
from Yorkshire to take part in the service. Some of my 'girls' had
volunteered to sing in the choir in Bishop Gundulph Church,
Chattenden, having turned up faithfully to choir practices to be
drilled by the local padre, a kind Australian called Ross Buckman,
and they also formed our guard of honour, wielding, instead of the
traditional swords, crossed sticks bearing the WRAC lioness cap
badge and the Welsh dragon, made by an enterprising draughts-
woman in my detachment. WRAC drivers drove the staff cars for us,
and the reception was in the very beautiful Royal Engineers'
headquarters mess at Brompton Barracks. A string quartet of
musicians from the regimental band added to the occasion. I insisted
on having Big Susan in the receiving line next to my mother, which
the mess secretary, a retired Sapper major, who ran the whole event
with meticulous precision, thought 'most irregular', and Miss West
came and gave me a fond kiss. Her wedding present, a stainless steel
carving dish, christened 'Miss West' by my mother, is in use to this
day. I guess that not every bride would want to invite her
headmistress, but DRW was a very special lady, who had been
immensely kind to me over the years.

Other CH friends included Mrs Kathleen Betterton, my beloved
English mistress, and Anne-Marie Braun, née Kelly, who, Mike told
me later, had fixed him with a ferocious stare at the reception and
threatened to do terrible things to him if he were ever to let me
down. She need not have worried, and in fact she and Christopher
became lifelong friends to us as a couple, and were almost the last
people apart from immediate family to see Mike before he died in
the hospice in Penarth, so gentle and sensitive with him, and full of

105

practical presents for the family like a casserole and Kate Hill's mother's famous fruit cake, known, I think, as 'Crack'. On hearing that Mike had been delighted by a pair of pyjamas I had got for him in Royal Welch regimental colours, described lyrically by a good RWF friend, Major John (JL) Evans as 'where the purple of the Merionethshire hills meets the blue of the sea', Anne-Marie had also made and sent in the next post a bag for his diamorphine pump in the same colours, which touched him greatly.

After our wedding on 14 April 1973 we flew out to the former Yugoslavia, to spend a blissful fortnight in snowy Plitvice, walking in the lakes and mountains. Already the economy campaign was on, so Zomba Mountain was out of the question, and Yugotours offered a very good deal, and left us to ourselves, so that we were not forced into any group activities. It is good to have discovered a beautiful country before all the political upheavals which plunged it later into a tragic war.

Settling down to married life was a joy. We rented Parc Llettis Cottage, a detached house about a quarter of a mile from the main road, near Abergavenny. Some army friends who came to inspect said it looked like a council house; to me it was paradise. Captain, later Major Ron Williams, Royal Regiment of Wales and his wife Barbara had kindly decorated it for us before we moved in, and although I heard much later from Colonel Jack Willes who had also lived there that it could be grim in winter, it was an ideal summer let. There was no gas, so we bought a Baby Belling oven from a Mrs Jones for £5. 'Mrs Jones' had many historic smells and a tiny, unreliable oven, with which I somehow learned to cook full meals. Everything was fun. If we let Brown Dog out at the beginning of the farm track he would chase the car, getting up to 40 mph. There was even a little back porch where he could dry off when necessary. We would take him for long walks in the fields round the house, and if we went into a clinch, Brown Dog would leap up and lick us both, not wanting to be left out.

Mike went off to Ebbw Vale Tech, as it was known locally, to finish off his A levels, and amazingly passed both with an 'A' for British Constitution, much to his tutors' delight, after only a few months' study. I would cheerfully wash and iron heavy old pure linen double sheets inherited from his family, heaving them onto the line in the back garden, the nesting swallows chirruping under the eaves. I took to domesticity with ease, so much in love that I just wanted to be a good wife, which must sound very old-fashioned now. By the time William had arrived, however, and there were three children under five, I was long past ironing sheets of any sort, and was more in need of cot sheets with a rapid turnover. Mike's elderly but very lively Auntie Gwyneth (*James*) in Aberystwyth offered to make some for me – by chopping up the old linen family heirlooms. Luckily, Father never noticed, and we certainly never told him! Gwyneth was from a family of three Rees sisters, herself, Ray (*Rachel*) and Olwen who had all gone to university – very enlightened and unusual for women in those days. She told funny stories of young men passing food up to her room in Alexandra Hall on the sea front in a basket – it was a strictly 'ladies only' hall of residence in those days. Olwen (*Story*), who was also very good to our young family, was to die in the Deva, only a few yards from Alexandra Hall, having made her century.

CHAPTER 19

Cambridge

WHILE AT PARC LLETTIS, I was applying for teaching jobs in Cambridge, and landed one at Chesterton Secondary School, so we moved at the end of August, Mike carrying me over the threshold of our solid three-bedroom semi out at Chesterton, within easy reach of the towpath. We had taken on a mortgage before Cardiganshire County Council notified him that his annual grant would be £50, and then Cambridgeshire could give us no more as he 'already had a grant'. He also had to pay all his own university fees, so it was a real struggle, and he nearly left Cambridge after the first year because of the finances, too proud to ask for any more help. I was determined, however, that he should finish his degree – he was so happy there, and we had invested so much in the enterprise already – and somehow we got through, even though I gave up my teaching job at the end of my probationary year when our first baby was on the way.

After the civilized life in the army, teaching was quite a contrast. As a form tutor, I was given my own classroom, drab and badly in need of decoration. There was a balcony outside where to my shock I found a heap of rotting Bibles. I asked the headmaster, 'Bruno' Brown, a TA colonel, who seemed to like me, if I could paint the room with my second form, 2E, and he agreed. The children and I had a lovely weekend together, although I should have listened to them and chosen a more interesting colour scheme. The youngsters were far more practical than I, and did the job beautifully. I had brought food for them, but, as so often happened in teaching with hard up families, I found that they had each been given far more money than I would ever have spent on lunch to buy themselves a takeaway.

With a freshly painted classroom I hoped that discipline would improve. I was wrong. Totally ignoring me, standing at the front trying to make myself heard, Bruno would come sweeping into the room in his gown (hence his nickname, Batman), yell at the children and withdraw, leaving me with my mouth open. My PGCE course had not prepared me for secondary modern youngsters, and my acting head of department, Kim, a young Cambridge English graduate with shoulder-length hair had greeted me on arrival with 'Yeah, yeah, do what you like. I'm not being paid for this.'

I was saved by Jackie Lawrence, my head of year, I think she was, who with her good solid teacher training sat me down and gave me some practical pointers on teaching English to less bright children. Tony Parrott, the geographer in the next room, who'd done National Service, was also supportive. I don't think he'd been commissioned himself, but when I explained that I really didn't want to play the big army officer, he understood. I soon longed for a sergeant or sergeant major to do the yelling for me. I tried to be kind to the children, thinking innocently that they would respond to be being treated well, and of course they took advantage, although I think I probably did have some success with real Special Needs children.

Another thing that saved me was music: I had volunteered for the school orchestra and somehow my cello survived, locked in a school cupboard when not in use. The head of music's strategy when teaching was to lock the children *in* and the headmaster *out*! Although pretty disorganised, he somehow managed with some talented pupils' help to put on good concerts, and even got us a 'gig' to play in the Minstrels' Gallery of Trinity College, for a boat club. I shall never forget the beauty of the tables before the meal started, or the chaos by the end. Unfortunately the boat club members, all men and not from the university, got extremely drunk, and as the umpteenth one got up and told a particularly obscene joke, a wonderful little boy's voice beside me piped up, 'The dirty old man!'

Several of the Chesterton senior staff were good to me, and miraculously I survived my probationary year and was re-appointed for when the school was to become a comprehensive, but by then I was pregnant with our first baby, so I handed in my notice rather gratefully, and had a nice letter from the Director of Education wishing me long years of health and happiness in the teaching profession. This seemed somewhat unlikely after that baptism of fire, although I'd loved those scruffy Chesterton children, however difficult some of them could be.

Home life kept me sane. We had such love and support from St Catharine's, Mike's college, and from our church, St Botolph's, across the road. Gus Caesar was the kindest of tutors, legendary meals being provided by his wife 'Chum' (*Margaret*) and daughter Pat, and Dick and Marjorie Gooderson also became lifelong friends, whose meals and parties at 1 Newnham Terrace, with their clever intellectual puzzle games were a delight. Dick was at the time president of the college, and a distinguished law don. Introduced by the lovely rector, John Long and his wife Rosamond on our first Sunday at St Botolph's, we were instantly invited over to Dick's rooms in college for a drink. Veronica Baker, whose father Stephen Lloyd had been padre to the Royal Welch Fusiliers' (RWF) TA battalion in Wrexham when Mike was a subaltern at the Depot there, took us under her wing, too, she and John, like Dick a brilliant law don at St Catharine's, offering us generous friendship and hospitality. Veronica and Marjorie became godparents to our baby Katie, along with the lovely Diane Burkham and the legendary Major Toby Kenyon RWF, and they have all been wonderfully loyal and kind down the years as have the godparents we chose for Ben and Will. Will's godmother Gentian Hodges, now sadly widowed herself, has remained a close and lifelong friend, while his godfather Patrick Holden has always been immensely generous and interested in all the family, and his godmother, my cousin Helen has made long journeys from her home in Germany to be with us for family occasions. We were touched that Ben's godfather Hugh Carson, by then a very busy headmaster, and his wife Penny, with whom I'd served, also made the effort to get to our silver wedding party and just a year later to Mike's funeral in Aberystwyth.

But all that was to come. Our first baby was due on Christmas Day 1974. By then the blood pressure had soared, and I was in Mill Road Maternity Hospital for rest, but let out for Christmas on the strict instructions that I was to do absolutely nothing. It was listening to the King's College Christmas Eve Nine Lessons and Carols in our west-facing spare bedroom which inspired the beginning of the poem 'Firstborn Son'.

The hospital said it was 'rather more convenient' if we didn't have a funeral, and not wanting to be a nuisance as my poor, stunned husband queued with the proud fathers to register our stillbirth the following day, he agreed. We did have a memorial service one cold winter's night in St Botolph's, beautifully taken by our rector, John

Long, and sang 'Give us grace to persevere' to make our friends smile, followed by several glasses of sherry in dear Gus Caesar's rooms, all of which helped enormously, but I kept thinking, 'Where is his poor little body?' We know that it was sent up to London for a post mortem and that he was 'a perfect baby, post mature and small for dates', and a nurse told me when I was in hospital antenatally again in the next pregnancy that they'd 'bunged him in an incinerator', but my obstetrician remained tight-lipped about it.

For us as Christians it was hard to have been denied both a christening and a funeral, and it is heartening to know that stillbirth and perinatal death are handled differently and more openly now, parents encouraged, I understand, to spend time with, and cuddle their baby who has died, and have a memory box prepared by the midwives to take home, and a hospital chaplain available, often in the middle of the night, to conduct a service of naming and blessing. There can also be a proper child's funeral afterwards; of course it all depends on the parents' wishes. The memory of babies who have died earlier in a pregnancy is also honoured here in Cardiff: at our local crematorium and cemetery at Thornhill there is now a garden of remembrance, the Ilex Garden, dedicated by the hospital chaplains on 29 July 2009. Each month a funeral service is held at the chapel at Thornhill, to which parents are invited, where a number of unborn babies are cremated together, and their ashes spread in the Ilex Garden. This garden, as the Rev Eric Burke said in his address, is 'where parents can . . . find a special place, a sacred space where they can come as part of their journey towards acceptance of what has happened in their lives . . . a dedicated and recognisable place for parents to visit and remember and feel near to the baby they have lost.'[1] By contrast, the only tangible reminder for us of our full-term John Gwilym back in 1975 was the little wafer box which we gave to St Botolph's, in use for Communion to this day.

Firstborn Son

December sun streaks low through apple boughs
And warms her under soft pink eiderdown.
The polished 'thirties clock sings three sweet chimes;
Across the Fens from flickering nave of King's
A single treble soars above the world.

Her own child stirred within her by his song,
She pictures Mary scared in cattle shed
And wonders how first giving birth must be.

Epiphany. Induction Day at last.
She wakens in the chill delivery room,
Still drugged and scantly clad in theatre gown
On hard, thin bed, equipment gleaming stark,
White sterile tiles symmetrical and dull.

She senses panic in young Houseman's voice,
Consultant summoned from his Sunday bed.
Her baby's head has fumbling clips attached
To monitor his heartbeat. Nothing heard.
A silence terrible provides the proof:
His brief life-struggle ceased within her womb.
She asks to have him christened. She's refused.
'You see, my dear, he's never breathed,' they say.

They all withdraw. Her husband stumbles in.
His old green suit with turn-ups puppy-chewed
Looks grey to her to match his grief-shocked face.
He crumples in her arms. She cradles him
As she would do their firstborn if she could.

He leaves. Two Sisters take up their positions.
Grimly they strap her up on either side,
Weak legs in stirrups, aching wide apart.
'Pant now.' 'Stop pushing.' 'Pant some more for me.'
She strains, obedient, to oblige them both.
She keeps her eyes tight shut as they advise
And feels the final wrench as he is born.

Stupidly she listens for the cry.
No cry. A quiet, cold, metallic snip
Snaps lifeline nurturing through nine long months.
They slip her son away, unseen, unheld
By her who carried him so full of hope.

No winter sun sneaks through grey frosted pane
To warm her voided womb where once he grew.

After John Gwilym, we had to pick ourselves up somehow. Mike was
deeply affected, but went silent in his grief; I was the opposite. My

poor mother came out in cold sores all over her face, distraught in her sadness for us, and in having lost her first grandchild, with me rejecting her tempting meals for ten whole days: I just couldn't eat. The churchwardens had instantly sent Mike a cheque for him 'to take Sue away for a few days,' and my instincts were to go back to York. We stayed in a B&B out in the country, where Brown Dog was made by the landlady to sleep in an outhouse. It was so cold even in the house that we were relieved to find him alive in the morning. We went to Evensong in York Minster, where I wept for the chorister that John Gwilym might have been, and Cliff and Marie Barker kindly invited us to their daughter Katy's Confirmation. The bishop just touched me on the shoulder after the service, and said, 'I am so sorry about your baby,' and I learned in that moment the importance of acknowledging a bereavement: it meant so much.

That was the turning point: I was able to eat Marie's celebration lunch, and I was on the mend. On our return to Cambridge, I saw an evening job advertised for a receptionist at a GP practice on the Newmarket Road. I went for interview, and just knew I had to go there. I went back to work for £10 a week – 50p an hour – and gradually the hours increased. It was one of the happiest jobs I've ever done. The staff were a good team, I grew fond of our elderly 'regulars', and I saw enough human tragedy there to put our own loss in perspective, as well as harassed mothers clearly ground down by poverty, who had to bring three or four young children to the surgery by bus. I saw that motherhood could be pretty tough.

I quickly found myself teaching English in a language school in Girton, and teaching a little boy with glandular fever at home, so I was soon doing three part-time jobs concurrently. When, after fertility treatment, to our joy I became pregnant again, the surgery job was the last I gave up. I had worked there for fifteen months, and taking my beautiful baby Katie, very much alive, back afterwards was a great moment. Dr Norma Rink, who I believe had lost a baby herself, just took her in her arms. She and I had a great rapport.

Note

1. Cardiff and Vale University Local Health Board: 'Hospital Chaplaincy Matters' Nov 2009.

CHAPTER 20

North Wales

THE FIRST FEW MONTHS OF parenthood were not easy: after the excitement of graduating, Mike had to find a job, and I was left alone with a colicky baby while he went for interviews all over the country. Some organisations said that he 'wouldn't fit into their career structure', in other words, at forty, he was too old. Having read land economy for his Part 2 Tripos, he was trying to find a place to train as a chartered surveyor in the Land Agency and Agriculture division. Then a trainee's job came up with a firm in Bangor, North Wales. He was warned by a friend that they could be tricky employers, but it seemed the best offer at the time, so he took it. We bought a house in Menai Bridge, and I found myself stuck at home with a three month-old baby knowing no-one, and not understanding the language, while Mike took the car for long days out to large estates which he was helping to manage.

Two things saved me: there was a good GP practice with a delightful health visitor called Ella Wyn Jones, who became a real friend to me. Then there was our church, St Mary's, Menai Bridge, the only Anglican one in the village – a shock after the plethora of churches in Cambridge from which to choose – but the people at St Mary's took us to their hearts. Very diffidently, I volunteered for the church choir, and got a real welcome, and I still go back to church and sing there when I visit my late mother's cottage. There were English and Welsh services when we lived there and sadly, the congregations rarely met. There was also a tiny, beautiful church, St Tysilio's, the present building thought to be fifteenth century, on Church Island, where we had our son Benedict christened, the sun beating down and the salt tang from the Menai Strait a reminder of my south-coast roots as I carried him along the causeway to the church, water glistening on either side. We sang unaccompanied, glad to have the beautiful voice of godfather Hugh Carson, who had been a Canterbury Cathedral chorister, to encourage us, and it was a joyful day, as Katie's christening in St Botolph's had been, with the added thrill there of being allowed to walk across the precious turf quad at St Catharine's for the lunch party after the service. What a privilege!

Ben's lunch party was a less grand affair, but we had the delight, thanks to our long 'through living room' of putting up the whole of the D-J family dining table with its ends attached, Glenys Ryan, the kindly lady who helped me in the house at the time, and I lovingly polishing the smooth mahogany surfaces in honour of the occasion. We had to borrow folding chairs from the church hall, not quite so beautiful, but there was a sense of continuity, somehow, in being able to use the table on which Mike had done his prep as a child. His father Gerald, by then totally blind, had come, and made a touching speech, wishing his grandson a happy life. Of course he couldn't see the table, but perhaps he smelt the polish with approval.

By the time Ben arrived, I had managed to persuade my mother to take early retirement from Social Services in East Sussex and move up to Anglesey with Big Susan. It was difficult for them house-hunting at that distance, and even harder for us trying to find a house that they might like. Eventually, we happened on an old detached cottage with a long, steep garden and a panoramic view of the Menai Strait with Snowdonia beyond. My mother came up on the train to see it, and was dubious, terrified that Big Susan wouldn't approve, but they bought it anyway. Meanwhile, heavily pregnant, I scrubbed out the indoor coal hole and we whitewashed it ready for conversion into a downstairs cloakroom, and painted Big Susan's room dove grey, just like her beloved bedroom in Worthing. It worked: as soon as the old lady walked in, she declared, 'Oh Susie, I'm going to be so happy here,' and we all breathed again. The gamble had paid off.

It is a delightful cottage, eighteenth century, with great thick walls and deep, solid windowsills in the original part, and open fires. It is actually two cottages knocked into one with an extension to make a third bedroom, and it's hard to imagine two large families living in it, especially before the extension. There was a back boiler in the dining room, and my mother and Big Susan put solid fuel central heating in which just about took the chill off if you worked very hard at stoking the open fire, which my mother certainly did. Every day she would clean out the fireplace, re-lay the fire, and polish her hearth with Cardinal Red, and the copper and brasses always shone.

After she died I put in storage heaters as well, the average tenant not wanting all the work that relying on solid fuel involved, but I have kept the open fires, and really feel nearer to nature when I go up there and work on the cottage between lets. With the children we always went 'sticking' on our dog walks in the nearby fields, drying off the twigs for starting the fire each morning, real Girl Guide stuff, and very satisfying, somehow. My mother always kept an old kettle handy, too, in case of a power cut. Being out in the country, the house has never had gas.

We lived about a mile away, an ideal distance, I thought, in our badly built but convenient modern house, and I would push the double buggy up Druid Road, sure of a welcome and food on arrival. Buggies seem to be built like battle tanks these days, but mine was a super-light aluminium one that I could just about manage to push and pull up slopes and steps. It was a very happy time, and we could all help each other out. We would come home from holiday to find a casserole waiting for us in the oven; when Big Susan had her first stroke, I knew where to get a commode in a hurry from the Red Cross on the island, as I had done first aid and home nursing courses with them, and Mike was able to get a bed downstairs for her. She would ring a little bell every time she needed help at night and my mother would come running down the stairs. Hospital was never once suggested – my mother did it all.

Imagine our devastation, then, when Mike was suddenly made redundant, and had to look for another job. Our children were both toddlers, so I had my hands full. I didn't know how I could tell them at the cottage. We had uprooted two ladies, both retired now, from a lovely house and all their Sussex friends, and now we were going to have to uproot ourselves again, and leave them stranded in North Wales. They took it stoically, but I could see how upset they were.

CHAPTER 21

Aberystwyth

BY GREAT GOOD FORTUNE, OLD family friends, John and Elizabeth Watkins, chartered surveyors in Aberystwyth, were looking for an assistant at the time. It was manna from heaven. Mike immediately enrolled on an intensive Welsh course, where a tutor told him he had a good accent, not realising that he was Welsh, and we started looking for houses. His parents had lived in Aberystwyth for years, and his uncle Malcolm, a retired brigadier, was still in Llanbadarn Fawr, a village just outside. For Mike it was like coming home. It was also not that far from Menai Bridge, perhaps a couple of hours' drive, and I got used to taking the coach up there when emergencies cropped up.

We found just the right house for us, Arwel, in Trinity Place, a typical Aberystwyth three-storey Victorian terraced house, just opposite the entrance to Holy Trinity church, where Mike's parents had worshipped. It was on the end of the terrace, with perfect views from our bedroom bay window of the tramps who would camp 'unofficially' in the church porch and uncoil themselves in the mornings from a mound of blankets. From home we could also observe weddings and funerals. The children were particularly fascinated by the coffins, and where the body went afterwards, and that helped us to explain to them in a natural way about burial and cremation. We little thought at that stage that when Will was still a schoolboy their father's coffin would be carried down those steep, awkward steps by the local Royal Welch Fusiliers Comrades, who had turned out faithfully some twelve years after we had moved to South Wales.

With Major Tim Bible, Mike had always remained a member of the Aberystwyth Comrades' branch, returning together each year for the St David's Day dinner. They were always given a tremendous welcome back, and when Tim died just a few months after Mike in 1999, the Comrades hired a minibus and brought poppies which were loosed, along with the ashes, into the Dovey estuary in

Aberdovey, his birthplace, at high tide, at sunset, as he had wished. Performed as a Church in Wales Burial at Sea, it was a touching ceremony, particularly as Edward and Henry, Tim's two sons, had to go through it without their mother Penny, too disabled then to make the journey from Romsey after a tragic accident to her legs years before. The regimental support must have been very important to them, as it has been to us as a family, especially since Mike's death. The Royal Welch Fusiliers really look after their widows. It is very much a family regiment, Mike having followed his father into it, and I think he would have been saddened by the recent amalgamation with the Royal Regiment of Wales, itself a hybrid created from the South Wales Borderers and the Welch Regiment, into the new regiment, The Royal Welsh, although I understand that the merger has gone well, and young soldiers joining now may hardly know the difference. For 'the old and bold', regimental loyalties understandably still die hard, families having grown up together through various postings at home and abroad. It has been a particular joy in recent years for our family to be invited to Henry and Edward Bible's weddings, both supported well by Royal Welch Fusiliers friends, their mother Penny making a wonderful effort to attend on both occasions.

I was determined to make the most of Aberystwyth, and loved being able to walk to all the shops there. With some friends in North Wales I had started a postnatal support group of the National Childbirth Trust (NCT) and was delighted to find an NCT antenatal teacher, Liz (*Todd*), who lived at the Centre for Alternative Technology at Machynlleth. Together we started the Aberystwyth and Mid Wales Group of the NCT, she as chairman and I as secretary, and I completed my training as an NCT breastfeeding counsellor. Quickly we established regular coffee mornings in each other's houses, and managed to get the use of the Postgraduate Medical Centre at Bronglais Hospital for evening meetings, inviting local doctors, nurses and midwives to come and give lectures on practical topics like, 'When to call the Doctor', thus managing to acquire some respectability amongst health professionals who had probably been pretty sceptical at first, although our own GP practice was kind and supportive. We were also delighted when health visitor and grandmother Betty Loyn and her anaesthetist husband Gren moved to the area from London, and Betty joined us in the NCT to train as an antenatal teacher. We sensed that some midwives were still not won over, however, and when I started in labour with Will I didn't dare admit to the midwifery sister on duty that I was NCT-trained until after I had been safely delivered. She hadn't realised how advanced the labour was because I was making so little fuss: she didn't know that I was 'breathing through' in approved NCT fashion, and Mr Geoffrey Williams, the much respected obstetrician who was supposed to be present for the birth was still in theatre when little William shot into the world, the October morning sun streaming into the delivery room.

One of the delights of our NCT group was making music together. Thanks to oboist Jackie Simm's inspiration, we organised 'toddlers' proms' in the Aberystwyth Arts Centre, where the tiny tots sat on the floor or in their mothers' arms, enthralled by live classical music. My moment of glory was merely tinging the triangle in Haydn's *Toy Symphony*, but I well remember a brilliant violinist handing over her baby to someone, picking up her violin and playing a Beethoven sonata exquisitely. I realised that musicianship and motherhood were not incompatible, and vowed to take up my cello again when I could.

We also started a local NCT newsletter, competently edited by a good Scottish friend, Norma Bordwell, and I began my *Diary of a Supermum (failed)*, to be continued intermittently over the years. For those of us stranded far away from any extended family able to babysit, the only hope seemed to be to help each other out and muddle through somehow. Any thoughts of being a perfect parent had long since evaporated, in my mind anyway, and I found that being able to laugh at myself was a great relief.

Those were the days when I could equally happily be typing an article or knocking up cakes or tubs of ice cream in our tiny kitchen at Arwel late at night. Miss Jukes, our fierce cookery teacher at CH would be astonished at what I managed to produce there. It took me seven months after moving in to persuade the gas board to re-connect us (not being able to make the request in Welsh was a distinct drawback, I felt), and I managed all that time with two electric rings kindly loaned by Elizabeth Watkins and an elderly solid fuel cream-coloured Rayburn which was either burning things or going out unexpectedly, and leaked acrid fumes. Its only merit was that like its big sister, the Aga, it gave off comforting warmth, and in winter we could move in the pet rabbits, somehow managing to negotiate round the hutch to get to the larder. How I loved that kitchen, the children, still very small, perched on our ancient utility chairs to stir the Christmas cake. I remember Marjorie Gooderson saying once that the kitchen was the most important room in the house, where all the best conversations took place, and she was right.

One dreadful evening, while Mike was in bed with 'flu, the boiler in the Rayburn burst, drenching the horrid multicoloured nylon carpet we had inherited, and flooding the kitchen. That was it – the old Rayburn had to go and we ordered a new gas one, brown and shiny, which also did the central heating. With a special aluminium flue it worked beautifully, a new gas hob was fitted beside it and we had the whole kitchen re-vamped. My biggest regret about moving in 1987 was leaving my new Rayburn behind.

CHAPTER 22

Army Cadet Force

ONE DAY I SAW A TINY advertisement in the *Cambrian News*: 'Men and women instructors needed for Dyfed Army Cadet Force'. It was to change my life. It was the first I had heard of there being any women in the ACF, and I was immediately attracted. I found out more. After some 125 years as a boys' organisation, a pilot scheme for girls was being set up nationally, Dyfed trying it in three detachments. They needed women to look after the girls. I took months to do anything about it, worried about the effect it might have on the family, when I had to go away on camps or training courses for a week or two at a time. I went to see the Rev St John Gray, Old Blue and ex-Royal Marines officer, who also happened to have five children. He and his wife Anita had become good friends, several of our children overlapping at Plascrug Primary School when St John was the minister at the URC Church in Aberystwyth. I knew that he would understand why I wanted to serve again, and he reassured me by saying that he thought children were fine so long as they knew what was happening. Then one day we happened to meet Brigadier Charles Hince, the 160 Brigade Commander in Brecon. When I asked if the ACF still needed women he sparked immediately. Next day, one of his staff officers was on the phone. I took the plunge and applied.

My first interview was not auspicious: Major Frank Edge MC, the Cadet Executive Officer, a retired regular army lieutenant colonel, came to see us at home. Will, still a toddler, crawled all the way up his smart grey suit and smeared mince pie all the way down it. However, I seemed to pass, and the next hurdle was for Mike and me to meet the Commandant, Colonel Trefor Walters, a lovely man from Pembroke with wartime service under his belt. I knew it was going to be all right. The paperwork took months to come through, but meanwhile I started the girls off in Lampeter, which already had a well established boys' detachment. Out of the twenty-five detachments in Dyfed, which comprised the old counties of Cardiganshire,

Carmarthenshire and Pembrokeshire, only three were allowed to have girls at first, and then not more than a third of the total detachment strength could be girls. The men were certainly erring on the side of caution, and it was a real struggle to get the girls accepted, not least because it was so difficult to get suitable women and any with Service experience in Dyfed to train as instructors at the time.

It was also difficult to get all the right uniform for the girls. The only item the boys had to buy was a pair of boots, whereas the girls were expected to buy boots *and* shoes, which would have been a real problem for some families. I wrote to the right people, and managed to get them WRAC drill shoes issued free. Those were pioneering days, and the first girls' weekend I ran in Saundersfoot, before mobile phones, I didn't even have access to the office telephone, and would have had to send a runner to a public telephone in an emergency. Fortunately I didn't need to, but I certainly felt the weight of responsibility at the time in charge of some thirty lively teenage girls.

At the end of the two years' pilot scheme, a meeting was held at camp and a vote taken amongst the senior officers in the county – all male – as to whether or not to continue with the girls. I was invited to address the meeting for five minutes. Being a mere lieutenant at the time, I was not allowed a vote. It was extremely galling but I managed outwardly to keep my cool. I made a little speech that I hoped was both rational and touching, aimed at the company commanders. My time up, I saluted and left. There apparently followed a lively discussion and it was decided eventually to keep the girls. We had won by a single vote. It was some satisfaction to me that by the time I left Dyfed to transfer to the Glamorgan Counties some twelve years later, both the Lord Lieutenant's Cadets in one year had been girls, Julia Turnock from Aberystwyth and Natalie Burrows from Ammanford, and I was with them when they escorted the Queen on her visit to St Davids with Prince Philip one radiant spring day, Natalie telling him firmly, 'We're the best cadets in the county, sir.' Now girl army cadets are accepted on an equal footing with the boys throughout the UK, and perhaps the early difficulties tend to be forgotten.

The girls were following the same syllabus as the boys for the Army Proficiency Certificate, and we as officers and adult instructors naturally had to learn the same skills as the youngsters – and how to teach them – in fast time. In those days, the 'basic cadre' lasted ten days. It was mostly infantry training, which even in the OTC I'd never had to learn, as all the girls at Leeds were in the Royal Artillery sub unit, and it was very demanding physically. I wrote an article for the *Army Cadet* called 'Mrs Worm's Eye View', based on the experience of being the only officer on the course along with twenty-six sergeants, ex-TA sergeant majors or potential instructors over Easter 1984, shouted at by fit young regular sergeants. By then I was thirty-six and Will, our youngest, was still only three. It was quite an experience being at the bottom of the heap again, and not very good at the practical skills required. I really hated handling weapons – I suppose being a mother had made me soft – but gritted my teeth and got through the course, and was grateful when later allowed to specialise in teaching first aid, and then press work and public relations, which took me out in the field with the cadets in all weathers in wild and beautiful places like the Brecon Beacons, the Preseli Mountains or Dartmoor. It was wonderful, watching the teenagers grow in confidence in challenging situations, gutsy and cheerful and full of humour, often with the rain driving down and no real shelter for miles.

The following is an imaginative piece I wrote as a short story on a Creative Writing course in Radyr, Cardiff in about 2001.

Ceri

It was a late afternoon in mid September, but it felt like November on the bleak Welsh mountainside. The rain was sheeting down, a vicious wind swirling round and through a huddle of eight teenagers in combat kit bent over a map. A tiny girl in the middle was clearly in charge – or trying to be.

'Think, Ceri, think,' Cadet Corporal Jones told herself fiercely. 'OK, boys, let's orientate the map again.' She was just fifteen, coming up to her GCSE exams, and she lived for the Army Cadets. This sort of exercise was her idea of bliss – or it had been up until now.

'Orientate the map,' piped up a husky young voice from the back. 'She doesn't know how to. Never trust a woman with a map. That's what my brother says.'

'Shut it, Griffiths,' snapped Ceri. The very mention of twenty year-old Jason Griffiths rocked her confidence. He was the one boy in Cadets who had ever scared her, and she, like the rest of them, had secretly rejoiced when the detachment commander had sacked him for bullying. And now they'd got landed with his little brother, Kyle, just fourteen. He had the same piercing blue eyes as Jason, the same close-cropped dark hair, the same shifty look. He had joined a year ago on his thirteenth birthday, and already he was getting a handful.

Ceri pulled on her beret more tightly. A good bit of kit, the beret. Even when it was rain-sodden it kept your head warm. 'Right, boys,' she tried again. 'That's where we did the river crossing, and it can't be much more than a k to the final checkpoint, as the crow flies.'

'But crows don't have to climb hills,' groused another. 'Look at those contours.' It was true: the wavy concentric circles were getting closer and closer on the route that Ceri and her second-in-command, a lanky lance corporal called John Edwards had marked out so carefully the night before. They had been climbing steeply for a good two hours, and all the time she had had a nagging feeling that they had gone wrong after the last checkpoint. Perhaps it wasn't the right hill.

'Right,' she said brightly, trying to assert her authority. 'If we look down there to the south-west, there should be a road, and a church with a spire and a telephone box.' They all peered into the distance, but all they could see was a thick, white mountain mist shrouding the valley. It would be dark soon, she felt sure. She tried again to sound cheerful. 'They'll have a good hot meal waiting for us back at camp.'

'I'm hungry *now.*'

'I'm frozen.'

'I'm knackered.'

'I'm sopping wet.'

The voices were growing insistent.

It was true. The ponchos they had been issued with to wear over their thin camouflage combats only kept off the worst of the wet. A raindrop seemed to hit the back of her neck every few seconds, and roll down the small of her back. Her backpack was beginning to chafe her wet skin, as was her rifle, slung across her chest. It must be the same for all of them.

'OK. This is what we'll do. See that hedge over there? It'll give us a bit of shelter. We'll take a NAAFI break there and have a brew. Last one to the stile gets to carry the radio.'

She and Kyle Griffiths set off enthusiastically, while the others broke into a half-hearted trot, slithering on the muddy grass. The cheeky little sod was going to beat her, she realised. A fitness freak like his brother, clearly. He clambered up and leapt into the air. Then there came a thud and a piercing howl of pain. By the time she got there, he was doubled up on the ground, moaning and swearing. His left leg had clearly hit a sharp boulder, and it looked as if his head had hit another.

Up to now, it had been a good week. She'd been awarded her second stripe and her Essentials of First Aid badge at the drill night on Thursday. She was particularly thrilled to be a full corporal, determined as she was to become the first female cadet RSM in the battalion. She also nursed a burning ambition, secret as yet, to go to Sandhurst and be the first army officer in her family. But right now, she began to realise the full responsibility of being a section commander. What had started as a small navigational problem, common enough, was suddenly turning into a crisis. Kyle Griffiths had gone eerily quiet. Their fellow cadets were gathering round, looking for a lead.

The Clansman. That was it – she'd radio for help. She was proud of her voice procedure. 'Hello zero, this is one. Message, over.' She fumbled with a shaking thumb, numb with cold, to press the Send button. A crackle, then silence. 'Hello zero, this is one. Radio check. Over.' Silence again. The bloody thing was U/S, after all those hours she'd lugged it around.

She turned to the casualty. He was very still. She wished he would start cheeking her again. Any sign of life would be better than this . . .

In reality on an exercise for Army Cadets, their own officers or adult instructors or regular army back-up would never be far away at the various checkpoints, and a search party would soon be organised, but I wanted to get inside the mind of young Ceri, experiencing for the first time the loneliness of command, and in what is essentially still a man's world.

The fortnight's annual camp each summer was the highlight of the year, and where the whole county came together. It was exhausting from supervising the excited youngsters on the coach journey to the end of camp, each day starting with a 6.30 reveille, and not finishing until the last lively teenager was settled, and sometimes as Orderly Officer I was on duty all night, based in the Guard Room and patrolling the camp, usually with a male sergeant instructor. Of course I had particular responsibility for the girls in the early days before we got more women officers trained, and was never so happy as when sitting in a barrack room perched on one of their beds, chatting, or making up a bed for a shivering child brought back to camp off exercise feeling unwell: there could be medical emergencies, some of them were homesick, and they all needed looking after. Of course the mother in me responded.

I enjoyed working with the padres, and in Dyfed each day started with a short Church Parade, the band leading the whole county onto the parade square. I thought it was wonderful. Even if children never saw the inside of a church for the rest of the year, they at least had this short time of communal worship, the padre on duty clearly reciting the Cadet Prayer, line by line, and everyone intoning it together:

> O God our Father, who has brought us together as members of the Army Cadet Force; help us to do our duty at all times and to be loyal to each other. May all that is good and true prosper among us; strengthen us to defend the right; and bless our work that it may be acceptable to You for Jesus' Christ's sake.
>
> Amen.

On the middle Sunday of camp, we would have a longer service, indoors or out, according to what was available, many of the cadets clearly unfamiliar even with well-known hymns, and I wrote the following article about one of our padres, Andy Herrick, whom I had first got to know when he served his curacy in Aberystwyth.

Padre Strikes the Right Note

Ceredigion boy and girl cadets had a bonus this camp when the new chaplain for Dyfed Army Cadet Force arrived to be their own Company Padre.

Aberporth Rector, the Revd Andrew Herrick, after a quick change into khaki from Air Training Corps kit, reported to Okehampton Training Camp all bright and shiny in Barrack Dress, sporting the badges of the Royal Army Chaplains' Department. Within minutes he was into lightweights, boots and puttees and off to the rock face at Meldon Quarry to go abseiling with the Cardi cadets.

As one of the adult instructors remarked: 'He was very, very good. He got cammed up like everyone else on exercise and even did the obstacle course where he got very wet, I believe. The cadets all like him.'

A former Youth Chaplain to St David's Diocese, father-of-three, the Revd Herrick made Church Parade go with a swing, switching happily from the organ to his guitar where appropriate. A Lincolnshire man who has chosen the Church in Wales for his ministry, he read the lesson for the cadets most beautifully – in Welsh.

His first reaction to life in the ACF? 'I really think the Army Cadet Force can do something to help young people today. What I thought was really good at camp was the positive way the cadets learned to work together as a team.'

1987. Reproduced by kind permission of the editors of the *Welsh Churchman*.

When I moved to serve with the cadets in Glamorgan, a much bigger county, the daily church parade couldn't be managed, but we still had one on Sunday, the Roman Catholic chaplain, Father Ray O'Shea, marching his flock to Mass in one of the Nissen huts which served as a simple makeshift chapel. When a much-loved company commander, from the Valleys, Major Mike Birch, died prematurely from lung cancer, his cadets turned out in uniform en masse, filling both chapels in the local crematorium, the girls all in floods of tears, and they have erected a memorial to him in the grounds of their weekend training centre. I felt that there was spirituality, if unstated, and a good-heartedness, in the cadets, boys and girls alike.

Although there used to be 'Padre's Hour' scheduled into the camp programme, I think that the padres often found it more effective joining in the training with the cadets, going out on exercise with them, and answering any questions about God as they arose. They also did hospital visiting at camp, and were always around as a friendly face and listening ear, a Christian witness even if the majority of cadets, officers and adult instructors had no formally acknowledged faith, and it is good that there was a padre allocated to each company or area, making a total of three or four in each Army Cadet Force county. Vicars would make huge efforts to get their parishes covered so that they could make annual camp, and one very keen padre of ours, Philip Gullidge, also looked after a TA unit in Cardiff for a time, earning his Bosnia medal to his credit.

The Army Cadet Force is a great family organisation, with the benefit of continuity not often enjoyed in my time in the regular army where postings were so frequent. A boy or girl could join Cadets at thirteen, stay in the same detachment until eighteen, and sometimes go on to train as an officer or adult instructor, like father or mother, having perhaps become a top 4-Star cadet and gained the Duke of Edinburgh's Award at Gold or Silver standard through the ACF. For one girl, Jessica, the future, sadly, was less bright, following a tragic road accident, and I wrote the following article in her honour in 2001, towards the end of my twenty years' service with the Army Cadets.

The Gold Badge of Courage

A former Gwent Army Cadet is to go to London next month to receive her Duke of Edinburgh's Gold Award – in a wheelchair.

Gaining the Gold Award is an outstanding achievement in itself, but for young Jessica Morgan of Tredegar, the story of her and her family's courage in the last few years is an inspiration.

Shortly after completing her Gold Award, and finishing her cadet service as a lance corporal, Jessica, then just nineteen, was knocked down by a car.

Three hospitals and two years later, Jessica was finally allowed home, but the accident has left her unable to eat or speak, confined to a wheelchair and needing constant care.

Jessica is now twenty-two and was recently well enough to go back to Gwent Army Cadet Force to receive her Gold Award. Her old unit laid on a party for her and her family at their Raglan Barracks headquarters in Newport as a welcome back.

At the parade, Major Keith Fulton-Forrest, Duke of Edinburgh's Award Officer and Adventure Training Officer for the Gwent army cadets read the citation, which stated:

'Being in the Cadets was a great part of her life. Jessica was a first class cadet and a credit to her detachment and her county.'

Activities covered for the award, he said, had included karate, a cadet leadership course at the Cadet Training Centre, Frimley Park, a tough expedition on Dartmoor and learning to drive.

Her Majesty's Deputy Lieutenant for Gwent, Brigadier John Hooper, in presenting her with her gold badge, said how privileged he felt.

Several officers and adult instructors who had known her as well as her old cadet friends were present at the ceremony to honour Jessica and her family, headed by the new cadet commandant of Gwent ACF, Lieutenant Colonel Mike Noel-Smith.

Jessica's mother confirmed how important the Cadets had been to her: 'It brought out such a lot in her and gave her so much confidence. Whenever there was an activity, she was off. She put her heart and soul into it.'

Former Sergeant Instructor Debbie Hopkins from the Royal Regiment of Wales Brynmawr detachment to which Jessica belonged, commented: 'Basically, she was an outstanding cadet.'

One action for which she is particularly remembered is when she used her first aid skills learnt as a cadet to take control of the situation and help a dying biker at a road traffic accident.

West Mercia Police wrote to thank her for all her efforts 'in difficult circumstances.' 'Such conduct serves to renew one's faith in human nature,' they told her.

Sadly, Jess is still suffering from the results of her own accident, but her Gold Award presentation with Gwent ACF was both a humbling and uplifting experience for all who met her and her family that evening and shared in their pride and delight.

Written summer 2001

Reproduced by kind permission of the editor of *Army Cadet*.

CHAPTER 23

The Welsh Question

MANY OF THE ARMY CADETS, particularly in West Wales, were Welsh-speaking, and Welsh was certainly widely spoken in Aberystwyth. Mike was determined that I should learn, and having got the first two children bathed, I would run round the corner to Yr Ysgubor (The Barn), also used as a drop-in centre, for evening classes, which I enjoyed. The tutors were keen to send Mike and me on a totally Welsh-speaking residential course, but when we discovered that we would be separated at night in dormitories, we drew the line. However, I was grateful for the smattering of Welsh that I had picked up in class when I later found myself filling in for nearly two terms at Penweddig, the Welsh secondary school, as a supply teacher. The teachers spoke only Welsh in the staff room, apart from my head of department, Mrs Ann Davies, who was kind, and talked to me in English so I could understand what she wanted me to do. I was allowed to speak English in the classroom, since it was my subject, but a child would often come round with a note on administrative arrangements written completely in Welsh. 'You read it, miss,' he would taunt me.

'No, you read it,' I would reply. 'You'll do it so much better.' The truth was, I could hardly understand a word of the instruction, so often hadn't a clue what was going on at the time. I had never really thought before in Britain about being different because I was English, and it was a salutary, but sometimes unnerving experience being a lone Englishwoman on the staff.

Although Mike was passionately Welsh, especially when it came to rugby, he didn't sound it, and of course we had both been in the British Army, so our difference in nationality had never really been an issue. He would describe himself on forms as 'British/Welsh', and I had an inkling of how important his homeland was to him three years into our marriage when we moved to Anglesey from Cambridge in 1976, and he announced that he wanted to die in Wales, which at the time I thought a bit 'previous'. He achieved his goal in

130

1999, and even then, would rather have died in Mid Wales, where his family came from. Back in 1976, stuck in North Wales, and missing Cambridge desperately, I would mutter jokingly to English friends, 'Drag me over the border to die,' but now I've lived in Wales so long I'm not sure where I would feel at home in England any more, and I think I would really miss Wales if I lived anywhere else now. I love Welsh warmth and kindness and expressions.

I think I'd even miss the Welsh road signs. It's good going on holiday to England, but there is a great sense of relief on the way back as I cross the new Severn Bridge and see the *Croeso y Gymru* (Welcome to Wales) sign. I'm home. I think, however, that there will always be a sort of inner restlessness. I remember saying to St John Gray once, 'Sometimes I panic inwardly about where I belong,' and he replied, 'So do I.' Perhaps it is something about having been in the Services, or even having boarded at CH, that you make your home wherever you happen to be at the time, while at the same time gradually growing away from your geographical roots. You feel an affinity with others who have been through a similar experience. And of course, I had moved to Wales, which is a rather different country from England. St John, like me a Londoner originally, did in fact move home to England with his family to look after a URC church in Dorset, back in Royal Marines country, but tragically developed a brain tumour shortly afterwards. It proved inoperable and he died at home. As we did for Mike, however, the family brought him back to Aberystwyth for the funeral. Only the eldest child, Andrew, was working by then, having joined the Navy, and Anita, amazing woman that she is, picked herself up, moved to Taunton and steered the other four children through school and university single-handed, the youngest, Thomas, gaining a place at Housey.

In Aberystwyth back in 1979, we already had to choose for our eldest, Katie, between the Welsh primary school and the English-medium Plascrug, where the nursery class took three-year-olds. We chose Plascrug, where I can still remember passing over our daughter to Mrs Steeds, who looked pretty fierce on first meeting, and I felt somewhat reluctant about delivering our little girl into the hands of Authority. I need not have worried: Rhiannon Steeds, ably assisted by Miss Rosemary, later Mrs Rosemary, a delightful nursery nurse, was an exceptional teacher, going on to become head of the whole school, and she and her husband David have developed into good friends. Benedict and William followed Katie to Plascrug, and it was a happy walk down Plascrug Avenue with Brown Dog once or twice daily over the years.

Then, one day, our lives changed forever: Mike had to be in Cardiff for the day for a job interview, and something drove me to go and see the Cathedral School, Llandaff. Like Katie, Ben was having free violin lessons at Plascrug, having been picked out with two others in the class as particularly musical. They were also singing in Holy Trinity choir. At the back of our minds was the possibility of a choral scholarship. I met John Knapp, the headmaster at Llandaff, and immediately liked him, as did Mike. The voice trial, held early every January, was imminent. Mr Knapp encouraged us to apply, stressing that nearly all choristers went on to win music awards to their senior schools at thirteen plus. 'If Ben gets this choral scholarship, Mr Knapp,' I said, 'sending him here will be a complete act of faith.' We had no idea how we could afford to put all or any of our children through independent education, but with a two-thirds scholarship, Llandaff would be just about possible for Ben, and we were pretty sure that Will was musical too.

The Cardiff job did not materialise, and we had to make a quick decision. We asked if we could bring Ben, then not quite eight, down to see the school and the cathedral, as it would be a huge upheaval for him to be boarding so far from home. The visit was readily agreed, and Christmas Eve was the only day possible. Rosie Knapp had made a magnificent chocolate cake, and Ben, who, exceptionally, had been allowed to attend choir practice in the cathedral song room, came back with eyes shining. He said he wanted to come.

Preparing for the voice trial, we were helped by his piano teacher, Dr Bernard Smith, who suggested 'Awake my soul and sing' as the piece to be sung, saying that that you couldn't go wrong with Bach. There would be an academic assessment and ear tests, like picking out the middle note of a triad, and Ben also had to play his violin. It was a little half size Lark, sold to us for £10 in the Plascrug auction by St John Gray, and shared at the time with Katie. We little thought when we bought it 'on spec' that it would lead them both on to music scholarships one day.

In order to get to the voice trial on time, we had to stay overnight, and squashed into a family room in Churchill's Hotel in Llandaff. The bathroom was separated from the bedroom by a thin partition, and when, sleepless with anxiety I got up to polish the violin for Ben in the bathroom, Brown Dog's tail pounded thunderously on the bathroom wall. It seemed that the whole family was in this venture together.

We arrived in the school dining room to find a mass of smart little boys in bow ties, all looking very confident, as did their parents. All were competing for a handful of places in the cathedral choir. I said to Mrs Knapp that I had no idea there would be so many candidates, and she just smiled. I had the feeling that they liked our little Ben, but the musicians, Dr Michael Smith, the cathedral organist, and school director of music Michael Hoeg were an unknown quantity, and then there was the Dean, the Very Reverend Alun Radcliffe Davies, who, we were told, had the final say in awarding scholarships. Were we completely out of our depth? Unlike for some other parents who did the rounds of voice trials in various cathedrals, this was our first experience. If we as parents were worried, however, Will, just five, was in his element, and when not eating, seemed to spend most of his time upside down on the wall bars in the gym.

We drove home to Aberystwyth and waited, for days, or was it weeks? At last the acceptance letter came and the die was cast: Ben had won a choral scholarship and was to start as a probationer at Llandaff in September. I was just so grateful that he hadn't been disappointed, but conscious that it would be a complicated undertaking for the whole family, with Christmas Day on the road for instance, all the boys in the cathedral choir having to be present for Choral Eucharist in the morning, even if, as probationers they were not yet allowed to sing.

Although Llandaff Cathedral years later started a girls' cathedral choir, when Ben joined it was very much the traditional set-up of men and boys. Katie was indignant: 'I'm just as good at singing as Ben. Ben's going to a *special* school. What about *me*?' I had some sympathy. What were we to do? We happened to be up in Denbigh one day, and let her spend some time looking round Howell's, a friendly, beautifully situated girls' school, about 320-strong, which took both boarders and day pupils. Miss Stubbs in the Prep School, a strict, traditional schoolmistress, put her through her paces, and pronounced her suitable, and Katie begged her Daddy to let her go there. She says now she thinks it was only the school ice cream that persuaded her, but certainly by the time we moved to Mid Glamorgan and she could have gone as a day girl to Howell's, Llandaff, she was determined to stay with her friends in Denbigh, and I think it really kept my mother going having her for exeat weekends in Anglesey. Katie still sees several Howell's friends frequently some fourteen years after they left school, which says something about the loyalties they developed there, and certainly replicates the experience of many Hertford Old Blues.

PART V

The Changing Years

47. With Katie (10), winner of the Prep School music competition, Howell's, Denbigh 1987

48. Move to South Wales 1987. With Alli the rabbit

49. *Katie's Confirmation at Howell's, Denbigh with godmothers Mrs Marjorie Gooderson and Mrs Veronica Baker, Mrs Enid Lloyd (Veronica's mother), brother Ben, father Mike, and her Granny, Mrs Eileen Wilson*

50. *Will's Confirmation. With his father at Shrewsbury School*

51. Susan Dipper 'Big Susan' in her eighties at Wrentnall, Menai Bridge

52. Early artistic promise: Happy Anniversary card by Katie Davies-Jenkins 1993

53. Church Island, Menai Bridge. Katie decorating Big Susan's grave. 1984

54. Sketch of Will Davies-Jenkins by his sister Katie

55. The Rough and the Surplus Cricket Club (Llandaff Cathedral Choir Association fathers). Mike D-J (kneeling, left). Standing far right: the Cathedral School's director of music, Michael Hoeg, now MBE and Edward Elwyn Jones (umpires), 1994

56. Gap year experience: Rachel Brown (21) of Llandaff; Ben Davies-Jenkins (18) of Groesfaen; director of the Right Hand Trust Mark Wright at Llandaff Cathedral 1996

57. *Will Davies-Jenkins. Marcello oboe solo at Shrewsbury School. 1998*

58. *Last day at school: Katie with her Granny at Howell's, Denbigh 1995*

59. Hertford Old Blue Anne-Marie Braun (née Kelly) with husband Christopher at their Silver Wedding party, April 1997

60. Hertford Old Blues compare notes: Lady Wendy Stone (née Lee) with Mrs Kathleen Betterton (née Baron), our CH, Hertford head of English, at the Brauns' Silver Wedding, April 1997

61. *Guernsey family at our Silver Wedding party: L-R Cousin Di (Lewis); Mrs Het Lane; cousin Lesley (Le Page) with her husband Nigel, April 1998*

62. *Silver Wedding party: Major Toby Kenyon, Royal Welch Fusiliers with his goddaughter Katie; middle distance: my cousin Helen von Hoyningen-Huene, April 1998*

CHAPTER 24

Howell's, Denbigh and Llandaff
Chorister Start

THE SUMMER BEFORE KATIE AND BEN were to start at their respective boarding schools was a race against time to get the last nametape sewn on. Katie's boarding house was called 'Bodgwilym', and every single item down to the last handkerchief and sock needed an extra long Cash's nametape with 'AK Davies-Jenkins Bodgwilym' and a laundry mark, a little yellow square of bias binding sewn on – a fiddly job. I couldn't help thinking that our parents had had it easier at Hertford where all the school uniform was provided, and usually just marked in indelible ink with our House and individual number.

The expense of the uniform could have been worse at both Howell's and Llandaff, as a second-hand system was in operation. Mrs Knapp at Llandaff ran the school shop most efficiently, and we could replace kit on the first day of term if necessary. I can well remember one chorister's father, Nigel Samuelson, sitting in the car sewing on the last nametape before saying goodbye to Robert, or 'Sammy' as he was always known. For the choristers we had to buy two distinctive pieces of kit – their mortar board, which just about lasted their four or five years in the choir, cardboard edges beginning to show through at the corners, and their red school cap which had an extra golden braid inner ring sewn on to mark out choristers from other Llandaff boys. They were trained to doff the mortar board to clergy and masters – mere mothers didn't count in the pecking order!

The most recognizable piece of Howell's uniform in Katie's day was a long Harris tweed cloak in grey with a maroon lining, which must have kept the girls cosy through bitter North Walian winters.

We acquired a second-hand one for Katie and she never grumbled about all the pass-me-downs. Neither did her brothers. They all realised that there was a tight budget and even declared that they really loved picnics when other boarders were taken out for meals by their parents in expensive hotels. I don't think ours felt deprived, and they were certainly far too polite so say so even if they *did*. In fact choristers often tended to come from large families in our day at Llandaff, so most of us were economising pretty carefully. There seemed to be far more wealth among the day pupils' parents, who of course were paying full fees, and those of children at secondary level.

Leaving Ben at Llandaff for the first time was particularly hard. I'd made a picnic for his supper after our two-and-a-half-hour journey. Mr Evans, the housemaster told him that they weren't allowed to eat in the Lodge, as the boarding house was called. I shot him a look. 'But if I turn my back, Ben . . .' he went on. A tall South Walian, he must have looked huge to a small boy, but at least there was a twinkle in his eye. We left Ben smiling and waving bravely at the school entrance in the golden September evening sunlight in his new school uniform, his father telling me simply, 'We have to let him get on with it now.'

'But I don't *want* to let him get on with it,' I thought, 'he's only eight,' and sobbed all the way out of Cardiff. I never really got used to the parting when any of my children had to go back to school, and saying goodbye to them is hard even now we're all supposed to be very grown up. I still have memories of boarding the Hertford East train at Liverpool Street at the beginning of term, my mother and I trying to be brave for each other.

We soon began to realise the administrative problems of having our three children in three different schools. Their term dates varied, complicated at Llandaff by the fluctuations in the timing of Easter, and we needed a different colour for each child on the year planner to see at a glance how to arrange holidays and each journey. We chose yellow for Katie, red for Ben and blue for Will – nothing to do with their politics! On one occasion the first term – it must have been their first exeat weekend – Katie was due back in Denbigh and Ben in Llandaff the same evening. I had to drive Ben back to Cardiff, unused to thrusting city traffic after the gentler pace of Aberystwyth. We arrived in the dark and got hopelessly lost round the docks somewhere. It was raining so hard that bleak October night that I could barely see through the windscreen and when a double decker bus was suddenly heading straight for us, I realised I must have turned into a one-way street the wrong way. I was terrified, but tried to reassure the rather quiet little boy in the back that all was well. We stayed in Churchill's again, knowing nowhere else, and I remember the net curtains in the dining room looking grey: it was a particularly glum breakfast, as we both knew the parting was imminent. I dropped him off at school and headed for home, my job done – until the next time. Whoever could say that sending children to boarding school was easy?

The new boys were not allowed to telephone home for the first few weeks, and then only with staff permission, 'to allow them to settle'. We were blessed, though, through the kindness of another chorister's mother, Penny Longmore, who lived locally and used to take Ben home for tea with her son Huw when they were let out for a few hours on Wednesdays or Sundays. To pick up the telephone in Aberystwyth and suddenly hear the familiar voice, with a cheerful 'Hi, Mum' was hugely reassuring, and I shall ever be grateful to Penny for her thoughtfulness to me, and for making Ben feel at home. When we moved down to South Wales ourselves it was a great joy to be able to help look after other choristers who lived at a distance.

There were about twenty boys on choral scholarships, of whom only fourteen to sixteen would be fully-fledged choristers. They all had to start as probationers. This time of waiting must have been a frustrating experience for the young boys: as probationers they had to attend every practice in the song room and then sit quietly through every sung service – seven a week – in their cassocks, not allowed to sing a note, unless, exceptionally, they were lent a surplice and allowed to fill in for a chorister who was off sick. The probationer period usually lasted about a year, but could go on for two years, and occasionally in this time a boy was asked to leave the choir, which could cause great heartache to a family, and feel like a bereavement, especially if they then couldn't afford the full boarding or day fees, and the child had to leave the school. Naturally, therefore, having a probationer son was an anxious time for parents, and we all longed for the great moment when the organist deemed a child worthy to be 'made up' to a fully-fledged chorister, and the ceremony was arranged with the Dean. This could happen at very short notice, and on one famous occasion I had just arrived at my mother's house in Anglesey when an excited little voice told me that he was being 'made up' the next day, and I had to hare back to Cardiff, another five-hour car journey.

In our day, for Ben and then for Will, who followed him into
Llandaff Cathedral Choir, there were junior and senior choristers, with
separate ceremonies for each promotion, as well as two head choristers,
or Dean's Scholars, as they were known. The juniors wore light blue
medallions and the seniors red, which they could keep forever, but
sadly, the Dean's Scholars did not have even a replica to keep of their
heavy silver badge of office. Ben became a corner boy and Will a Dean's
Scholar. Ben's godfather Hugh Carson told me that he still had his silver
corner boy's medal from Canterbury, so cathedrals obviously differ
slightly in their traditions. I think that for most children it is a matter of
immense pride to have been a cathedral chorister, and my mother had
wooden carvings made of the Llandaff badge, on which Ben and Will
hung their medals in their bedroom at home. To that Ben added a
purple-ribboned medal when he was awarded the Bishop's Certificate
for singing by Lichfield Diocese in his first year at Shrewsbury.

The 'making up' ceremony was a real rite of passage, and the only
difference in the ceremony for choristers nowadays at Llandaff is that
the distinction between junior and senior choristers seems to have
been abolished, so that only the Dean's Scholars have a badge of
office. The donning of the surplice is therefore the critical moment
for a new chorister, whereas in our day the appropriate medallion was
also placed round his neck. Picture the scene at Evensong for a
probationer's 'making up': perhaps only two or three boys, aged only
nine or ten, their families watching tensely, each boy waiting in his
dark red cassock, shoes polished and hair combed, for his big moment
and standing in the centre of the cathedral under the 'Majestas', the
Epstein sculpture of Christ. The ceremony runs as follows:

> The Organist presents the boy to the Dean, saying: 'Mr Dean, I
> present to you . . . to be admitted as a chorister in the choir of this
> Cathedral.'
> The Dean then addresses the boy saying: 'Do you promise to serve
> faithfully and well as a Chorister, and to sing the praises of Almighty
> God in this Cathedral Choir?'
> He replies: 'I do.'
> The Dean then says the following prayer: 'Most merciful Father, we
> pray You to send this chorister Your heavenly blessing; that he may
> sing to Your glory and serve You joyfully all the days of his life.
> Though Jesus Christ our Lord. Amen.'

The Dean then takes the boy by the hand saying: '. . . I do here in the presence of God, admit you as a Chorister in this Cathedral Choir.'

The Dean places the surplice on the boy: 'And may Almighty God endow you also with the ornaments of His grace, through Jesus Christ our Lord.'

And the boy replies: 'Amen'

The Dean leads the boy to the Choir Stalls, he takes his place in the choir and the Dean says the following prayer: 'Almighty God, send Your blessing on all Your servants who minister before You in the choir of this Cathedral. Give them the spirit of faith, reverence and joy, and lift their hymns and their lives to You. Through Jesus Christ our Lord. Amen.'

This solemn ceremony effectively sealed the fate of a boy for another three or four years, as he was technically 'bound' to the cathedral until he was thirteen and a half or his voice broke, whichever was the sooner. Already, he was used to a very tough routine, starting with half an hour's instrumental practice before breakfast (they were mostly learning two instruments) and choir practice in the cathedral before morning school, and another choir practice before Evensong every day except Wednesday. At Llandaff, they covered a huge and ambitious choral repertoire chosen by Dr Michael Smith, so their sight singing had to be pretty accurate. Then, thanks to Michael Hoeg's inspired leadership there were the various music groups in the Cathedral School like the orchestra, and, particularly prestigious in our boys' time, the Chamber Choir, trained by Alun Jones, who went on to Howell's, Denbigh, whose beautiful Chapel Choir in our Katie's time won the Classic FM Choir of the Year under his directorship.

The choristers joined in every facet of life at the Cathedral School, and some were very sporty too, although the Cathedral Choir could be used as an excuse on occasion for getting out of unpopular activities, and evening prep after Evensong was often skimped by tired little boys. However, they learned to work under pressure and use their time well, and were generally bright children, who did amazingly well all round, many of them achieving academic as well as music awards to their public schools.

There was still Saturday morning school for most of our sons' time there, and dedicated schoolmasters like Tony Phillips would give extra Latin lessons on Saturday afternoons to prepare boys for academic scholarships – not always appreciated at the time by his pupils! I think the fact that they were all boarders really put less strain on families than nowadays where all Llandaff choristers are dayboys, and have to be delivered to the cathedral very early every morning for choir practice and picked up after Evensong, with prep and instrumental practice presumably having to be fitted in often at home. It takes a different sort of dedication for parents today than for us parents of boarding choristers, many of whom faced long journeys frequently every term. Of course homesickness could be a problem for the younger boarders, but with warm, cuddly matrons like Heather Jenkins, and headmaster John Knapp passionately committed to the Cathedral Choir, he and Rosie unfailingly kind and courteous to us supportive parents, most of the boys flourished as boarders, and absolutely loved 'Choristers Only' weeks before Christmas and Easter when the other pupils had gone home, they had the run of the school, and were invited out to parties every evening. It made them feel very special, which they were.

CHAPTER 25

Move to South Wales

WE LASTED JUST A YEAR DOING the five-hour round trip from Aberystwyth to Cardiff before Mike got a job with the NHS in Cardiff and we moved to what was then Mid Glamorgan. Will became a dayboy for a short time at the Cathedral School before winning a choral scholarship and joining Ben as a chorister. We moved on Will's seventh birthday, a difficult drive as Alli the rabbit crouched in a laundry basket beside me, quivering with fear. We had found an old mid-terrace cottage to rent in Groesfaen with a beautiful landscaped front garden, and we had to get permission from a rather unpredictable young lady landlord to keep Alli there. The rear garden was wild, a child's delight, and backed onto fields. The Calor gas heating was exorbitant to run, and I was glad of the open fire in the kitchen as we got through our first winter. For me, it was a delightful woodsmoke-and-wellies existence as we adapted to life in South Wales, which, I soon realised, thinks of itself as rather 'posher' than Aberystwyth. Even the very young mothers from the Valleys, I noticed, would teeter into the surgery in Talbot Green on uncomfortably high heels pushing their buggies, and in a time when many women wore tracksuits to pick up their children from school, some Cathedral School day pupils' mothers wore designer models, gold jewellery and lots of makeup. In that way I think I always felt a bit different. 'Aber' had been a very sensible and down-to-earth place to bring up children where much of the time we had to dress for the rain and the cold. I had a wonderful 'Paddington Bear' rain hat and a long, padded, turquoise oilskin mac, totally waterproof. It felt stiff and almost squeaked as you moved, and when I walked into the Bursar's office at Llandaff wearing it one unusually wet day, I could see him wincing, terrified that I would spray water onto his precious computer.

Amazingly, he still gave me what I wanted: a decent buffet lunch for a large number at a reasonable price. The occasion was John and Rosie Knapp's farewell, and we managed to keep the party a complete surprise from John. By then, Mike and I had been running Llandaff Cathedral Choir Association for about four years. This was largely a support group, completely self-funding, for choristers and parents alike, and we took over from Gerard and Elisabeth Elias who had run it magnificently, and even organised a choir tour to Sweden in their time. After strenuous efforts, the most ambitious one Mike and I could manage was a West Wales Tour in 1993, and we learned the negotiating skills needed to deal with musicians and clergy, who didn't always see eye to eye. Then there were the gentlemen of the choir, whom we knew less well, but who also needed to be kept onside to make a successful tour, or any other event involving the whole choir.

One of the big fund-raising events would be an evening of carols for 'the great and the good' of Cardiff at the Mansion House, hosted by the Lord Mayor, but with us choristers' parents producing a hot buffet. It was great fun, but pretty complicated, as all the food had to be prepared at home beforehand by busy mothers who had volunteered to help. I can still remember superchef Erica Austin taking charge of an oven and emerging flushed but triumphant with a giant lasagne. She was magnificent.

Then there was the washing up. Curiously, there were no dishwashers installed, and it says much about John Knapp that he was deep into the kitchen sink in his dinner jacket at midnight, leading from the front. It was a huge team event for mothers and fathers working together, and choristers' sisters helping out as waitresses.

When we heard the news that John Knapp was leaving we were stunned: as headmaster, he had been a vital part of our lives. We knew that generations of choristers and their families who had been at Llandaff in his time would want to contribute to a leaving present for Rosie and him, and so Mike and I wrote secretly to as many as we could trace, inviting them to a party at the school. The response was as we had thought, and I was particularly touched by cheques from hard-up undergraduates.

We had had a huge sponge cake made, decorated with an outline of the school, and it was only as I was trying to slip it into the school building that I was caught by John Knapp and he wondered what on earth was going on. 'Don't even ask, Mr Knapp,' I said firmly, and it was wonderful to see his face when he eventually was led over from his house by Rosie, who of course had to be in the know, and saw all the former choristers and their parents, as well as the current generation, there to honour him. He was clearly delighted.

By then it was 1992, and Will was on his last lap at Llandaff, Anthony Evans standing in as acting headmaster. We had already had to make the decision on where to send Ben when he left the choir in 1991. I had spoken to Admissions at Housey, hoping that they might have a place for him, but because he would have had to start at thirteen plus instead of eleven like all the other boys, they said that whilst they would love to admit choristers, they thought that they wouldn't fit in with the rest of their peer group. It was a great disappointment, and the rules have now been changed to take in choristers on deferred entry provided that they pass the entrance examination along with the other candidates.

CHAPTER 26

Shrewsbury School

T HIS LEFT US HAVING TO find somewhere else. After exhaustive research and visits to various public schools, we had found Shrewsbury, and felt instantly at home there. A couple of Mike's delightful and independent-minded Royal Welch Fusilier friends, Major Tim Bible and teacher and writer Michael Hodges, were Salopians, which undoubtedly influenced us, and helped us to choose a House. Unlike at CH, Horsham and Hertford, the Houses were all very individual architecturally. They also varied in character, of course, according to who was running them. We looked at Rigg's Hall, and liked housemaster Stewart Roberts, a physicist, and his pianist wife Anna, instantly. It was also conveniently close to the Music School, a practical consideration for Ben on such a huge site. Director of music John Moore tipped us off that the headmaster, Ted Maidment, was a singer, and finally meeting 'Big Ted' clinched it for us. He was extremely welcoming, and genuinely interested in Ben and all his music. He clearly approved of cathedral choristers and wanted to recruit them, especially for the chapel choir.

Ben and then Will won enough in awards for us to feel brave enough to send them to Shrewsbury, and each in turn became School Captain of Music, a credit to the teaching in their formative years at Llandaff, both in the Cathedral Choir and in school, and to the musical interest fostered earlier at Plascrug. Love of music is part of life in Wales, and it was good to see music encouraged and respected at Shrewsbury, as indeed it is very much at Christ's Hospital.

We were exceptionally lucky in Rigg's, in that when Stewart Roberts left to take up a headship, he and Anna were succeeded by David and Sue Aston. They were particularly good to me, and of course to Will, I'm sure, having me to stay before Speech Day, just weeks after Mike had died, when it was all very raw. It had been dreadful sending Will back to school immediately after his father's funeral, but I think he was supported both before and afterwards by quiet and unobtrusive kindness from many of the Shrewsbury staff,

146

from Big Ted downwards, and not least from his personal tutor, Christopher Argent. It was a humane touch, I thought, that the sixth form boys were allowed to choose their own tutor. Both Will's and Ben's, artist Caroline Pringle, were known for their culinary skills, which may have had something to do with their selection!

I wrote the following piece after our first Shrewsbury Speech Day, which I really don't think changed very much over the years; some traditions are worth preserving. This is a shortened version of the article I wrote to *The Salopian*, the Shrewsbury School newsletter, and appears by kind permission of the current editor, Richard Hudson. I asked for it to be published anonymously at the time, for fear of embarrassing Benedict aged fourteen.

The headmaster at the time was still Cambridge historian and inspired bass baritone, Ted Maidment, known affectionately as Big Ted, and we also had an immediate rapport with his senior master, Colonel Stephen Caney and his wife Elizabeth, partly because of the army connection, and also because they had gone to university at Aberystwyth, which is where all our children had grown up. Ben's housemaster Stewart Roberts and his wife Anna became firm friends, and Stewart was assisted in Rigg's Hall by linguist Chris Etherington, a house tutor. (Every member of staff was attached to a house, and in Will's day Mr Maidment volunteered as a house tutor for Rigg's, which must have been quite a challenge for new housemaster David Aston). The dynamic director of music was John Moore, and directing the chapel choir was kindly Welshman Richard Dacey. The Chaplain was a lovely, gentle Mirfield-trained priest, David Allcock, who was said to encourage his Confirmation candidates to leave a letter to God on the altar before the laying on of hands. I couldn't help wondering about the postal delivery system!

First Shrewsbury Speech Day – An Appreciation

School Speech Day is a wonderful institution. It may vary considerably in style from place to place but it always has, one suspects, the same aim – to send parents out filled with pride and delight and conviction that they have made the right choice of school for their child.

This, our first Shrewsbury Speech Day, had a quality all of its own. In fact, it started for us the night before with the *Musique sans Frontières* concert. Arriving breathless as usual, after a frantic journey from Mid

Glamorgan, just before 9 o'clock, one could sense the anticipation, marquees and beer kegs everywhere, trumpeters warming up nervously outside The Alington Hall. We slipped upstairs to the gallery from where we could just make out our third-form son, combed and serious at the back of the stage, making his début in the Symphony Orchestra. Beside me sat our eleven-year-old, enveloped in his big brother's Shrewsbury rugger shirt, cocking a critical little ear.

From the first blare of the trumpet prelude he was riveted, caught up in the sheer verve and excitement of the live performance. He launched into the Latin and heel-stamping of the 'Carmen' as if he had known it all his life. By the end of the 'William Tell Overture' he was bouncing with delight. The String Orchestra then provided a gentle contrast and who could fail to be impressed by the warmth and breadth of tone of the legato piece or the delightfully varied dynamics of the 'Pizzicato Polka'?

John Moore's sense of humour showed through in a charming selection of songs for the new Chamber Choir, the animal noises being particularly memorable. After this came another change of mood: the house lights dimmed. Big Band was ready for blast-off. The impact of the first note almost knocked us off our bench (could it be that one or two rather senior masters had already made their escape?). Once we had recovered from the initial shock, though, we began to enjoy it. I shall never hear 'The Pink Panther' again without thinking of James Harries, apparently effortless, holding the audience with his tenor sax solo. And to think that only a few weeks ago he had done the same with his clarinet. Only that time it was Mozart. What versatility!

What could possibly follow Big Band and not be an anti-climax? Answer: the Jazz Band. It was fascinating for its movement and confident improvisation, the young pianist particularly stunning with his rhythm and fluency. Chris Etherington, the bearded master in charge, looked in his element with his grainy voice, strumming away in his multicoloured open-necked shirt, slinking across the stage amidst his younger fellow musicians.

Next day, Ascension Day as it happened, we began Speech Day itself with the Junior Commemoration Service. The Chapel, always well cared-for, looked especially beautiful, the russets and golds in the new altar kneeler blending perfectly with the altar flowers, while the deep blood orange shine of the Sanctuary tiles reflected years of loving attention.

Mr Godwin was well into his stride. The television screen danced in the organ loft beside him. The trumpeters were preparing for action, John Moore in command. Richard Dacey smiled encouragingly at his choir. The Chaplain's warmth and obvious sincerity as always set the tone. A third-form chorister read the Ascension story with impressive clarity and confidence, delighting in every word with the unselfconscious enthusiasm of the young.

The word 'frailty' in J.M. Peterson's Founder's Hymn struck a note of humility, echoed in the simple prayers. No excuse here for complacent triumphalism, more the sense of generations of Salopians working together, doing their best in this beloved place.

Too soon, the final hymn was over, the organ voluntary was crashing out, the Chapel Choir bowing to the altar, carefully together, only to repeat the performance a few minutes later for the senior service. It is said that the Chaplain later ate his dog collar in appreciation of their double efforts.

The rest of the day passed far too quickly to be able to take in the whole range of exhibitions and activities on offer. However, 'Chemical Magic' more than lived up to expectations for the children while we enjoyed the warmth and fun of our house 'At Home'. Whatever was the 'pick-me-up' it worked wonderfully and we queued for our lunch (which proved well worth waiting for) in a happy glow.

We enjoyed seeing some of the exhibitions and meeting our son's teachers who all made time to talk about him. Each of the staff, masters and mistresses, showed delight in his or her own subject, and expressed satisfaction with the equipment available to teach it. One even heard frequent and unsolicited praise for the Head.

Of course it was for his report for which we had really come. Beforehand, The Alington Hall stage looked rather bleak, bare apart from a single huge flower arrangement, a table and lectern against a black background. Suddenly, with no fanfare or retinue a gowned figure appeared. From the rear of the gallery it looked curiously small but when 'Ladies and Gentlemen' filtered through the microphone, the hall was filled with the headmaster's familiar voice. He didn't need to raise it, such was his own instant authority. We could each have been sitting face to face with him in his study.

The journalist in me itched to record every word, but after his stern warnings I desisted from grabbing my pencil. This was not for publication, for an outsider, a cheap hack to get hold of and distort. This was strictly for us the parents, we were told. Suffice it to report that he was compelling, at times provocative, and very funny. For thirty-odd minutes we hung on his every word. I even forgot about tea.

I think what epitomised for me the spirit of Shrewsbury that day was head of school Ed Lewis, trying solemnly to take Call Over under a huge golf umbrella, held obligingly, it is said, by his deputy, while the heavens descended, the slightly ragged-at-the-edges Royal Standard flapping above him, brilliant against the blackening sky. The boys were getting sodden, lightning was streaking over the marquees and everyone was laughing. What a finale!

What is it about Shrewsbury that sets it apart? What gives it that unique blend of kindness, friendliness, formality and fun? Is it the sharp intelligence and practical good sense of the masters' wives, combined with the ready wit and quiet courtesy of the typical Salopian master? Even the rather more casual good manners of most of the boys hold a sort of charm. Could it be the unobtrusive, underlying, but one senses very real self discipline (despite the famous 'Salopian saunter') that makes the whole place work with such a sense of purpose? Is it the sheer beauty of the site which gives it such allure?

As for me, our first Salopian Speech Day has simply confirmed me in my belief that Shrewsbury is a very special school.

Speech Day at Howell's, Denbigh followed a similar format, in that there was a service in St David's, the school chapel, in the morning, and the chance for families to picnic on the school fields. I particularly loved the Chapel Choir, as it reminded me so much of CH, Hertford. The purists in cathedrals will still maintain that there is nothing like the sound of boys' voices, but I think that the sound of well-rehearsed, and therefore confident girls singing in harmony has a quality all of its own, and of course the Howell's choir which included girls right up to the sixth form had some well developed voices.

Although it was much less strict, there were other similarities with Hertford like the politeness of the girls, who would all hold open doors for staff or visitors, and of course the schoolgirl humour which doesn't change much over the years. The Howell's girls were perhaps a little braver in their naughtiness than we were: on Speech Day there was an immensely formal ceremony after lunch called 'Walk Down', where the whole school processed, hair tied back and shining, little ones' socks carefully pulled up, down stone steps outside St Andrew's House and converged in front of the main school building while the Bishop of St Asaph and members of the Drapers' Company took their place centre stage. It must have been at the time of the American presidential elections that Miss Penelope Dixon was Head. A good Roman Catholic, who had previously headed a convent, she couldn't quite get used to our feisty Howellians after her nice Catholic girls, and when a girl attached a big, bold 'Penny for President' sticker on the rear of one of the banners in the Drapers' procession, she failed to see the joke: the culprit was found – and expelled – on her last day at school, or so the rumour went. It must have all been too much for poor Miss Dixon, who left shortly afterwards herself. Miss Martineau, the long-serving school chaplain, however, knew Howell's girls better, and it was said that she had a supply of the letter 'D' to stick on at the last minute, should the Drapers' official banner have been tampered with by any practical joker.

It never quite rained for 'Walk Down', and the simple outdoor service was very beautiful, and always went without a hitch in the end, with the unaccompanied singing of 'I will lift up mine eyes unto the hills'. Doubtless the girls resented the time spent in practising for the occasion, but it was worth it, the pursuit of excellence and a piece of tradition worth preserving.

Mrs Mary Steele became Head for Katie's last few years, a wise and kindly lady. Katie was also blessed with an excellent art teacher, Ms Roberts, which led her on to Glasgow School of Art, although she was still considering reading archaeology up until she left school. The range of universities and courses must have seemed bewildering for sixth formers then, and is even more so now, I think. It was much simpler in our day at Hertford when we had fewer choices to confuse us and tended to accept Miss West's advice on where to apply. Getting into university at all was so hard then, back in the 1960s.

For us as parents, sending the children off to university was quite a wrench after all the contact with school staff both at Howell's and Shrewsbury. As Mike commented, 'I do rather miss the end of term report.' By the time Katie went up to Glasgow in 1995, my mother's health was failing. Meanwhile, I had just started a job as a year tutor in a tough inner city school in Cardiff, when I started getting messages from a neighbour in Anglesey that my mother wasn't eating. The stress was impossible to deal with, and I resigned before Christmas. This was effectively the end of any full-time teaching career, but I shall ever be grateful that I was able to be available for my mother during that last year of her life: it is a time that you can never get back.

CHAPTER 27

My Mother's Passing

BECOMING AN ORPHAN, EVEN when you are quite grown up, is a painful rite of passage. My mother died in hospital in Bangor on an acute medical ward in Ysbyty Gwynedd. It had taken nearly ten weeks, and despite having my husband and children in South Wales, I had spent nearly all that time with her, the old lady having no other relatives close enough to visit regularly.

She had made friends with the young, very caring hospital chaplain, Kathy Sandells Rees: 'Lovely face, lovely legs, doesn't look like a parson at all,' as she described her delightedly to me – and told her that at eighty she'd had a good innings, so I think, really, that she was ready to go.

The following is what I wrote in a fuller letter for friends, dated 28 October 1996:

The local vicar, an ex-army chaplain who had visited her regularly, offered to take the funeral for us, his last one before he retired, and he did it beautifully. He asked for her V.C. 'or should I say C.V.?' he mused, and included below is what I wrote for him, he adding the comment about Big Susan's grave.

We started with three short prayers outside her beloved cottage, the rain just holding off, her faithful dachshund Fred yapping inside, as if he knew, and we were then driven behind Granny at a good Welsh funeral pace in an ancient black Mercedes, holding hands together, over the old Telford Bridge to the crematorium, which is lovingly kept with shrubs and trees. We processed in to 'Jesu, joy of man's desiring' and the organist played 'Nimrod' slowly and quietly at the end. The committal itself was dignified, happy almost, the coffin sinking gently into the floor, our last glimpse the simple bunch of roses picked that morning from the Wrentnall garden. It was just as it had been for Big Susan.

The children said it was a lovely service, and afterwards we came home to a wonderful spread of buttered Bara brith (another Welsh funeral tradition), sandwiches and cakes prepared by Mummy's next door neighbour, Helen. Deep into the nosh, our Will announced contentedly, 'I feel better now.' I think we all did, and Mummy would have loved having so many people home, brasses gleaming (courtesy of Great Aunt Jean) and dining room fire blazing as she had always kept it.

Mummy's ashes will be buried in December, as soon as we can get the family together again, next to Big Susan's on Church Island, at the children's request. It is a quiet and beautiful resting place.

Eileen Louise Wilson
15 April 1916 – 21 September 1996

Address given by the Revd Canon Richard Jones, Vicar of St Mary's Church, Menai Bridge at the Service of Celebration and Thanksgiving at Bangor Crematorium on Saturday 28 September 1996. Canon Jones was assisted at the service by one of Eileen's neighbours, a former schoolmaster and Suffolk rector, the Revd Alan Caldwell.

Eileen (Lane) was born on 15 April 1916, in the East Ham district of London, the middle child in the family. She won a scholarship to her local grammar school, where her English mistress gave her an enduring love of the English language . . . Sadly, she never quite got to grips with Welsh!

She trained as a nurse at the London Hospital in Whitechapel and was a staff nurse when the Second World War broke out. She volunteered as soon as she could for Queen Alexandra's Imperial Military Nursing Service, nursing British soldiers in England and then in India.

After the war, she ran a home called Beach Court for twenty-six children in Lancing, Sussex, with another London Hospital nurse and ex-QA Susan Dipper, who was quickly christened 'Big Susan' by the children. You can find the place where her ashes are buried here on Church Island. This has solved a mystery for me as many, many people have asked me over the past seven and a half years, 'Who is this Big Susan?' and I have now found her name in the parish records.

Eileen and Big Susan ran the children's home together for fifteen years until Big Sue finally retired. Beach Court had been full of warmth and love and laughter, a happy place for Baby Sue to grow up.

After Beach Court they moved to Denton Cottage in Worthing, and Eileen began a new career with Brighton Children's Department, looking after all the children's homes there. She took a Diploma in Social Work on day release and was appointed Assistant Director of Social Services. Her last post involved responsibility for all the residential and day care centres in Brighton for geriatrics, mental health and her beloved children.

She took early retirement in 1977 and she and Big Susan moved up to Menai Bridge in time for the birth of Eileen's third grandchild, Benedict. Ben and Katie and William are all here today. Eileen nursed Big Susan at home in their cottage in Druid Road until she died in July 1983. At this stage, she might have been expected to put her feet up and enjoy a well-earned retirement. But it was not to be: just one week after she had said goodbye to Big Susan here in this building she had a first painful bladder operation. She battled through, and even volunteered to work regularly in the WRVS Hospital Shop in Ysbyty Gwynedd, a commitment which she kept up for nearly ten years, and where she made many new friends.

We are all here today because we loved her, and to give thanks for a wonderful character, and for a life of service to others.

We all have our own memories, but perhaps what we most valued about her were here absolute integrity, her courage, her kindness, her humour, her marvellous cooking, and her passionate loyalty to her hospital, to her country, to her family and to her many friends.

CHAPTER 28

Adjusting to Widowhood

MIKE HAD BEEN PROFOUNDLY affected by my mother's dying, having missed his own mother's because of army service, and I was so grateful to have him with me at the end. After the funeral, my Aunt Jean from Suffolk, who had been a wonderful support, spending time with me in the cottage in Menai Bridge, told me firmly, 'You'd better get back to Mike, my girl, or you'll be losing your husband as well as your mother. He looks ghastly.' She was right. Mike was losing weight inexplicably, and getting desperately tired. Blood tests followed, and we waited a difficult month for the results.

Non-Hodgkin's lymphoma was confirmed, and our GP had already warned me that lymphoma could be 'pretty grim'. We decided to transfer to the University Hospital of Wales to haematologist Dr Jack Whittaker, who was unfailingly kind, and said that in fact the lymphoma was a low-grade one that might never need to be treated. Nevertheless, Mike decided to take early retirement a few months later. We were overcome by the generosity of both office staff in the Family Health Services Authority and local GPs in collecting for his leaving presents. I was tearful at his leaving party, but for him, clearing his office was just a relief. No more battling daily with the Cardiff traffic; at last he could enjoy pottering in the house and garden and we could take our time over school and university trips to see the children, even splashing out on a pub lunch or a night or two in B&Bs. We had time to enjoy each other.

I feel sorry for couples who find retirement so difficult. For us, perhaps because we realised how short it might be, every day together was precious. We had a conservatory built, mainly to keep art student Katie and Ben's oils out of the house, and their father would relax in it for hours, snoozing contentedly with *The Times* on his nose.

Insidiously, however, he was losing strength, and he knew it. He made a supreme effort to get to see Katie in her final year at Glasgow School of Art, perhaps with a premonition that he would die before her degree show. She was living so far up on the top floor of a flat in Hillhead Street that the cars parked below looked like Dinky toys. Uncomplainingly, he carried Katie's huge canvases up the sixty-six stone steps for her. That was the kind of man he was. Katie rustled up a cup of tea for us, and as her flatmates returned, one by one, each young woman would forage in her personal cupboard and start munching an apple or a carrot. We were too exhausted to face the stairs yet again to go out for a meal so the students, whom I was delighted to meet again ten years later at Katie's wedding in 2008, kindly pooled resources and concocted something savoury and delicious, all of us squashing into the kitchen together to share it. The system now is so different from my own student days at Feversham Crescent, where Wilsey, Isabel and I would routinely share meals we had cooked together, often with friends. The cost of anything that one of us had bought was deftly divided into three by Wilsey, and we always squared up instantly. We would never have thought of having separate food cupboards for each of us.

Tragically, the next time I was to see Isabel after leaving York was at Wilsey's funeral. Wilsey, by then Dr Paren, and in the Careers Department at St Andrew's, and a very experienced mountaineer, had fallen to her death roped up to a twenty-one-year-old girl in Glencoe. The only daughter of a widowed mother, Mrs Violet Barnett, Wilsey herself was only thirty-one. I managed to get in touch with Isabel, by then a PhD at Bristol. We agreed to meet at Birmingham New Street, and to wear our York scarves, dull orange wool with a brown stripe. Mine had got the moth, but I darned it carefully in Wilsey's honour. The emotion for us of losing the first of our generation can be imagined, but Mrs Barnett was magnificent. I realised what comfort it must bring, going through such an ordeal, to be known and loved in your own parish church. The crematorium, by contrast, was grim on a bleak, grey winter's afternoon, the rain driving down onto the huge, swaying trees and the stark chimney. Inside, the St Andrew's colleague next to me had to remove his spectacles to wipe away the tears. Clearly, Wilsey had touched many hearts.

The funeral tea at her home in Edenbridge Road was unreal, as these occasions always are, the house full of photographs of a bright, smiley girl with a mass of curls and her Welsh good looks. I found that I had to write a poem about the funeral, sadly lost now in one of our moves. I sent it to Kathleen Betterton, who was kind. Later, Mrs Barnett was to send me a boxful of Wilsey's precious things for my own children, including a large, old-fashioned pink doll in Bakelite, with very blue eyes and fluttering eyelashes. I cannot imagine the depth of grief of that poor, brave mother.

Many years later, on holiday with the family in St Andrew's, I sought out Wilsey's colleague whom I'd met at the funeral. It seemed important, somehow, to see where she had last worked. He told me that a bothy had been erected in her memory, but sadly, I've never yet managed to make that pilgrimage back to her beloved Scottish hills to find it.

I think all this was in my subconscious during our trip to Glasgow and Edinburgh in that raw November weather. There is something haunting about the memory of your own student days, particularly when sadness has followed, and a feeling of fragility and loss that you no longer have the good health and energy you took for granted as an undergraduate. In Mike's case it was particularly poignant, remembering his time at Cambridge when we were newly-weds, and he and I so fit with all our lives together ahead of us, or so it felt then.

While in Glasgow, we visited the art school, conscious of its reputation, and whilst he tried to be polite about Katie's work in progress, which frankly neither of us quite understood at the time, what really thrilled her father was the woodwork room, where all the students' stretchers for their canvases were individually made. I'm afraid that this comparison was not lost on our daughter!

From Glasgow we went on to Edinburgh College of Art. The work there was generally a little more conventional and comprehensible than at Glasgow, and therefore perhaps rather less exciting. Nevertheless, we could see that Ben's unique style was developing, and what a privilege to work in that huge, well-lit studio, with a full view of the castle beyond. It was then that we stayed with Richard and Elisabeth Seton-Browne, old army chums, in their elegant town house. As always, they were kindness itself. It was only weeks after the nephro–ureterectomy operation – a urologist had eventually found a kidney tumour – and I'm sure that the nurse in Elisabeth could read the signs. We could not pretend that all was well: however Mike tried to face the world bravely, and he always did, he was clearly going downhill. It is interesting that in our Christmas letter that year he was still sounding upbeat. Perhaps we were both still trying to hope.

In fact, he had only a few months to live, the cancer having spread elsewhere, including to the liver. In March, Dr Whittaker found a bed for him on the haematology ward, with its young men, totally bald from chemotherapy, but by then Mike's condition was beyond any medical treatment or surgery. It turned out that we had just three weeks left. The Palliative Care Team took over, Chris Lloyd Richards, a thoughtful Macmillan nurse proving a comforting listening ear, as did her hospital chaplain husband Robert; a bed came up miraculously quickly at Holme Tower, the Marie Curie hospice in Penarth, and we were urged to take it. Once there, Mike just flopped into bed gratefully in that tranquil, loving atmosphere, boats dancing on the sunlit water beyond. 'This is wonderful,' he sighed. And wonderful it was.

The Royal Welch Fusiliers rallied round magnificently. Friends travelled great distances to see him. There were cards and books of poetry, and farewell letters to Mike, each clearly very painful for the writer. Morgan Llewellyn, whose best man Mike had been, and who had been ordained after leaving the army, came over several times from his home near Brecon.

By the grace of God, it was the Easter holidays and all the children were home, so they were able to spend time with their father and help to nurse him, as well as field telephone calls at home. Towards the end, he was moved into a side ward looking straight over the Bristol Channel. Volunteers kept it beautiful with flowers; there was a spare bed so that the patient need never be alone.

It was Friday, 2 April 1999. In the morning we sang the Welsh National Anthem, Mike just able to mouth the words. I said I hoped Wales would win the England–Wales rugby international coming up. He smiled, and they did – by one point. By lunchtime he had slipped into unconsciousness. At three in the afternoon, all his suffering was over. It was Good Friday.

Afterwards, we drove back in convoy with Morgan to Groesfaen. It was a perfect, sunny, calm spring evening, and it felt surreal. Once home, we demolished a huge chocolate cake, very real and delicious, freshly made for us by fellow chorister's mother Erica Austin, and drank more tea. We found a date for the memorial service, at which Morgan was to preach. The Dean of Llandaff at the time, John Rogers, had generously offered us the cathedral for the service. We had already asked our vicar from Aberystwyth days, Bob Capper, now my vicar here at St Mark's, Gabalfa, if he could take the funeral for us at Holy Trinity, Aberystwyth, as Mike had told me firmly, 'Take me home to Aber.' Graham Jones of Llanidloes who had buried both his parents, was to do the same for him. Blessed with those precious last few days at Holme Tower, we had discussed everything together, pretty well down to the last reading, hymn and prayer, and I know that it brought him comfort.

There was a very good turnout at Holy Trinity. Bob Capper, whose churchwarden Mike had been, struck just the right balance for me between the pain of our loss and the Christian hope of joy through the Resurrection; people were touchingly generous in the collection for Holme Tower. Mike would especially have loved the panoramic woodland view from the plate glass window at Aberystwyth Crematorium. Mary and Arthur Jones had laid on a fortifying funeral tea at Llety Gwyn. It was another perfect evening for the drive home to South Wales in the setting sun, the road curving round the huge grassed mass of Plynlimon which Mike and I had climbed with Brown Dog soon after we first met. Somehow, there was a rightness about it all.

Next day, there was a daffodil card from Rhiannon Steeds in Aberystwyth hoping we'd had a good journey home. It is small kindnesses like that which mean so much. In the afternoon, we buried the ashes at Llandaff Cathedral, described in the poem below. The following day, the children all had to go back to school and university, poor Katie to produce the final work for her degree show, and Will to tackle his A levels. I was left alone at home with Fred the dachshund. Of course I missed the children dreadfully, yet with the messages of sympathy still arriving I felt loved, as well as thrilled by the obvious affection and respect that so many people expressed for 'D-J'.

I threw myself into work again, and started preparing for the memorial service. We in the parish choir at St Catwg's, Pentyrch practised hard for the cathedral service, and I shall always be grateful to my friends there and to our choirmaster John Gough for the effort

they put in. The Shrewsbury School organist, Christopher Argent, at
the time, of course, Will's tutor, who himself was to die from cancer
tragically young, was meticulous in helping me to get the music and
order of service together, accompanying the choir so sensitively on
the day. Our Cadet quartermaster Danny Donovan's daughter
Elizabeth was the soloist in Mozart's *Laudate Dominum*. An ex-
Llandaff chorister friend, Edward Elwyn Jones, played his trumpet in
'Thine be the Glory', and it is lovely to know that both Elizabeth
Donovan and Ed Jones are now enjoying successful careers as
professional musicians. Katie, whose Glasgow graduation ceremony
she missed that day, Ben and Will sang with me in the choir at the
service, along with our friends from young to middle-aged; Morgan's
address was just right; the sun streamed into the cathedral; it all felt
very proper and beautiful.

Then, of course, friends and relatives scattered to their own homes.
First the dying, then the funeral, then the memorial service –
everyone had been so kind. But finally I realised that the man we had
been honouring was never coming back. Our children had lost too
young their beloved father, and for me, the long, bewildering slog of
widowhood had really begun.

The title 'Buried Treasure' was a gift from tutor Susan Morgan's
Creative Writing at the Museum course in 2004, some five years into
widowhood. It has taken another five to try to recall the events in
prose.

18 January 2010

This is an excerpt from a letter to all the singers who had come from
afar to make up a choir of more than fifty for the memorial service.
There were friends of Katie's, colleagues of mine and ex-choristers,
their sisters and parents augmenting our own parish choir. To my
shame, I never quite managed to send the letter out and I feel that
my gratitude needs recording here.

The letter is dated 17 October 1999:

> I have been meaning to write to you ever since July. Please forgive my
> tardiness, and my resorting now to the word processor . . . When one's
> weary and busy at the same time, everything seems to take so long.

Thank you very much for coming to sing at Mike's Service of Thanksgiving on 2 July. It was a real thrill for me to be able to play my small part alongside so many accomplished choristers like you, and wonderful for Katie, Ben and Will to have your support, too, to help them get through what was bound to be something of an ordeal. It was actually more difficult to face in some ways than the funeral.

I have had many letters and telephone calls about the Llandaff service, and all have mentioned the beauty of the singing. One old friend of Mike's, who doesn't admit to being a Christian any more, wrote, 'Rarely have I felt so uplifted by a service.'

As I told John Gough, our conductor, getting the choir together was an act of faith, and I don't think he could believe his luck on the day when he saw and heard everyone in the Song Room! St Catwg's Church Choir had been rehearsing hard for weeks, but it was brilliant to have professional reinforcements arriving on the Thursday and Friday. Thank you so much for making the effort to be there.

Mike would have been thrilled to see everyone getting together, and honoured – puzzled even – that people should go to so much trouble on his behalf. The cathedral meant a great deal to him, as you can imagine. Nothing will diminish the sense of loss for us as a family, but it is good to have positive memories both of his funeral in Aberystwyth and the service in the cathedral, and to know how greatly loved he was . . .

Buried Treasure

She lost her treasure five long years ago.
They'd loved each other twenty-six brief years.
Now he lies buried in an unmarked grave:
The Garden of Remembrance has its rules
That none may mark the spot where loved ones lie,
Not even with the tiniest of plants,
The Church indifferent to the pain it brings,
Uncomprehending of the human need
To etch the name in marble, brass or stone
And trace with loving fingers where it's carved
As if to make the person real again.

The kindly dean in surplice of starched lace
Recites the burial service perfectly,
As Haydn mass through thick cathedral stone
Rehearsed in slow yet joyful dignity

Brings solace to a grief-shocked family,
A mother, daughter and two big, brave sons,
The younger only eighteen precious years.

The wooden casket sits by waiting hole,
The treasured name engraved on glinting brass,
Modest and unassuming like the man.
The dean runs out of words, the casket left
Unburied on the bright green April turf
As virger trundles wheelbarrow away,
'Til mother intervenes and he returns
To make the simple ritual complete.

And there her treasure lies unrecognised,
Six paces in, six paving stones along,
How can a human life be thus reduced
To such a hidden anonymity?

She lost her treasure five long years ago,
The lithe, athletic body that she'd loved
Incinerated to amorphous ash,
Never to warm and comfort her again.

His stubby hands so capable and strong
Were trained to grip a rifle in his youth,
Machine guns, rocket launchers, live grenades.
Thank God he never had to kill a man:
He was devoid of any ruthlessness.

In later life he loved to work in wood.
Stretchers he made for children's canvases
And taught them how to make each separate joint.
A knitting needles box with graded drawers,
Planed smooth and varnished to a glowing gold
Delighted an old lady with the gift.
The Baby Cupboard, carefully designed
With hand-height dropdown wooden central flap
Formica-lined to make a useful shelf
In time for firstborn son, alas stillborn
And later used for all the other babes.
Too large to fit into her present house,
The garage houses it for odds and ends,
Old Thermos flasks and welly boots and string.

She cannot bear to lose that work of love,
Reminder of impending parenthood
And more than two decades of children's lives,
A treasure beyond any earthly price.

His treasure lay in simple piety,
Although he rarely put it into words,
Was never sanctimonious or dull,
So gracious, courteous, full of kindliness,
Yet able to direct a firm rebuke
If any of the children misbehaved.

His blue eyes sparkled with infectious fun,
Until they clouded grey towards the end.
His cheeks felt downy as a puppy's fur,
His lips so gentle in their first, shy touch,
And every kiss right up until the end.

Her treasure's buried in an unmarked grave,
But his true worth lives on through memory,
The legacy of love he left behind.

15 June 2004

PART VI

Later Writings

CHAPTER 29

Creative Writing at the Museum

CARDIFF UNIVERSITY'S LIFELONG LEARNING department offers a range of courses for adult learners. Naturally, I was drawn to writing, and the Creative Writing at the Museum one particularly appealed. I have already referred to it in the chapter 'Adjusting to Widowhood.' Probably the tutor, Susan Morgan, expected some story about hidden artefacts when she gave us the title 'Buried Treasure', but then I've always thought that treasure lay in *people* as much as in objects. Not for nothing would a lady in my youth refer possessively to her cleaning lady, or charwoman, as she would more likely call her then, as her 'treasure'! And I too have had a succession of treasures who've helped me in the house and with the children over the years, like Glenys Ryan in Menai Bridge, who also looked after my mother, and died far too young from cancer. Then in Aberystwyth there was the incredible Mrs Wood followed by the gentle Mrs Pugh, another victim of cancer, who loved our little Will so much, taking him out in his buggy to 'kick the bar' at the end of the prom., while Debbie Annersley, then an English student who did so much to beautify Holy Trinity for its centenary, now the Reverend Larkey and a mum herself, will always have a place in my heart. Mrs Mary Pothecary, born in Petticoat Lane, much to my Londoner mother's delight, helped me for years at our home in Mid Glamorgan, and became part of the family, while in recent years I've had several excellent students from St Mark's to help me – just some of the treasures in my adult life. As for my childhood at Beach Court, Mr Cook, or 'Cookie' as I always called him, 'Nearnie' (Miss Earnshaw) our cook for a time, and the legendary Mrs Trott, 'Trotsky', or 'Trottsy' as she called herself, were each a pearl beyond price.

At the National Museum in Cardiff I particularly enjoyed meeting the 'treasures' on the staff, whatever their job there. Whether it was in the library or the Glan Ely Gallery, the Mollusc Collection or art restoration, they were all so helpful, and enthusiastic about their work. Susan Morgan had carefully arranged for us to see behind the scenes each week, and exploring the collections through the writing course sparked all sorts of ideas. 'Childhood Experiences of Non Fiction', another of her titles, has been included in the early part of the book as an early Christ's Hospital memory, and I have selected further pieces here.

Turning in their graves?

Written as a response to a lecture given by Archaeology Education Officer Kenneth Brassil at the National Museum of Wales:

What would the museum's Victorian founding fathers have made of this twenty-first century archaeologist, one wonders? They in their stiff white collars and dark three-piece suits, he in a greenish dark jacket and grey sporty trousers, they, one imagines, in highly polished black leather shoes or boots, he in fawn Hush Puppies. They have all made their fortunes in South Wales; he prides himself on his Welsh-speaking, Vale of Clwyd roots. They all look so rigid and respectable in their formal Victorian camera poses, while he in the flesh is wiry and radical. Would they be shocked?

Perhaps what unites these leading lights of different generations is more than what sets them at odds with each other – their Welshness, and their vision for a museum and art gallery worthy of Wales. The founding fathers were probably in their way equally passionate about the honour of the Principality, but then as wealthy men, they were probably also pillars of the British Empire, influential figures in trade or industry. Wales had no capital city then, and the only representation it had with the rest of the United Kingdom was through its Members of Parliament at Westminster. It is ironic, too, that it should be two North Walian MPs who in 1903 mooted the idea in the House of Commons of a national museum for Wales, yet it was Cardiff, thanks to South Wales money, which won the bid for the siting of this new national institution.

If one studies the Victorian characters a little more closely, they emerge as rather more complex individuals. It is difficult to imagine William Menelaus, for instance, in the heat and sweat of his Dowlais steelworks. He has a fine, slightly wistful, sensitive face, and clearly had an eye for a powerful picture, like Tissot's 'The Parting'. His bequest to the museum in Cardiff of thirty-six paintings was really the beginning of the art collection today.

63. 'Costume Drama'. Glasgow School of Art Degree Show piece by Katie Davies-Jenkins, 1999

64. *Glasgow School of Art graduate Katie Davies-Jenkins after her father's Memorial Service. Llandaff, Cardiff, 2 July 1999*

65. *Fine art and history of art with distinction MA, Benedict Davies-Jenkins with Edinburgh 1st Class psychology MA, Nicola Pritchard. Edinburgh, 12 July 2002*

66. Ben and Nicola's Wedding, Durham Cathedral. 16 August 2003

67. Michael and Gentian Hodges at Ben and Nicola's wedding

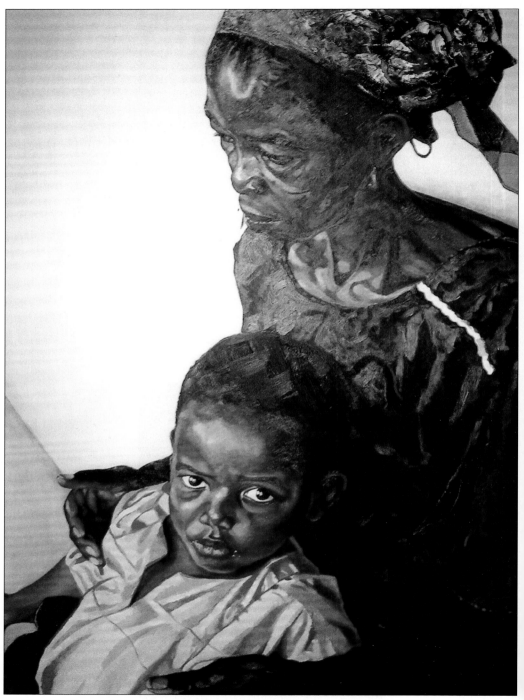

68. *'Akosikya and his unknown grandmother' by Ben Davies-Jenkins. Wales Portrait Award 2007*

69. Marriage of Katie Davies-Jenkins to Jack Goolden at St Mark's, Gabalfa. With L-R Rosie Goolden; Amy Goolden; Eve Yagual Goolden; Will and Ben Davies-Jenkins. 4 July 2008

70. Mother and daughter: with Katie on her wedding day

71. *MSc with distinction in transport planning: Will Davies-Jenkins with Mrs Penny Longmore. St David's Hall, Cardiff*

72. *The grandchildren: Cora Hope Davies-Jenkins (2) with her brother Jacob Michael (5 weeks) and their cousin Ella Munro Goolden (5 months). Edinburgh, 2 July 2010*

73. *At CH, Horsham: the Treasurer of Christ's Hospital, Susan Mitchell (centre) and other Hertford Old Blues read 'The Spirit of Susannah' by Miss DR West in Big School. L-R: Miriam McKay (née Radley); Kerren Simmonds; the Revd Judith Thompson (née Lillie); Susan Mitchell (née Hamilton); Diana Gould (née Robinson); the Revd Dorothy Green (née Steel); Jean Hayes. 27 April 2002*

74. *Christ's Hospital today: Members of the famous Christ's Hospital Band*

75. My first Christ's Hospital Presentee: Dominic Parker from Gwalchmai, Isle of Anglesey.
September 2002

76. My second Christ's Hospital Presentee: Charity Griffiths from Rhandirmwyn near Llandovery,
Carmarthenshire. September 2006

James Pike Thompson, with his extraordinarily clear, serious eyes, was much more than just a wealthy corn merchant. Perhaps it was his Unitarian faith that gave him both his independence of spirit and belief in the arts as well as his generosity to the fledgling museum and art gallery. It cannot have been easy in the days of a powerful established Anglican church to deny the existence of the Trinity – he surely was not a typical Victorian establishment man. Moreover, he clearly had an eye for good art in a variety of media from etchings to oil paintings to porcelain, both British and continental.

It seems that it was Pyke Thompson's breadth of vision which caused the museum to adopt a twin-track approach, to collect not only the best of Welsh art, but 'the very first painters of the day.' Doubtless he was influenced by his friend and executor, the *London Standard* art critic Sir Frederick Wedmore, who became Art Advisor to the Welsh Museum. Wedmore looks a shrewd, tough man, and he certainly hedged his bets, asserting, 'We exist, it is admitted, not only to show what good art Wales may have produced, but also to represent Art generally – whether English, or even Foreign.' One can imagine the fur flying in a museum Court of Governors' session when the Keeper of Art, Isaac Williams, 'vehemently opposed' the purchase, recommended by Wedmore, of Sickert's 'Eglise Saint Jacques, Dieppe' as 'an example of the extreme impressionist school which Sir Frederick seems to admire so much.' One guesses that the Davies sisters, with their love of the French Impressionists, found in Sir Frederick quite a kindred spirit.

It is interesting that the Welsh sculptor, Sir William Goscombe John, a founder-member of the Court of Governors, while advocating in 1913 the museum's 'concentrating on the purchase of art connected with Wales', had, perhaps a little grudgingly, acknowledged like Wedmore the quality of some foreign art, advising that the museum 'should buy occasionally, for the purposes of comparison and study, works of art of various kinds by distinguished artists of other nations, both British and foreign.' Surely even such a loyal Welshman as Goscombe John could appreciate the brilliance of a fellow sculptor like Rodin, and be glad that Gwendoline Davies had lent it for the 1913 Loan Exhibition in City Hall. Indeed, it was probably her vision, and that of her sister Margaret, and their determination that Wales should not have to look to London for a good art collection, which caused their anonymous loan of so many continental pictures to that 1913 exhibition to be hailed by the Bath Menstrie Gallery curator Hugh Blaker as 'the greatest artistic event in the history of Wales.'

Here was the central dilemma, even at the inception of the museum, and highlighted so vividly by the modern-day archaeology education officer, Ken Brassil, of how to make the National Museums and Galleries of Wales, as it is known today, truly representative of Wales, yet with an international appeal, 'telling the world about Wales and Wales about the world.'

It was not only in painting and sculpture that the new museum achieved international and professional recognition: largely thanks to Wilfred de Winton's collection of British and international porcelain, added to the museum's collections of Welsh porcelains and ceramics and British ceramics generally, Bernard Rackham, Keeper of Ceramics at the Victoria and Albert Museum was moved in 1919 to remark: 'It is no exaggeration to say that students of continental porcelain must make a pilgrimage to Cardiff . . . the Welsh Museum is to be congratulated on having a collection worthy of a national collection.' Study de Winton's portrait, and one observes sharp, shrewd eyes and a determined mouth. He looks like a pretty tough character, but Wales must surely be grateful for his contribution to establishing the National Museum's reputation, as it must be to another Victorian, E. Morton Nance, a rather jollier-looking man, some twelve years his junior, Cardiff-born author of *Pottery and Porcelain of Swansea and Nantgarw* for his bequest in 1952 of his own important collection.

One can imagine the founding fathers all vying for position at the laying of the royal foundation stone in 1907, and again at the final opening of the National Museum some twenty years later. They may all have expected to be introduced to His Majesty. Perhaps Alderman Cory and the Marquis of Bute were rivals in their claims for influence on the museum's development. One may criticise, like the modern-day archaeologist, its siting on marshland, or its neo-classical, un-Welsh architecture, but whatever its politics, whatever its short-comings in accentuating Welsh language and nationhood, as he would naturally like to do, the great building in Cardiff still stands, and it is loved by Welsh people, as are the other museums like St Fagan's, Swansea's Maritime Museum, Caerleon and Big Pit and the National Library in Aberystwyth.

The collections, growing and evolving all the time, be they art or archaeology, industry, science, natural history, maps or books, attract streams of visitors from Britain and throughout the world. The rather stiff, formal Victorian founding fathers and the wiry, enthusiastic archaeologist today can each claim credit for the museum's development and its success, and the people of Wales of every generation can truly feel proud of their heritage.

25 May 2004

The brief was to write up an imaginary interview, perhaps travelling back in time. There could be an authority figure or victim. We were told to decide on the tone, being empathetic or keeping one's distance. We were told not to be too nice – there could be some tension.

I knew that we were going to have the chance to interview a museum assistant, and I tried to imagine how a writer might be viewed. I must stress that what I wrote is entirely fictitious. The lady I actually interviewed subsequently (I've called her Cheryl) was pleased to chat, and was very happy in her job.

The imaginary interviewee here is a Londoner by birth of Welsh extraction and he's married a Cardiff girl.

Museum Assistant's Account

I've had a terrible day, love. I could murder a cuppa. There was this woman, English, posh, all cow-eyed and caring, said would I very kindly tell her all about me and my job. Said she was doing a creative writing course, or something. A bit old to be a student, I reckon.

The only good thing was that I got to take the weight off me pins for an hour. A whole hour. And who was guarding *my* patch then, that's what I'd like to know. It's me who'll be for the high jump if anything's gone missing. The boss'll have my guts for garters. Some of them little sods from school would nick anything. One got away with a whole stuffed fox under his jacket one day. D'you remember? And the French kids are worse.

'What qualifications did you have for this job, Mr Morgan?' she asks, peering at my ID tag, 'or may I call you Dai?' Cheek, I call it. Hasn't known me for five minutes.

'You learn on the job,' I mutter. I'm not telling *her* I left school without so much as an O level when Mum needed another wage earner after my old man kicked the bucket. Learnt everything I know in the university of life, me. And I haven't done so bad, have I?

'And what do you think of these wonderful French impressionists? Or isn't that your particular field?'

'Madam,' I says, 'I don't have a particular field. I go where I'm sent each day, anywhere in the museum. I pick up a bit about the exhibits wherever I go.' I'll give her field. She should try tabbing round Sennybridge in full kit in the middle of winter when it's tipping it down and the fog comes in and you can't see a bloody thing. And I bet no-one's ever fired at *her* in anger.

Then she leans forward, all confidential, a bit too close, if you ask me, so I gets a whiff of some classy scent, and I can see the make-up caked on her face. 'And what bugs you most about the job, Dai? The repetitiveness, the rotten pay, the *boss*, perhaps?'

I ask you, how could I tell *her* that the pay's lousy, and I've got a God awful boss half my age, an art history graduate, if you please, and I was sweating my guts out in Borneo when he was still in nappies, and I only stick this job to help our Cath and the tiddlers after that no good man of hers went AWOL. I don't know who this woman is, do I? For all I know she's some undercover reporter. She insisted on taking my picture, too. I could be splashed all over the *Echo* tomorrow. You can just see it, can't you? 'I'd quit if I could: War Hero slates Museum Top Brass.'

No, it's more than my job's worth to tell her the real story, and how fed up I get just standing there day after day, with me knee giving me gyp – damned shrapnel – and having to be polite all the time to that wet-behind-the ears arty farty boss, and the great British public, and all them foreigner visitors, not to mention the likes of *her*. Where's that cuppa, love?

Cheryl – a museum assistant (a real interview: only the name has been changed)

She is petite, and impeccably groomed, her short golden hair in a bob, dangling gold earrings, neck chain, bracelet and rings all feminising the rather austere uniform. The wide collar of her pure white blouse sits neatly over the collarless jacket of her plain black suit. She looks alarmed when asked for an interview. Clearly she has not been briefed properly.

'Well, I suppose it's all right, as long as I keep walking. No, I'm not allowed to sit down. I cover here, on the corridor, and all through there. What's this *for*? To give you practice in writing interviews? All right then. Yes, I'm a part-time paid worker, not a volunteer. What got me interested in the job? Well, I was a cleaner here for ten years before I got this job. No, I never came to the museum as a child. I can still remember coming here for the first time for my interview as a cleaner fourteen years ago. I was so nervous. Walking up the white steps at the front? Oh, yes, I think I did. I remember sitting on that bench over there, where they interviewed you. I was so nervous. But they were very nice, and it went well. I *loved* the cleaning job. It was seven to eleven every day.

'They're doing a curatorial course at the moment. I did it a couple of years ago when I came on to warding. Warding really appealed. Why? Well, it's three days a week, Tuesdays, Wednesdays and Sundays. I look after my granddaughter the other two days. She's four. Yes, it's always the same days I work. Yes, exactly! I can plan the work round my family.

'Yes, we *have* the uniform, white blouse, black jacket and skirt or trousers. You can have what *you're* wearing, yes, that's right, a fleece, but I think the jacket's smarter. Thank you. I do feel smart in the uniform. I'm fifty-eight, you know. I don't look it? Really? Oh, thank you.

'No, I don't feel it's a posher job than cleaning. I *loved* being a cleaner. It isn't a dirty job, you know: all the cleaners are immaculate. They're immaculately dressed. They have a uniform too. The days of the turban is over, don't you think? But I don't know, your lifestyle changes as you get older, doesn't it? The early mornings aren't so appealing.

'Yes, we used to be called warders. What do I think about Museum Assistant? Maybe the title sounded more friendly. After all, we're here to help the public. Yes, we move around every day. I like that: it breaks the monotony.

'We've got a lot of people retiring. Yes, we've got four ex-police. They're more experienced than me on the security side, of course. Yes, we have walkie-talkies in nearly all the galleries. Sometimes we meet the people who set up the exhibitions, yes, if we happen to be working in that part of the building at the time, but not very often.

'Yes, we get lots of children. The children *love* the museum, of course. Mostly primary and students. Yes, we get French students too, but they're not so well behaved.

'Yes, we do get questions. What if it's a difficult one? I endeavour to help, but if I don't know the answer, I tell them I don't know, and I can call a colleague.

'Years ago, the museum never used to open until the afternoon. No, the cleaners never work in the mornings where the public are. Since the museum's been free, you get a lot more people. Yes, it's a very nice place, but working here all the time, it's funny, you don't appreciate it. We went on a fire drill to St Fagan's, too. That's a wonderful place.

'Yes, some people do ask me if I speak Welsh, but they're very nice about it. My granddaughter's teaching me!'

17 May 2004

CHAPTER 30

Family Life

T HOSE PENETRATING LITTLE VOICES (copy of letter to the *Church Times* dated 29 September 1989)

From Mrs Susan Davies-Jenkins

Sir. How much I agree with a fellow mother-of-three, Dorothy Jamal about children in church. I remember stopping a dinner-party conversation thirteen years ago by saying that since our baby daughter had gone to church with us for nine months before she was born it seemed only natural that she should continue to come with us now she'd arrived. Indeed, I should have felt desperately isolated as a new mother if I had been unable to get to church myself.

Of course there were rough times, when we've gritted our teeth and considered fleeing from disapproving fellow parishioners half-way through a service. The turning point came at the end of one very long Eucharist when Katie's brother Benedict had yelled all the way through. Worn to a frazzle, we got up to leave, with my husband whispering through clenched teeth, 'I'll never, never bring that child to church again'. The cuddly, rather senior mother turned round from the pew in front and beamed: 'I do love to hear their little voices.' William (no. 3) was equally a yeller but we were almost immune to frowns by then. We always took them all up for a blessing, and although there was a lot of activity in the back pew, miraculously they never let us down at the altar rail. They all joined the church choir very willingly when they were six or seven, and our two little yellers are now cathedral choristers.

The week that this letter appeared in print, I bumped into the Dean in Llandaff Cathedral. He gave me a very sideways look!

CHAPTER 31

New Year's Day 1992

Diary of a Supermum (failed) cont.

DEMOCRACY IS A MIXED BLESSING in our family, I've decided: New Year's Day being Daddy's day off, 'Where shall we go today?' comes the cry. I groan inwardly. The Family Outing in prospect feels like a public duty. How I sympathise, Your Majesty.

In no time our efficient daughter has rung round to see what is open and solemnly organized a ballot. Penscynor wins so after a hasty baked beans lunch we are on the motorway heading for Neath. The sky looks grey and bleak and when we arrive the normally crammed car park is almost deserted. As we leave the warm fug of the vehicle I can see why: a chill, damp wind assaults us and even our hardy Katie shivers in her jeans and cotton jacket. 'The things we do for fun,' I mutter to myself. Still, at least the entrance fee is reduced today.

I consider myself somewhat of a veteran of zoos and wildlife parks having been dragged round them for the last fifteen years in England, Scotland and even France by our animal-mad offspring. Penscynor has a simplicity and charm all of its own after the size and sophistication of some of the others. Here even some of the signs are handwritten, with spelling corrected here and there by helpful visitors. The official metal signs are beautifully engraved but today are so muck-encrusted that they need a good scrub to make them legible again. This is definitely off-season. All the ice-cream booths are boarded up, the alpine slide looks derelict, much to little William's disappointment, and the children's playground is empty. Our three race off to clamber up a monstrous plastic-looking animal. Could it really be a pink elephant?

I take shelter in the marmoset house and almost choke from the acrid stench. And they're behind glass. What must they smell like close-up? I am soon fascinated, though, by their alert little faces and we play games with each other bending from side to side. Katie joins us and holds a class of five tiny marmosets riveted to her Usborne

Zoo-Spotter's guide which she presses open for them against the glass cage.

In another cage, a baby monkey with translucent pink protruding ears darts around its seniors in sheer joie de vivre while another outside, missing its footing on a perch, looks embarrassed, scrabbles up the wire cage and wiggles its bottom at me. But the king for me is a black ape with massive muscular shoulders who decides apparently in mid-flight which hand to put out to catch the next parallel bar. Utterly casual, supremely confident, he lollops from pole to pole giving a whole new meaning to the monkey bars on an assault course. We humans look so clumsy in comparison.

Feeding time for the penguins. A tall young man hands out the fish to each penguin while a cheeky little one nips round behind his back and grabs an extra silvery ration. The man works in total silence while a huge white pelican 'revs up' for several minutes, flexing its cumbersome wings. Suddenly with a whoosh it is airborne, floats majestically for a few feet and descends to another rock. The penguins are totally unimpressed.

The Father Christmas Grotto looks somewhat incongruous in the aquarium. It is strange how sad Christmas decorations look barely a week after the great day. The fish look happy though.

Ben, our elder son nuzzles up to a dirty white billy goat and I wish I had my camera: they look content in each other's company like two old men not needing to speak.

The café bears a sign: 'Don't panic! The Copper Kettle Coffee shop is open.' The thought brings some comfort. Meanwhile outside two little girls munch sandwiches glumly on the picnic table beside them while Dad positively chortles over a prostrate babe. I notice the dirty nappy and wonder if he would do the same on a busy day.

Katie suddenly produces her sketch pad in the rapidly dwindling daylight. William and I retreat to the warmth of the shop. It is full of the usual trash, expensive but appealing to young children. I dissuade him from getting a huge inflatable frog and after an agony of indecision he settles on a fat, multi-coloured stick of rock. It is past closing time and the middle-aged couple in charge seem to be the only other humans in the place. The children slip off in the semi-darkness for one last look at the animals and we chase after them, the alluring light in the coffee shop looking tantalizing as it, too, is shut. I make one desperate attempt to prise the children away. 'Quick, or we'll get locked in for the night and we've got nothing to eat except William's rock.'

'That's MY rock and I paid for it with my own money,' comes the instant reply. Whatever happened to democracy?

Note: I had been bitten before Christmas by our rapidly growing Border Collie pup Trog at my mother's cottage in Anglesey. I forgave him at the time because I felt that he had been provoked into snapping when my mother's dachshund Fred growled at him under her kitchen table. Unfortunately, my left leg happened to be in the way and was caught by the full force of Trog's jaws. The wound took three months to heal. He proved unreliable with other people and we had to have him put down in the end.

January 1995

Sunday 1st

Managed to get Will down to breakfast by 11 a.m., still looking pale and full of sleep.

James (*Lu*), Ben's sixteen-year-old Taiwanese chum still with us. He has beautifully shiny black hair, standing up in natural spikes like an elongated crew cut. In a black woollen cap comforter and climbing boots he could easily be mistaken for a Sherpa. His idea of dressing up against the bitter Welsh January air is to don an extra checked shirt, open at the front. He has a wonderful spontaneous guffaw and asks questions all the time. I think he is very bright.

He accepts eagerly his third helping of roast beef and listens intently to the Cathedral School's CD of 'Let all the world', suddenly surprised by the high notes. I tell him how much I enjoyed hearing Shrewsbury School's Chamber Choir singing in the last concert, and he admits he was 'faking' at the time, unable to sight read the music and have it ready to perform in two days flat, as required.

We hurry to Cardiff Central to find that the 1505 isn't running. A BR lady in black boots and matching BR maroon hat and coat tries to help. She gets a man with some important-looking gold braid to help. They are apologetic, and once the computer has stuttered back to life, the chap writes out the new train times for James.

Station almost deserted. Everything looks at half cock in the grey wintry afternoon, the light beginning to fade. Happy New Year!

Monday 2nd

Beautiful morning. Ben came back from walking Trog suggesting walk by reservoirs in Brecon Beacons. Agree. Spend rest of morning trying to get picnic together.

Leave eventually at 1240, Daddy announcing that the Beacons are OFF and we're going to Aberdare.

We drive through drab, deserted Valleys towns, shops boarded up in honour of the bank holiday. Wonderfully sensitive war memorial in Tonypandy would have been worth stopping for, however. It showed a soldier holding a rifle in one hand and a woman with the other. The woman is cradling a baby. Quite the most moving war statue I've ever seen.

Arrive at forestry site high above Aberdare. Even driving onto the track is tricky in the packed ice and snow.

Have picnic ridiculously in the sun on a wooden table, ridiculous because we are all shivering in the icy wind.

Coffee tastes deliciously hot. Glad I heated the milk. We all stuff chocolate into our pockets and set out. Mike has thin navy jacket, no hat or gloves, and the hole made from his wellies in his old green M & S trousers. No wonder he's cold.

Zip car keys into my old Ventile anorak. Can't afford to lose another set after the Boxing Day disaster in Llantrisant woods.

The sun is quite warm on the back and the views are glorious. Trog's belly looks a dirty cream against the brilliant blue-white snow and he stumbles through and over long grass savouring the sensation of snow on his paws. Once called, he scurries down the icy road towards us at impressive speed.

We turn back for the car on Will's directions, just in time. The wind is biting in the shade as the sun slips almost perceptibly lower.

We drive off, the setting sun pinking the edges of the Brecon Beacons. 'Aren't we lucky to live in such a beautiful place!' says Ben.

Tuesday 3rd

Saw Ben off for his first day of work experience at Rookwood (our local rehabilitation hospital – he was considering medicine as a career at the time) looking casual but tidy with shiny blond hair, new baggy blue jeans, navy sweatshirt and new, clean trainers size 9.

Got to surgery late and Pearl (the lovely practice nurse) came to view wound. It now looks bigger and damper and altogether nastier, with a little greenish crust in the centre. She calls district nurse colleague in who says it is worse than when *she* last saw it, now ulcerated and infected. Suggested taking a swab and trying Comfeel again.

Will v. sweet and agreed to make supper. Katie concerned for me, but more concerned to sort out her open days for next term. Work and panic catching up with her.

Ben in good spirits after his first day. Not deterred by a black gangrenous toe, or several limbless patients. Dr (*Harry*) Baker had been quite kind to him, by the sound of it.

Caroline's (*Erskine*) birthday, so put Katie on Radyr train to meet her and Will and I knocked up a dark chocolate cake for her which we eventually ate about 10.30 p.m. after Jane's (*Caroline's mother*) excellent garlic and herbs basted chicken. Boys very enthusiastic.

Got my feet up on sofa for a few minutes. Bliss. Legs v weary going upstairs today.

K. got AAB offer from Edinburgh (*for archaeology?*) and sank into further agonies of indecision.

Thursday 5th

John Gwilym would have been 20 today. Surprisingly, I haven't shed any tears this anniversary. Perhaps just too tired with this choking cough.

Ben had a good day at Rookwood – made beds then tea, but then did a ward round with Dr Williams, senior registrar, a nice-sounding lady who explained things as she went along.

Katie and Daddy to Newcastle Emlyn to see Bardy (*Mrs Barbara Jones, Mike's cousin*). Will and I had a quiet day at home. Made a triple quantity of Rayburn carrot soup – a great coup with Katie who doesn't realise that its deliciousness lies in the butter base.

Saw programme on RM (*Royal Marines*) officer selection and wished I could be as young and slim as the WRNS (*Women's Royal Naval Service*) personnel selection officer.

Friday 6th

Picked Clint up. At fourteen, he is scrawny and his speaking voice sounds uncertain, as if it is breaking again. On his top lip are the fair, downy sproutings of a moustache.

Clint clearly unsure about carrot soup and granary bread, but dug eagerly into the chocolate ice cream. Declined fruit and a drink.

Ben finished his work experience this afternoon, and seemed glad to have had the experience. Hair tousled, shirt pocket button undone and shirt twisted over at the waist, his appearance could do with a little more attention to detail, as the nice RM lieutenant told the Malvern officer candidate on the box last night. Don't think CCF inspections can have made their mark on our Ben. At least he doesn't squeeze into the stereotypical public school mould, and flak from the ward sister today about going to boarding school seems to have bounced off him almost innocuously.

Saturday 7th

Washed and ironed for Katie all day. Got the last load of washing out of the machine at 11.30 p.m. All she is bothered about, however, is *Bluff Your Way through Archaeology*. She can't sleep until it's found, she says. What an end to the last day of her holiday.

Sunday 8th

Trog attacked me on the landing tonight as I was drying my face with my big pink towel. There is something about wiping things that upsets him. I fended him off with the towel, and both boys rushed out, grabbed him and smacked him hard. They are far braver with him than I. Don't know how long I can go on living with this unpredictable hound. Perhaps more obedience classes will do the trick.

Boys did the evening dog walk for me and noticed tall man with stubble and a funny hat, Ford engine running, down in the usual suspect place. Will took great care to see they weren't followed home.

Boys put up a spirited defence of Trog when I said we might have to give him away to a farm. I agreed that he had generally got a little better. Then he chewed my Barclaycard bill until it was almost illegible tonight.

Tuesday 10th

(*Note: Emma (Mansfield) was the only daughter of our neighbours in Redgate Terrace, Groesfaen, Marilyn and Simon, who had been exceptionally kind to us on our big move from Aberystwyth to South Wales, and I had grown very fond of Emma, who attended the local Welsh secondary school. Simon worked for Mr Henry Jones, the legendary family butcher in Pentyrch. Simon had died just a year before his wife, so suddenly, poor Emma was an orphan. We knew Clive and Cheryl Milsom through Llandaff Cathedral Choir*).

Took lemon cake round to Emma and beat a hasty retreat. She gave me a lovely smile. Marilyn's funeral clashes with Clive Milsom's. Both announcements in the *Western Mail* today. Feel very empty for Cheryl.

Interviewee's Mother's Morning

Katie heard from Cardiff Institute this morning – accepted for their art foundation course. Could she let them know as soon as possible? It will boost her confidence for her interview today at the Mid Glamorgan College of Art, Design and Technology.

Bleak, soaking morning. We arrive early, having taken the turn for the cemetery by mistake. College building looks stark and uninviting, the wet accentuating the harsh, bright redness of brick. Hope Katie isn't too put off by first appearances.

We drive up the road to kill time, parking in a lay-by on the mountainside above the town. 'Please don't say anything,' she says firmly, 'I like to be quiet before an interview.'

We get back, five minutes early, and she almost skips up the steps through the great turquoise swing doors, despite the weight of her bulging portfolio, scratched on the bottom from its journeys on London tubes. Still no news from Central St Martin's, but I think she's rather written that one off after an awful group interview with about fifty of them all together. It's Emily's (*Hughes*) first choice, though, and she can live with Auntie Eunice.

I nip in to spend a penny. Atmosphere is warm and welcoming, beautifully mounted work around, parquet floors gleaming.

I note that various students have BA placements at Cardiff, Coventry, Nottingham *and* Central St Martin's. Poodle (Katie) might end up there.

After 11.30. A couple of youngsters slip out smiling, clutching portfolios. Poodle's is quite the largest I've seen today. At Cardiff they told her she was 'post foundation standard'. Dying to know what they thought of her here.

CHAPTER 32

Christmas Letters – Extracts

Christmas 1990

I SOMETIMES WONDER IF LIFE, whatever that's supposed to be is passing me by (how do other women cope with a family and a full career?) but find that most of the time I'm just gasping to keep up. With Mike so busy in his job I feel really needed to keep things going on the home front. I've decided that my real vocation in life is probably to try and keep other people happy. A modest ambition, but then we can't all be P.M., thank the Lord.

Christmas 1991

We had a good Scottish family summer holiday near St. Andrew's and then in the Highlands followed by Sue's having to charge down to cadet camp in Devon the day after we got back, which probably undid any good which the holiday might have done. The 'great nametapes battle' was resumed in the few precious remaining days with mum still sewing in the car up to Shrewsbury. Ben was unpacked immediately by the older boys while the new parents were plied with a 'very innocuous' drink by all the House staff. Ben was whisked away with the other new boys to sign on formally with the headmaster leaving mum with an ache in the pit of the stomach wondering if we'd done the right thing. It was almost worse than leaving him at Llandaff five years before!

Mike staggers on with his workload uncomplainingly and mutters about retirement every so often. Sue is learning to live with chronic asthma but is much better after six days on a medical ward this autumn gave her a jolt and forced her to re-assess her priorities. Number One must surely be to keep a happy home: We find our teenage children need us emotionally as much as ever. They eat a lot, too!

Christmas 1992

Well here we are still, Mr and Mrs Stodge, as Mike once christened us, staggering through our twentieth year of marriage together, mercifully content in each other's company. Stodginess has its advantages! We stagger only in trying to keep up with our three ever-lively, but not yet driving offspring who want transporting with their ever-increasing kit to and from Denbigh, Shrewsbury and Llandaff. William is due to join Ben at Shrewsbury in September 1994, when, we kid ourselves, life will be easier.

We must record that Ben got a free biology trip to Paris on a *L'Europe des Fleuves* international conference. His main scientific contribution appeared to be wading in the Severn and counting the ducklings, recording his findings on impressive-looking graphs.

Katie braved a huge mixed *lycée* near Rouen with an unforthcoming girl rejoicing in the name of Angélique for a week at Easter. Being vegetarian, her main horror was trying to be polite in French about a whole *fruits de mer* dinner produced in her honour by Angélique's mother. Angélique was less polite about good old British grub when she came back for the return match and her reluctance to speak any English did wonders for Katie's French!

Fetching Katie from Dover gave Sue a chance to walk along Lancing beach and show the children her first home. She stood and howled with nostalgia. It was the first time we'd been back to Beach Court in twenty years. The old place looks sadly run down but the verandah is still there and the courtyard, concrete uneven and cracked now, where 'the Beach Court kids' spent so many happy hours, and Sue got black and blue learning to ride her first bike.

Katie started the summer holiday with an army family in Berlin. Mike and Sue drove her to Birmingham Airport, most convenient from here, and clutched each other as her aeroplane lurched into the sky, unprepared for the emotion of letting her fly alone. She was duly signed for by Major Mike James (her friend Laura's father) and they gave her a tremendous week 'doing' Berlin. We suspect that the Genesis concert was the high spot!

William, meanwhile, nipped off to America with the Cathedral School's chamber choir for a fortnight's tour. They did a US aircraft carrier, Washington (where they sang in the cathedral), Chocolate

World and several concerts, amusing their homestay hosts as they went along. We think the professional baseball game was pretty important as far as Will was concerned, and the boys enjoyed being mobbed by an American teenage audience at a music summer school.

Christmas 1998

Our milestone this year was our Silver Wedding Anniversary in April when we were delighted to see many of our friends and family to remind us of the past, and to have Katie, Ben and William with us as evidence of twenty-five happy years together so far. The celebration for Sue and Mike was the high point of the year.

Mike and Sue had a very welcome week's holiday in May when we went back to Guernsey. Sue discovered more of her Guernsey family who gave us a grand welcome, as they always did her little mum, which is a comforting link.

It was as well that we did take the holiday then because we had to cancel the August one at the last minute. Mike had to go into hospital to have a nephro-ureterectomy, (work that one out!), 'which rather mucked up the family arrangements,' as he puts it. Feeling fitter, he is very nearly back to normal now, he says. His remaining kidney seems to be functioning well, and Sue does her best to keep up his haemoglobin levels by feeding him properly. He has been a very brave patient, and hasn't even grumbled about spinach!

26 November 2001

Dear Friends,

I thought we should resume the tradition this year of some sort of family report, particularly as we so much enjoy having news in similar letters from many of our friends. Twelve months ago I must admit that I would readily have cancelled Christmas, had it been possible, a sentiment shared by many bereaved people, I gather, but of course in the end we enjoyed Christmas Day, and the last thing that Mike would want is for us to be miserable for ever.

Christmas 2003

The big news here is that Ben (twenty-five) was married to Nicola (Pritchard) on 16 August in a stunningly beautiful service taken by her father, Bishop John. They were able to have the Galilee Chapel in Durham Cathedral (do go and enjoy the peace there if ever you're in Durham) and St John's College for the reception. Nicola, always beautiful, looked especially lovely, as did all the flowers that her mother Wendy had grown for the occasion. Wendy had planned the whole wedding brilliantly, the college staff were lovely, and the big day went perfectly. Will was the best man, and both he and Ben made very funny speeches which would have made their father happy and proud.

Ben and Nic have known each other for more than six years, through the Right Hand Trust working for the church in Uganda, and then at Edinburgh where Nic did an MA in psychology before primary teacher training in York. She's now working with children with problems in several Edinburgh schools, mostly secondary – not the easiest of jobs. She and Ben are cosily installed in their lovely third-floor flat near the city centre, with views across to the Fife estuary, and Ben is using the second bedroom as his studio. He works on his art full-time now – producing often big, usually bold figurative pieces with strong colour mostly in oils, or sometimes black and white, often with a touch of gold or aluminium leaf. You may recognise Katie or Will whom he finds useful models. He's also done some beautiful portraits of Nic.

Extract from a letter to Mrs Chris Bailey, one of my mother's social worker colleagues in East Sussex, now over eighty, who has faithfully kept in touch.

3 November 2003

Dear Chris,

Your lovely letter of 12 September cheered me enormously – thank you so much, and for your card. I'm embarrassed that it's taken me so long to reply. I'm very sorry.

Ben and Nicola's wedding on 16 August was quite wonderful . . . Nic's father married them – he's the Bishop of Jarrow – and took the service most beautifully. They had really funky music from a band with distinctly African rhythms on the drums – shades of Uganda – but the 'Be still for the presence of the Lord' just before they took their vows was breathtaking.

Will was best man, and although I had dreaded getting through the whole thing without Mike, having Will snuggled up beside me in the pew in 'a nice bit of Moss Bros cloth', as his granny would say, proved an enormous comfort.

The weather was perfect, and the reception in the college dining hall, and later in the garden, great fun. Ben and Will made very funny speeches, and I was just sad that their father wasn't there to share my pride – and amazement! – that our little boys had grown up into such poised young men. Bishop John and Wendy looked after me with such thoughtfulness.

After a family lunch at the Pritchards' home in Gateshead, a retired GP friend, Jenny (*Holden*) kindly put me up in her gorgeous renovated cottage in Weardale . . .The cottage is absolutely lovely, and surrounded by her own fields. Her priority was to get an Aga fitted, and then she slept by it while the rest of the house was gutted! She now has about seven rescue cats as well as a sweet little terrier called Millie, and it did me no end of good to go for walks with them all.

I'm pretty sure I heard from Jeanne (*Wall*) and Anita (*Carey*) but can't quite put my hand on their card at present. Would you please give them my love and pass on my news. I've spoken to Margaret (*Hulmes*) on the 'phone so she's a bit more up to date.

Much love, and thank you again for taking the trouble to write.
Sue.

Christmas 2004

I do hope this year has been as happy for you as it has been for me. Of course life will never be the same without our lovely Mike, but I'm sure he would be glad to see all the family living it to the full.

Katie is still living in Bristol and working for the Children of the Nineties research project. She's also had an art exhibition in Clevedon with a school friend, Emma Wright, where she surprised herself with how much she sold. She's been working mostly in pastels, not quite brave enough to get back to oils yet, and has done several commissions. She keeps up her Ultimate Frisbee and a hectic social life, still very loyal to old school and university friends now widely scattered, and yet finds time for her old ma, bless her. She is off to Ghana in March to see Ben and Nic with her new boyfriend Jack, a website designer and Frisbee international (respect!).

Ben and Nicola having settled happily into married life in their Edinburgh flat, decided to do their missionary bit again before they became too cosy, and found themselves at the end of August on a USPG placement in the Ashanti region of Ghana. They are living and working in Mampong Babies' Home, where the electricity supply sounds to be erratic and running water even more so. Taken under the kindly wing of Auntie Mabel, a local retired midwife who runs the home, they try to keep the tiny tots, some of whom have been very ill, fed, watered, clean and amused. They are also doing some teaching in the local schools, Nic primary, for which she's trained, where her beautiful white face proved such a draw that the class suddenly swelled to seventy, and unofficial pupils had to be beaten off by the headmistress with a big stick! Ben teaches English in the girls' secondary school where his zero tolerance approach to cheating earns him some unpopularity in which he revels, he says.

Christmas 2005

My year has been dominated by the passing of a young Nigerian/ West Indian friend Ngozi, leaving a husband, Andrew, and Zoë (nine), Joshua (eight) and Immanuel (two). Ngozi was one of the loveliest, funniest and most gracious people I've ever known, and the courage and dignity, as well as the deep Christian faith, with which she faced her cancer, were humbling, all reminiscent of our darling Mike. It was a privilege, as well as poignant, to play a small part in nursing her. Just five days before she died (in her own bed, as she'd wished) she made a supreme effort to come downstairs, resplendent in bright blue Nigerian robe and headdress, to witness Zoë's baptism, her lips silently forming the words to the hymns and prayers. It was one of the most moving services in which I've ever taken part. I was asked to be a sponsor, so now have in Zoë a delightful 'godchild'. People came from across the world to the funeral, our church packed to overflowing, and then of course the hard time for the family of coping without Ngozi began. Andrew is managing brilliantly with the children, but there are times when one of them suddenly goes sick and he needs to get to work that I become quite a useful unofficial aunt. In fact, I reckon that professional gap-plugger is my new occupation, and it helps to reconcile me – just! – to middle age.

Christmas 2006

The most satisfying new thing I've done this year is to train as a chaplaincy lay visitor in the University Hospital of Wales. Apart from the ongoing training – I'm currently working for a Certificate in Chaplaincy Studies – we're asked to give an afternoon a week to one of the wards. I've been allocated the renal transplant and nephrology ward, and although it's draining emotionally, I absolutely love it. Because it's a specialist unit, patients come from as far as Chepstow, Fishguard or Abergavenny, and so it's really hard for relatives, particularly those with no transport, to visit often. I feel as if my thirty-three years' experience of living in Wales has prepared me for this, somehow.

Christ's Hospital still plays a big part in my life, and I'm enjoying following the school careers of Dominic from Anglesey who's becoming a real star of the stage, as well as little Charity from near Llandovery who's just started there, joining her brother Oliver and sister Emily who went in as sixth formers. They all seem enormously happy there, and are doing very well.

I've also found myself even busier in church, appointed as assistant warden, and no, I certainly didn't volunteer for it, but it does bring the satisfaction of helping our hard-pressed clergy on the admin side. I still host a homegroup for prayer and Bible study, and what with singing in the worship group and all the other parish activities, find my church, St Mark's, Gabalfa, along with my own family, of course, together with my deepening faith, the most important things in my life.

Christmas 2007

To our delight, Katie (thirty-one), now in her final year of her occupational therapy degree at Cardiff University, got engaged to Jack Goolden in August. Jack, a Bristol boy, is a self-employed website designer and photographer.

Will is still working as a transport planner in Portishead and shares with Katie and Jack a good group of friends, mostly based on the Ultimate Frisbee community, from what I can gather.

Next week Ben will have survived his first term as an art teacher — all nineteen weeks of it! — and is enjoying it apart from the inevitable fatigue at this stage. He's very happy in the school, Knox Academy in Haddington, East Lothian, but will have to apply for another job to start after his probationary year. He's had a solo art exhibition this summer, in Lichfield Cathedral.

Davies-Jenkins Family Update Christmas 2008

This has been an exciting year for the D-Js, dominated first by the safe arrival in Edinburgh on 3 June of Ben and Nicola's beautiful baby daughter, Cora Hope, and then Katie and Jack's marriage here on 4 July, to which Cora was a vocal witness!

I suppose that of all the happy life events a mother might anticipate in middle age, seeing a daughter married, and becoming a first-time granny are about as huge as it gets, and I'm thrilled to bits on both counts.

Katie and Jack chose to be married here at St Mark's by our lovely vicar, Bob Capper. He had known Katie since she was a little choirgirl at Holy Trinity, Aberystwyth, and also baptised Will in 1981 and taken their father's funeral service there in 1999, so there was a real sense of continuity.

Apart from guests who had come a very long way, we also had great support from my St Mark's friends. Jack had used his design skills on the invitations and order of service; it was all very personal. A poignant moment for me was when Katie was given away by her brothers, they steering her firmly down the aisle, one on each arm. How proud their father would have been of them all.

The reception was at Aberdare Hall, a Victorian hall of residence at Cardiff University. Its dining room has comforting light wood panelling, we had live music with flute and harp, and the very helpful catering officer, a good Bala girl, took care of everything for me. It was appropriate to go there as we were also celebrating Katie's degree results from Cardiff as well as her qualification as an occupational therapist. It had been a tough three years for her commuting from Bristol mostly by train and bicycle, and she achieved a First, and also won the Research Award for her dissertation.

The wedding weekend culminated in a frisbee (what else?!) 'tournament' on the Sunday morning after camping, for all Katie and

Jack's young friends, based at the Glastonbury Leisure Centre. They had first climbed the tor in torrential rain, Katie in her simple silk wedding dress, on the Saturday, with champagne at the top, and enjoyed an excellent party in the evening, all organised by the bride and groom. Ben (thirty) and Will (now twenty-eight), made star appearances, Ben reciting his own fairly rude and very funny poem about his sister, and Will singing with his tuneful barber shop quartet. It was lovely for me, too, to have more time to meet Jack's family.

We were much saddened in August by the passing of John Knapp, the boys' headmaster at Llandaff during their time as choristers there, but it was good to catch up with old friends at the very beautiful and dignified memorial service in the cathedral, a fitting tribute to a lovely man.

I am so grateful to have had better health this year. I'm enjoying my hospital chaplaincy visiting, church activities, acting, singing and playing my cello, Christ's Hospital – Charity's Confirmation there was a delight – and, of course, our growing family. Now I *must* finish *Hang on Tight!* One slight excuse for the delay is that a gammy hip is slowing me down a little. Roll on the operation . . .

CHAPTER 33

Miscellaneous Pieces

APART FROM ALL MY PROFESSIONAL press work, I've always tried to record important events and interesting activities. This is a selection.

St Paul's Spotlight for Llandaff Cathedral Choir

Tuesday, 18 May 1993 was an exciting day out in London for Llandaff Cathedral Choir. They were singing at an important civic service in St Paul's Cathedral, and there among the 3,000-strong congregation to hear them was our own Archbishop of Wales, the Most Reverend Alwyn Rice Jones.

The preacher was the Archbishop of Canterbury, Dr George Carey, who described the singing of the three visiting choirs invited for the occasion, (Wells, York Minster and Llandaff), together with St Paul's own choir as an example of what could be achieved 'when ability is honed with practice.'

The service was to celebrate the 339th annual festival of the Corporation of the Sons of the Clergy, a charity set up in the seventeenth century to help clergy families in need, and which also helps to fund ordinands today.

Like each visiting choir this year, Llandaff had the awesome responsibility of singing an unaccompanied anthem under the vast gilded dome of St Paul's with its slightly unnerving echo. Llandaff's Cathedral Organist and Master of the Choristers, Dr Michael Smith, had chosen 'O Lord, arise into thy resting-place' by Thomas Weelkes, and the sixteen young choristers, backed firmly by the gentlemen of the choir sang the challenging seven-part setting with commendable confidence.

Dr Smith has a family musical connection with St Paul's. He is the second closest surviving relative of Sir George Martin, a former organist of St Paul's Cathedral who was knighted in 1897 following the Diamond Jubilee service for Queen Victoria. Dr Smith was able to show the choristers his ancestor's tomb in the Order of the British Empire Chapel in the crypt of St Paul's. The boys also sang some of 'Uncle George's chants' in their psalm settings back home at Llandaff.

Family support

Some of the gentlemen brought wives and families on the choir coach while parents, grandparents and friends gathered from as far apart as Yorkshire, Hertfordshire, Dorset and West Wales to catch a glimpse of the Llandaff choristers aged between eight and thirteen. One mother from Brecon even made a special return journey from France.

Supporters were not disappointed. They were able to see clearly the Llandaff boys processing solemnly in their familiar red cassocks and pristine ruffs and surplices amidst a colourful array of clergy and City liverymen. By tradition, the Lord Mayor of London attends the service, and accompanied by the Sheriffs, processes with the Archbishop of Canterbury in state.

According to the Service Paper the Festival Service has always two main elements – 'the invitation of a distinguished person to preach the Sermon and fine music'. The musicians of London Brass contributed to the excitement and drama of the whole occasion and perhaps the most enjoyable part for the Llandaff choir was when all four choirs faced the congregation and joined in a thrilling centenary performance of Parry's anthem 'Hear my Words, ye People' which culminates in the familiar hymn, 'O Praise ye the Lord.'

It was a day that sixteen young boys from Llandaff are likely to remember for the rest of their lives.

Reproduced by kind permission of Mr Tony Phillips, editor at the time of *The Llandavian*, the journal of the Cathedral School, Llandaff.

The following piece is history now, as, sadly, the Right Hand Trust no longer exists.

Llandaff Youngsters Lead the Way in Overseas Mission

Two South Wales missioners have been selected to serve overseas with the Right Hand Trust in 1997. They are: Durham University English and Theology graduate Rachel Brown (twenty-one) of

Llandaff and ex-Llandaff Cathedral chorister Benedict Davies-Jenkins (eighteen) of the Parish of Pentrych near Cardiff.

Rachel and Ben followed the Right Hand Trust's director, Mark Wright in giving a talk about the work of the Trust to interested parishioners in the David Chapel, and Mr Wright then held the Llandaff Cathedral Parish Youth Club riveted with his stories of life in the Third World. An Anglican Lay Reader for the past thirty years, he has just 'retired' from teaching to concentrate on the expanding work of the Trust, which he founded in consultation with USPG five years ago. The Archbishop of Wales is Patron of the Trust.

The Trust aims to provide an Away Year challenge for young people between the ages of eighteen and thirty through placements with the Anglican Church in Africa and the Caribbean. The link dioceses involved with the Trust so far are in Kenya, Uganda, Zimbabwe, Swaziland, the Gambia, Malawi and the Windward Islands.

Although all these dioceses to which the missioners are sent are Anglican, the Right Hand Trust appealed to Rachel because it is an ecumenical group: the volunteers come from a variety of denominations ranging from Roman Catholics and Anglicans to Methodists and members of the Salvation Army, and share a common faith in Christianity. They each have to express their Christian commitment in writing as part of the selection procedure when they apply, and interestingly, Mark Wright reports that of the application forms sent out to youngsters, only one in ten is actually completed and returned.

The Trust aims to provide a life-enriching experience for the successful applicants in their overseas placement, and in doing so, to forge personal and corporate links between Christians in Britain and Africa and the Caribbean. The vision is to match the needs of an under-resourced Church overseas with the time and talents of the young people from Britain seeking wider horizons and spiritual development. In practical terms, they join in the work of the local Church, using whatever skills and interests they may have in teaching, health or social work without pay. As it works out, most school leavers find themselves teaching, and experience of facing a Birmingham primary school class is part of their training course in December before they have to jump in at the deep end overseas. Missioners go as guests of the Church to share a simple life in a rural area and they keep in touch with each other and with their home parishes through prayer cards and through the *Bush Telegraph*, the Trust's own newspaper, to which every missioner contributes regularly. Each young man or woman is sent out with a 'mission partner' of the same sex, and the Trust's director tries hard to meet individual preferences for particular countries, as well as matching personalities as far as possible. The mission partners may well be the only 'Brits' for miles.

So what persuaded Rachel and Ben to volunteer? Rachel, an active Christian at University College, Durham was attracted by literature about the Right Hand Trust in her university careers library. She also met a young man in his first year at Durham who had worked in Uganda with the Trust as a school leaver. 'He had had such an amazing time,' she says, 'even starting a candle-making business while he was out there, and he really convinced me that the Right Hand Trust was a good organisation. There were other links, too, like the fact that Mark Wright was a Durham graduate himself and was also Church in Wales. I thought, it's got to be right for me.'

Ben found out about the Trust in his last year at Shrewsbury School when looking for something worthwhile as well as interesting to do in a gap year before university. The school had sent out two RHT volunteers in 1996 and Ben was encouraged to apply by his housemaster and the school chaplain as well as by the careers master. That his mother had spent her gap year teaching on a USPG mission in Malawi thirty years earlier as a VSO cadet volunteer is purely coincidental!

Rachel and Ben begin their eight-month projects early in the New Year: Rachel is off to the tiny coastal village of Chateaubelair in the Windward Islands with its rugged, volcanic terrain where, by mid-October, building on the house for her and her mission partner, a Bristol graduate called Gail, had not yet been started (it is not impossible for missioners to have to build their own on arrival). Rachel knows that her tasks as a lay minister will include helping with Sunday school, visiting the elderly and 'the lapsed', and youth work. A keen Guider, she hopes to get permission to set up Guide and Brownie units locally. She has even been asked to start a guild for the over forties!

Ben is going to Nyaruhanga, 22 km west of Kabale (by dirt road) in the south west of Uganda, in the diocese of North Kigezi, in hilly, open countryside with gorillas close by. He will live and work with Sussex boy Giles Seaford (nineteen) in the local high school, where they expect to teach, as well as helping out in the parish. The school has 300 students going up to A level and the boys' RHT predecessors there, two graduate girls, describe the African staff as 'brilliant'. Ben hopes to teach some biology, music and art. Like all the 1997 missioners, he has also been encouraged by Mark Wright to get some practice in taking an active part in services in his home parish, as he may well have to lead them at Nyaruhanga. As far as teaching aides are concerned, keen rugby player Giles will go armed with a rugby ball, while ex-music scholar Ben thinks that his clarinet and a harmonica will be his most useful tools. Their house was specially built for the Right Hand Trust and has a bedroom each for them and a spare room, a sitting room, and even a shower room and kitchen, but no electricity or running water. The boys will have to do all their own cooking on a charcoal stove. Their lavatory is a 'long drop' some distance from the house.

The 1997 RHT youngsters have had two training weekends at the Trust's mid-Wales base in Llanfair Caereinion, meeting the enthusiastic newly returned 1996 missioners in September. Their last hurdle, apart from medical checks, is an intensive eight-day course at the United College of the Ascension in Birmingham run in December with USPG, culminating in a moving commissioning service to which parents, parishioners from home and past missioners are invited.

Rachel and Ben have both been working hard to earn the £3,000 needed to fund each project, and are also receiving great support and encouragement from their parishes at home. Mark Wright's visit to Llandaff Diocese in October was part of a UK-wide tour to the forty-six parishes of all the young people going out to Africa and the Windward Islands with the Right Hand Trust in 1997. In his 1996 annual report he pays tribute to the missioners: 'Without their enthusiasm and dedication there would be no Trust; we are delighted that yet again this year there has been a 50% increase in the number of young people coming forward for this exhilarating, but often daunting experience where much is expected of them.' If Rachel and Ben were looking for a challenge, it certainly looks as if they have found one.

Last Supper with a Difference in Chaplain's Easter Triptych

Step into the thirteenth century chapel at Christ College, Brecon, and you are in for a surprise. Between the altar and a conventional

Victorian crucifixion window, you will find a twenty-first century Easter triptych in oils, its colours brilliant against the background of dark oak panelling.

Come a little closer to examine the central panel depicting the Last Supper, and you will notice several unusual features. Despite the traditional middle Eastern clothes of the times, the faces have a twenty-first century look, one is clearly a woman, and if you count carefully, you will find only ten disciples seated around the figure of Christ, standing chalice in hand, while another figure, 'slightly snakelike in shape', representing Judas, is seen leaving the room and slipping out into the darkness.

The artist, the Reverend Morgan Llewellyn, who was the school chaplain at Christ College when he painted the triptych, explains:

> This is reminiscent of the account in St John's Gospel, in which he (Judas) went out, and it was night. The other Disciples are of all ages, all colours and races . . .The space between the two apostles in the foreground, one young one old, and from which the picture is viewed indicates that you, the observer, are also a disciple and welcome at the table and included in the invitation to drink.

Centre background on a distant hill, stark against a darkening blue sky, stand three empty crosses – 'waiting' – as the artist says, an ominous reminder of what is to come.

The left panel of the triptych depicts the crucifixion, and the right one the resurrection. Both show extraordinarily vivid use of light. We are spared none of the agony of Christ's suffering on the cross, yet, as Morgan Llewellyn says, 'Low on the horizon, the white light beneath the lowering clouds promises eventual release from the overpowering gloom.' Look right to see Christ rising from the tomb, which is already 'too small to hold the body of God incarnate . . .With the calm sky of dawn and Jerusalem golden behind him . . .the light of the world shines past the young girl (Mary Magdalene), and falling on the steps, leads out of the picture and towards us.' The artist says it all – through this powerful and symbolic piece we are drawn irresistibly to both the tragedy and the joy of the Easter story.

6 April 2003

Young Edinburgh Art Graduate Makes Wales Portrait Award

A promising young Edinburgh-based artist and former Llandaff Cathedral chorister, Benedict Davies-Jenkins (twenty-eight) is spreading his wings, and one of his paintings is showing in Cardiff now.

After leaving Shrewsbury School where he was school Captain of Music, and played violin, viola, clarinet and alto sax, as well as singing in the school Chapel Choir, Ben worked in his gap year with the Anglican church in Uganda though the Right Hand Trust. Here he met his wife-to-be Nicola, younger daughter of the new Bishop of Oxford, John Pritchard.

After Uganda Ben took up his place at Edinburgh University and Edinburgh College of Art, gaining his MA with a 2:1 with distinction in fine art and art history.

After marrying Nicola, and beginning to establish himself as a painter in Edinburgh, he took a career break with her in the Ashanti district of Ghana on an eight-month voluntary stint through USPG. Here they lived and worked in a babies' home in Mampong, under the auspices of the local Anglican diocese there. They also taught, Ben in the local girls' secondary school.

Out of the Ghana experience has come the impressive portrait in oil on canvas, mysteriously titled 'Akosikya and his unknown grandmother'. This will now hang in St David's Hall, Cardiff until 17 February as one of only fifty paintings selected from artists of all ages for the prestigious Wales Portrait Award.

Ben recently completed his first portrait commission for a bishop: the sitter was former Bishop of Ely the Rt Revd Stephen Sykes, on his retirement as Principal of St John's College, Durham, and he apparently expressed approbation when he saw the finished work. Now Ben has an exhibition coming up in Lichfield Cathedral.

Ben lives with Nicola in Brunswick Terrace, Edinburgh, and is currently training to be an art teacher at Moray House.

Written 2007.

Learning the Cello

'You're not keyboard-minded, Susan, but you're not unmusical.' The kindly piano teacher, Miss Cordery, has spoken. Grade 3 is clearly Susan's limit. 'How about another instrument?' The teacher does some ear tests and suddenly gets excited. 'Have you got perfect pitch?' The pupil doesn't understand the question, but it seems that she has done something right. 'How about the cello?'

Next hurdle is the headmistress, who happens to be a cellist, and tells her to spread out her hands, paint-spattered from an art lesson. The stretch is declared good enough for the cello.

A school instrument is found for her in a heavy old wooden case. It stands in a corner in a dark little practice cell next to an upright piano.

The first sweet, exotic whiff of rosin is intoxicating. Miss Hughes is young and encouraging. Practices can be frustrating though, trying to tune up by twisting the stiff old wooden pegs – no adjusters in those days – the child fearing that she'll get it too tight and a gut string will snap and fly whipping into her ear. Lessons, however, are a delight, when she realises that she is in tune with the piano as she and Miss Hughes romp through pieces together. Isn't Telemann fun! For a few precious minutes each week, she feels transported.

Then one day Miss Hughes tells her that she is leaving. Desolation sets in; tears flow. The pupil is assured that the new teacher, Mrs Jen Lynch,[1] is very nice, and indeed she is, but by now for the young Susan A level studies are taking hold and there is little time to practise. She longs to be as good as brilliant violinists at school like Elizabeth Onley or Judy Douglas, or Pam Henson on her oboe, but for her School Orchestra is hard, and at the dreaded Speech Day performance she always feels under-rehearsed, and daunted by the audience, the Lord Mayor of London and other civic dignitaries in their finery, and all the Christ's Hospital Almoners and Governors. Hiding behind future professional cellist Christine Clemetson on the stage, she is still too terrified to play the first few bars. Poor Miss Barratt conducting looks scarcely less terrified herself!

Making quick progress in her cello lessons, however, Susan is put into Grade V theory class, but there Miss Barratt despairs of her. Rules of rhythm and harmony, which come so easily to some, perhaps more mathematically inclined girls, are a mystery to her.

What a pity to have missed the first four grades. She is quickly encouraged to drop the theory – better, presumably, than failing the exam.

But she still has her cello (German, about 1870) bought for her by her generous mother, and she vows that one day she will go back to it. Impossible to take it to Malawi, or up to York, doing the journey alone from Worthing by train, kettle and climbing boots already dangling from her kit, and anyway there are hugely talented musicians there like Moray Welsh. As for the army, they would just laugh at her with a cello! She must wait.

Suddenly, it seems, she has three children and discovers that they are all musical, and she is determined to try again. She gets the old instrument, not particularly valuable, but precious to her, done up and her husband buys her some lessons for her birthday. Unfortunately, the teacher recommended is a supercilious young man who tells her he thinks she has more in her head than is coming out in her fingers. He is probably right, but she is not encouraged.

She tries again in South Wales and is just getting to know her new teacher, Adrian, when his wife gets pregnant again and he is needed for babysitting duties. He no longer has time to teach her.

On the fifth attempt she strikes gold. A Welsh National Opera cellist of some thirty years' standing, with a delightful violinist wife Elizabeth, Andrew Elliott is all that a keen but struggling pupil could wish. For by now it *is* a struggle with arthritis making even short practices hard, and concentration not what it was, but it's worth all the effort. Indeed, one of her daughter Katie's fellow occupational therapy students, Luke (*Macfadyen*) even interviews her for his dissertation on music as therapy. For her these days, music really *is* therapy. It keeps her thinking, and when occasionally in a lesson Andrew exclaims, 'Beautiful!' she immediately goes wrong from the shock of having got something right! He helps her to aim for exquisite phrasing in Vivaldi sonatas; they can agree unselfconsciously on the beauty of minor keys. Enormously patient, he always, always, finds *something* to praise – surely the mark of a good teacher – and his absolute seriousness about the music and her attempt to play it makes it always worthwhile.

Moreover, she is surviving the chamber orchestra (*St Edward's*). Boosted by Cardiff music students, it is blessed with some excellent soloists, and they tackle brilliant music together like whole Mozart or Schubert symphonies, or the Rutter 'Requiem' or a Hadyn mass with the church choir. Thanks to the tolerance of her fellow instrumentalists and their enthusiastic young conductor, Alison Dite, who like Andrew is encouraging to adult learners, she doesn't get totally lost any more, and is even enjoying it now!

February 2010

Uncle Malcolm

This is a mini-saga that Helen Dunmore encouraged us to write at our Community workshop. The story had to be compressed into fifty words. This is what I came up with to describe the life of Eric Malcolm Davies-Jenkins, OBE, late Royal Welch Fusiliers and Welch Regiment, one time High Sheriff of Cardiganshire.

Uncle Malcolm

He was born the youngest of three brothers, and the most ambitious. Educated at Bedford School, joined the army and travelled the world. He won medals for boxing, shot lion and tigers and became a brigadier. He terrified most people, but underneath he was kind and shy.

He never married.

1983

Note

1. Jen Lynch, now in her eighties, is still teaching, at Benslow.

CHAPTER 34

Leading Intercessions

ONE OF OUR JOBS AS SENIORS in the House was to lead prayers every day, all thirty-six girls kneeling up on the hard Dayroom floor in front of our beautiful trestle tables, polished daily by us, and still bearing marks of the boys' hobnail boots in the ridged bar underneath. In the evening we would sing a hymn, too, and we would say together our Ward Two Prayer. I have it to this day, printed in green, our House colour:

> Grant, we beseech Thee, that Thy Spirit may so dwell within us, that we may go forth with the light of hope in our eyes, and the fire of inspiration in our lives; Thy word on our tongues, and Thy love in our hearts, and that we may do Thy will in service to all mankind, this day and evermore.

We also had a tradition in our House to read from Dorothy L. Sayers' radio play cycle *The Man Born to be King* every Christmas, all sitting at the same long tables, and I loved it.

I loved choosing the prayers, too, although they all came from a book, and I don't think any of us would have dared make one up in those days. All these years later it has been a privilege to lead Intercessions at our wonderful parish church here, St Mark's, Gabalfa, where it is considered quite normal to write our own prayers to reflect the concerns of the day. I have included a small selection here. As a traditional Anglican by upbringing at CH, I am gradually getting the hang of evangelical worship!

Prayers – 14 August 2005

Enable with perpetual light
The dullness of our blinded sight.

Lord, we try to imagine the terror and confusion of Saul of Tarsus, up until then so powerful, cruel and feared by the Christians, suddenly blinded, vulnerable and totally dependent on others, needing to be led by the hand to Damascus.

We may be fit in body, but we acknowledge our own vulnera-
bility to temptation and to sin. Teach us to depend on You, and be
led through Your Holy Spirit to do Your will for the rest of our
lives.

Lord in Your mercy: **Hear our prayer**.

Lord, we haven't all had blinding conversions like Saul, and we
probably don't expect to die for our Christians beliefs. Perhaps we
are quiet believers, not wishing to impose our faith on others, or just
not brave enough to speak out about it.

Give us, we pray, new courage, like the newly-converted Paul, to
spread Your gospel, especially in difficult situations, for instance with
work colleagues or friends or family who are not believers. Help us
to find the right opportunities and the right words, and if words do
not come easily, to be shining examples of our Christian faith
through loving actions to bring others to You.

Lord in Your mercy: **Hear our prayer**.

Perhaps, Lord, like Ananias we are sceptical or even afraid of
sudden conversions, especially if the new Christians until recently
denounced or ridiculed our faith. Help us to believe that as in Paul
You can work miracles even in unlikely people.

We bring to You particularly the work of prison chaplains and
those working with young offenders, that those previously without
hope or self respect or respect for others may have their lives
transformed by the knowledge of Your love and be given a second
chance when they return to the community.

Lord in Your mercy: **Hear our prayer**.

We bring before You, Lord, all those *young* people whose lives are
ruled by boredom, violence, drink or drugs, that we may find ways
of reaching out to them through Your gospel and helping them to
find new meaning in life.

Acts Chapter 9 tells us that the early church had a time of peace
after Paul's conversion. Guide us, Lord, to enable Your church *now*
to grow in numbers, through Your Holy Spirit, and to live, like the
early Christians, in true reverence for You.

Lord in Your mercy: **Hear our prayer**.

We pray especially at this troubled time for all who bear heavy
responsibility in government and the judiciary, that they may strike
the right balance between protecting the public, and tolerance of

other nationalities, races and religions, and we ask You, Lord, to continue to give us guidance whilst trying to spread Your gospel, in promoting harmony in our land and in the wider world.

Lord in Your mercy: **Hear our prayer**.

In our own parish, we thank You especially for Bob and Roz, Melanie and Darren, Ken and Rosemary, and all our lay readers, and pray that we as a church community may find ways of perhaps sharing the burden or easing their workload in practical ways in the face of further clergy cuts in our Deanery and Diocese.

Lord in your mercy: **Hear our prayer**

We remember, before You, Lord, all those known to us who are sick at this time, especially . . .

We also bring to You, Lord, the bereaved family and friends of . . .

Lord in Your mercy: **Hear our prayer**.

Finally, we remember before You, Lord, all clergy working in hospitals and hospices, ministering to the sick or the dying, that patients' faith in You may be sustained or rekindled, and that they, and we, may find peace at the end.

Lord in Your mercy: **Hear our prayer**.

Amen.

Prayers for 24 July 2005

We come to You today, Lord, shocked and frightened by the bombings and attempted bombings in London in recent weeks, and now by the devastating explosions in Egypt yesterday.

We cannot understand the minds of those who commit such atrocities, Lord, yet we acknowledge that we are all sinners capable on occasion of hatred and of the desire to hurt others, whether in word or deed.

We pray for peace, Lord, in our fallen world, and we pray that we as Christians may do all we can to promote good relations amongst those of differing race and creeds. We thank You for the example of leaders of the major faiths coming together to express solidarity after the London bombings. Help us, Lord, to look for the good in others, and to find opportunities in our own multi-cultural community of Cardiff, to show Your love towards those whose beliefs we cannot share, or do not fully understand, or who have no faith, so that we may be positive witnesses to You, and bring our children up to live in harmony with others.

Lord in Your mercy: **Hear our prayer**.

We are overwhelmed, Lord, by the images of the children starving in the famine in Niger. We pray for all the relief workers, that food may get through more quickly, and as we have declared our intention to make poverty history, help us to back that up by more generous giving to those in such desperate need.

Lord in Your mercy: **Hear our prayer**.

We bring to You, Lord, at this difficult time, all those trying to protect the public, especially those working in the police and the security services. We remember before You particularly our armed police officers in the split-second decisions that they have to make in stressful situations, that they may always act with professionalism and sound judgement.

Lord in Your mercy: **Hear our prayer**.

We remember before You Lord, all those injured or emotionally damaged in the recent bombings, and the families of all the victims.

Lord in Your mercy: **Hear our prayer**.

In our own church community, we bring to You all the sick and suffering, especially . . .

Lord in Your mercy: **Hear our prayer**.

We also bring to You the families and friends of the recently departed, especially Vi Hulme's daughter Mary, and Ken White and all Norah's family.

Lord in Your mercy: **Hear our prayer**.

We thank You, Lord, for this holiday time, and pray that all teachers and teaching assistants and school support staff may enjoy the break, and come back with energy renewed to look after the children again in September.

We pray for all our young people on Christian summer camps, and those helping to run them, and for the chaplains of all our Cadet Forces away on camp with Royal Marines cadets, sea, army or air cadets, that they may find opportunities to spread Your gospel to the young people and their leaders in a meaningful way.

Lord in Your mercy: **Hear our prayer**.

And as we enjoy our own holidays, Lord, we pray that we may

find time to stand back, take stock, and return refreshed, ready to making serving You a priority above all else in our daily lives.
Lord in Your mercy: **Hear our prayer**.
Amen.

Perhaps the greatest privilege was to lead the Intercessions for my daughter Katie's marriage to Jack Goolden at St Mark's on 4 July 2008. What I came up with is an amalgam of the prayers from the Church in Wales marriage service and what I thought most appropriate for them both and their families and friends.

Prayers for Katie and Jack's Wedding Friday 4 July 2008

Would you please sit or kneel, as you feel most comfortable.

Almighty and everlasting God, strengthen these Your servants Katie and Jack with Your grace, that they may keep the promises they have made in Your presence.
Lord in Your mercy: **Hear our prayer**.
Let Your peace be in their home, and Your blessing upon it.
Lord in Your mercy: **Hear our prayer**.
Bless their marriage with the gift of children. Help them to be responsible parents, and give them wisdom, love and patience to bring up their children in the Christian faith.
Lord in Your mercy: **Hear our prayer**.
Make Your love known through them and their home, that Your holy name may be glorified.
Lord in Your mercy: **Hear our prayer**.
Now the prayer of St Francis of Assisi:

Lord, make us an instrument of Your peace.
Where there is hatred, let me sow love;
where there is injury, pardon;
where there is despair, hope;
where there is darkness, light;
and where there is sadness, joy.

Divine Master,
grant that I may not so much seek
to be consoled as to console,

to be understood as to understand,
to be loved as to love.

For it is in giving that we receive,
it is in pardoning that we are pardoned,
and it is in dying that we're born to eternal life.
Amen.

And now a prayer for *all* our homes from the ancient monastic evening service of Compline.

Visit we beseech thee Lord, our homes, and drive far from them all the snares of the enemy.

May Your holy angels dwell therein to preserve us in peace, and may Your blessing be upon us evermore.

Amen.

Shall we sum up all our prayers by saying together the Lord's Prayer.

Our Father, who art in heaven,
Hallowed be Thy name;
Thy kingdom come;
Thy will be done;
On earth as it is in heaven.
Give us this day our daily bread.
And forgive us our trespasses,
As we forgive those who trespass against us.
And lead us not into temptation;
But deliver us from evil.
For Thine is the kingdom,
The power, and the glory
For ever and ever.
Amen

Perhaps before I ever started leading Intercessions at St Mark's, possibly I should have read John Pritchard's book *How to Pray*. I did the next best thing, and wrote a book review for our parish newsletter, *Roundabout*.

How to Pray

If you find prayer difficult, as I do, this book comes as a joyful discovery. Bishop John Pritchard's *How to Pray* is exactly what it says, a practical handbook, and in simple, direct language, it tackles how to go about praying whether in church, outside, or at home.

While scholarly in its many references, it is thoroughly unstuffy, often moving, sometimes funny, and full of humanity. It has chapter headings like 'How to Slow Down' and 'How to Start Saying Something' where the 'Thank you. Sorry, Please' formula really seems to work.

John Pritchard tackles head-on the problems of fitting prayer into the hectic pace of modern life and the devastating effects on prayer of burn-out. He deals honestly with relationship problems, terminal illness and violence. He includes a haunting prayer for forgiveness found by the body of a dead child in Ravensbrück, where 92,000 women and children died. He never pretends that prayer is easy, but he encourages us to 'plod on' even when we don't feel anything at the time. 'Faithfulness matters more than feelings,' he asserts.

There is also plenty of joy in this book, and the uses of music, poetry and the visual arts as well as the Bible are explored as an aid to prayer. Touching stories and beautiful prayers from throughout the world are included, different prayer traditions are explained, and the 'Try This' sections in each chapter provide a practical resource.

Do try this book. It could transform your life.

CHAPTER 35

Recent Poetry

I DID IN FACT GET AN EXCELLENT new hip, in May 2009. Unfortunately I also had serious medical complications afterwards. As always for me recently, illness seems to fuel a furious spate of writing. Indeed, it was in sleepless nocturnal hours due to chest problems early in 2007 that the idea of this book was conceived, and much of the writing for it achieved its first draft. I really did feel at the time that I was hanging on tight!

I have included these recent poems in the order in which they were written, which also reflects my gradual recovery. I'm sure that the writing itself was therapeutic.

This next I wrote in honour of a lovely lady who nursed me the night I was diagnosed with two pulmonary embolisms, when not surprisingly, I got no sleep. I was enormously grateful for her cheerful nature and her practical kindness, and when she told me she'd been in the WRAC, I that felt that as Girls in Green we were kindred spirits.

Ode to a Senior Healthcare Worker
or
The Rise and Rise of Private Wendy

Once there was a girl in green
Served her country loyally
In the W-R-A-C[1]
Did Wendy.

Specialised in stores, and now
Does the same on S-A-U.[2]
Big and buxom, heart of gold
Is Wendy.

Once she wore a beech brown stripe:
Lance Jack, put the fear of God
Into privates, girls or men
Did Wendy.

Fell from grace with one right hook:
Hit a sergeant, got the book
Thrown at her, and busted, she,
Was Wendy.

Now she's still a girl in green.
Treats each patient like the Queen.
Still a smasher, patient's dream
Is Wendy.

10 June 2009

Diagnosis

Andreas Scholl and Bach: the perfect combo
For people braced to tackle shocking news.
That's what I recommend for frightened patients
Like me with D.V.T., through one small clot
Which sneaked, insidious, upwards from the calf,
Then split in two, formed clots on my right lung:
These embolisms, source of instant peril
Until dispersed by Warfarin and jabs
Of Heparin each morning in the tummy.

The gentle German doctor looks distracted:
(I know him from our parish church, St Mark's,
Young Marcus and his doctor wife and children)
Thinks how to tell this granny trapped in wheelchair
What she's already seen, a fuzzy patch
Of black which keeps recurring on each shot
On V.Q. scan in Nuclear Medicine space.
'Now come on, Dr Trautner,' I encourage,
'Give it to me straight now, I can take it.'

'How are you?' he begins. I know at once:
A doctor being nice to me means trouble.
'I'm very much afraid to say I can't
Rule out a pulmonary embolism.
We need to do another scan to check.'
So kind, so troubled in the telling, he,
I speak in German, aim to comfort him.

He tries, and fails, to slide a needle in.
'There is a thrombus,' gently he explains,

Then probes again, towards the wrist this time.
I try to make it easier for this father,
Who's now a budding radiologist:
'Send for a nurse!' I tell him jokingly,
'That's what you need for needle sites and vomit:
You doctors really want to run away.'
I'm teasing him because the situation
Is far too serious not to crack a joke.

He leaves, and suddenly I am alone,
Huddled in wheelchair with my two-week hip.
Desperately I fumble in my handbag
Locate the fine white lead and tiny earplugs
And slim–line turquoise lifeline – MP3,
Given by all our children for my sixtieth.

Instinctively I scroll with fumbling thumb,
Search for Andreas Scholl, another German,
After the gentle radiologist,
And press the flat white circles in my ears.
Then I'm transported to a peaceful world:
Exquisite counter-tenor fused with Bach,
Soothing baroque makes perfect symmetry.
If this is heaven, I think it can't be bad.

But then the tears start pricking down my cheeks.
I love this world too much to leave it yet.
My children! How to break the scary news?
I love them all so much, I ache to hug them
As heaven beckons perilously close.
O God, please let this embolism vanish,
Dispersed by Warfarin or Heparin.
Anything, Lord to cling to precious life,
And loving of my daughter and my sons
And baby granddaughter in Edinburgh.

I try to pray for them and make my peace
And beg forgiveness for unhealed hurts
That I may leave behind me if I die.
Father forgive: I know not what I do.
My life is in Your hands and in the medics'.
Time to amend it, that is what I crave.

Please give me strength to fight this dreadful weakness.
I have so much to do, Lord. Grant me time –
A book to finish, grandchildren to cradle.

Whether we live or die, we are the Lord's.
In my Father's house are many mansions.
I know the Christian theory, but right now
I want my modest semi in the Heath,
And garden. Let me live and love, and sniff
Velindre rose bursting with fat pink bud,
Its very first, in memory of Ngozi,
My precious friend we lost to bowel cancer,
Ascites-swollen stomach so obscene –
Reminiscent of my poor, brave Mike's –
It snapped off short bright medic in her prime,
With pain beyond the point of human bearing,
Yet somehow borne by her with Christian joy,
Dying as she chose in her own bed.
St Mark's was overflowing at her funeral
With Cardiff folk and friends from overseas.
To grieve with family so torn apart,
Young Poppy nestling on his father's shoulders,
The singing soothing desperate disbelief:
It is well with my soul, it is
Well with my soul, it is well
With my soul, it is well. Amen.

Precious, heavenly Daughter, Violet called her,
Robbed of her PhD by vicious fate,
Leaving behind three children under ten,
To brave this world so young without their mother,
Zoë, Joshua and little Poppy,
Heroic husband Andrew stunned with grief.

I want to see those children growing up.
Big Zoë, Joshua and Immanuel,
O God! An elder daughter and two sons,
Same as my own, my gentle, frightened children,
Katie and Ben and Will and baby Cora.
I long to hug them all and not let go.

My fighting spirit's back: I'll beat this illness
And swim again and sing and play my cello,
Visit my patients on the renal ward.

Andreas Scholl and Bach: the perfect combo.
Thank You, dear God for music, love and life.

14 June 2009
Cardiff

The Best Medicine

Soldier Sue is fighting through,
Crutch her only weapon, too,
Soldier on – so much to do.
   Hurrah!

Singer Sue keeps smiling through.
Could have died, I tell you true.
Sing, not cry is what she'll do.
   Hurrah!

Granny Sue is praying through.
Christian friends keep praying, too.
God is good: she's pulling through.
   Hurrah!

20 June 2009
Cardiff

By 23 July 2009, I was feeling so much more positive about life,
realising how happy the writing was making me, that I wrote:

The Goodie

Don't panic, Major Sue, Ma'am:
Mr Jones is on the case.
Renowned for playing rugby,
As orthopod he's ace.

Soft speaking, gentle Welshman,
A gentle giant he.
With courtesy he treats you,
And wouldn't touch your knee:

For hips are what he's good at,
A champion, I ween.
He leaves a lovely hip scar
And treats you like the Queen.

Three cheers for Stephen Jones, yes!
Three cheers, and three more cheers.
This patient, she salutes him
For he's conquered all her fears.

8 July 2009
Cardiff

Note: It didn't occur to me at the time of writing that there could be any confusion with our Wales rugby fly half of the same name!

The first draft of the following started with 'She was only a dull old major'. I'm still not sure which version I prefer!

Middle-aged Writer's Breakout

Her son couldn't quite understand it:
It wasn't like Mother at all.
He thought she was getting eccentric.
In fact, *she* was having a ball.

23 July 2009
Cardiff

Notes

1. Women's Royal Army Corps.
2. Surgical Assessment Unit; Lance Jack: Lance Corporal; Hit a sergeant: A woman sergeant! (from the WRAC); Busted: Reduced to the Ranks.

CHAPTER 36

Conclusion

I THOUGHT I SHOULD END this book with contributions from two friends with first-hand knowledge of Christ's Hospital from the past, and from Dominic, my first Presentee, who has just left Housey as a Grecian (upper sixth pupil), so it's still very fresh in his memory.

Mrs Judith Hepper (née Heaven) taught me at Hertford, of course, and it is she who has helped me so much with *Hang on Tight*. I thought it would be fun to get a view of the school in my time from a staff perspective.

The White House, Fore Street, opposite the main gates at Hertford, was a bolt-hole for the four young teachers who lived there in spartan bed-sits. We saw it as a centre of subversive thought, if not of action – though we were proud of securing our first teaching posts at Christ's Hospital. But we were constantly blotting our copy-books! School Chapel, for example, was sternly compulsory for staff. But so were 'Chapel Hats'! and it was not unknown for hats to be mislaid – so that hasty borrowing or even improvisation had to be employed to save the situation . . . ! I remember how, one hot summer's day, one of our merry band made the mistake of wearing open sandals, thus incurring the deepest opprobrium: a series of 'appropriate footwear' notices swiftly appeared on the staff room notice-board. End-of-term report writing was another nightmare. Each document had to be perfect, naturally. If you were the last to enter your remark and made one fractional error so that all the columns had to be re-written, you were unlikely to be forgiven by your elders and betters. My worst moment was when I collected a pile of exercise books from DRW, who regularly checked her young teachers' work. In an otherwise impeccably-marked set of essays, Miss West's eagle eye had spotted one uncorrected spelling-mistake, in the title above a long offering on the dramatic qualities of 'Julius Caesar' (alternatively, 'Caeser'). I was in deep trouble.

But of course Christ's Hospital was a good place for a young teacher. There was plenty to learn from the experienced staff. My own head of department, Kathleen Betterton, was an inspiration and a comfort. I quickly realised that many of my pupils were dauntingly bright and therefore very exciting to teach. I enjoyed their dramatic, musical and artistic talents and many have remained friends to this day. It is strange that the very children who arrived in my English lessons in floods of tears after the dreaded needlework hour have become successful writers in a variety of fields!

Now I too can forget the bleak hours of games duty and winter walks, and remember the fun of pancake parties in the Red House and invitations to coffee parties in the Wards, exciting involvement in productions of *Tobias and the Angel* and *The Magic Flute* and an English Department trip to see Laurence Olivier's *Othello*. There was the privilege of being chosen to attend Speech Day at Horsham and the St Matthew's Day service in the City. I was even allowed to chaperone my Form on their visit to Cambridge, where a generous Governor had arranged for them to be shown around the Colleges by indulgent Old Blues. As for 14 July 1967, when we had a day off to celebrate Miss West's twenty-five years as headmistress . . . Not only were the hard wooden chairs in the dayrooms transformed overnight by soft, brightly-coloured cushions, there were also games organised by Miss West, a special lunch for us all, and an entertainment by every form for teaching and domestic staff in the evening. It was a happy day, and a generous and imaginative gesture by Miss West.

Eventually the White House was demolished, and I graduated to being a married staff, eventually leaving to have my first daughter, who is now married to an Old Blue (Julian Dye: Thornton B 1971/8). I have had a varied and privileged teaching career, and I hope that it has reflected the qualities that I observed at Christ's Hospital: a love of my subject, a sense of purpose, high expectations and exacting standards for myself and my students, and concern not just for academic excellence but for every aspect of a pupil's development.

But – I have to confess – I never wear a hat to Church!

Judith Hepper

Of course, Christ's Hospital, Hertford is no more. In order for readers to understand something of the ethos of Housey, who better than a Horsham Old Blue contemporary of mine who went on to teach there? Here Robin Case, now the registrar at Shrewsbury School, describes the Housey Leaving Service, and how Christ's Hospital has left its mark on him for life.

Extract of letter from Robin Case

Of course, you don't just go to one Leaving Service at Christ's Hospital but at least five. Even the first makes a big impression: the scale of the event, the looming Brangwyns, the singing, Ecclesiasticus, and above all the injunctions: . . . the good name of Christ's Hospital . . . to help others enjoy the same advantages. And then there is the last: to walk down the steps to the aisle and wait to receive the Bible and the prayer book from the headmaster. Privileged, humbled, awed, nervous, excited, proud, grateful, certainly I felt that I had taken part in something significant. And as ever the significance is felt along the blood, part of the tradition – it is something that happened, not something you looked in on, and something shared between boys and staff. Only afterwards, walking out into a sunlit evening did we greet our parents, and wait for the band to march into the quad. Every year I was amazed by this, and can still feel and hear and see the band weaving its patterns on the grass; 'Abide with me' from the organ – a stillness at the centre – the drums beating the retreat, and the march away. Every year for five years. I carried this away as much as I did my trunk, holdall, the extra rug on my bed, and my cricket bat. And this held as powerful a spell for me as a teaching colleague for five years as it did for me as a boy.

I was of course privileged to have my second job at Shrewsbury – a wonderful school with a good heart, sound values, a lack of pretension, where individuals are taken seriously and where the relationship between boys and staff is of vital importance, as at Christ's Hospital. But when I arrived in 1980, there was no Leaving Service, the boys just leached away after A Levels and were not seen again. There was, however, 'Bump Supper', for which many of the boys returned. In Ingram's Hall, of which I was Housemaster from 1988, we held the Bump Supper as a bar-b-que in our garden: prize-giving, speeches, thank-yous, presents, farewells, strawberries and cream, more-or-less alcoholic. It didn't take me long to realise that it lacked a centre, so as dusk fell we gathered round the piano wheeled out for the purpose to sing 'Abide with me'; the Head of House read from Ecclesiasticus, and I charged the boys never to forget the great benefits they had received in this place. A little part of Christ's Hospital lived on in our garden until I stood down in 2001.

In fact, by our sons' time at Shrewsbury, a Leavers' Service had been introduced in Chapel (perhaps Robin Case had leaned on the headmaster, Ted Maidment!), and while there was no presentation of a Bible, and no reading of the 'Charge' in the service, it proved a solemn occasion, tall, athletic leaving Salopians (and their mothers) fighting back the tears. Clearly, Robin Case's CH experience has now left its mark on generations of Shrewsbury boys, and the profound effect that Christ's Hospital had on him both as a pupil and a member of staff demonstrates how strong the bonds with CH can remain, for boys as well as girls, as young Dominic Parker also graphically describes here:

Life in a Grecian Pod by Dominic Parker

Having already spent six years living in a house full of boys, fast becoming men, whom I count among my close family, I could not have been looking forward more to Grecians' life. Having seen the coeducational houses, large rooms, installed kitchens, giant social areas and independence, I was really unsure of what to expect. Arriving on 1 September, lugging all of my baggage up three flights of stairs, I thought that I could get bored of this very quickly. Having said goodbye to my parents, and then another hello to all of my friends, I realised that it would not get old. Moving into a 'house' with sixty of my fellow Grecians was at first, a daunting prospect – I constantly thought of the creation of social cliques, and the exclusion that would be possible. In fact, to my surprise, the opposite happened. We all lived under one roof, by one set of rules, and became simply one family, regardless of how we had behaved in the past. I spent my Grecians' life on a floor with my best friends, Alex, William and Ryan. It was exceptionally different to the house life we had before, as in the mornings, we had a rota. Sounds scary, but simply, one person would make the teas and coffees and toast eight slices of bread before rousing the floor for lessons. We would have a communal (if somewhat sluggish) breakfast, a shower, and then off to lessons with us. We came to be known as the married pod, as the one phrase constantly heard was: 'Cup of tea, dear?' It may also have had something to do with breakfasts in bed, or the fact that we all cared enough to always be there for a friend. I had fallen upon family hardships in December, and the people who really got me through it all were my brothers and sisters at CH. As for the workload, obviously nothing comes for free. I spent at least three hours at my desk most days, completing essays, coursework tasks, and further assignments. You always knew, though, that it could never get you down, as you could walk less than ten steps to relieve some stress. I cannot quite recall every weekend evening, however, so this obviously pertains to the fact that we weren't being worked too hard to have fun. My housemaster, Mr Walsh, is one of the most understanding and open people I have ever met, and easily approachable with problems, teenage, work-related, family-related . . . the list doesn't end. I could not have asked for a better year in social conditions.

Another major part of my year was in extra-curricular activities. I will start with the CCF – this year, I was promoted to WO1 (warrant officer first class) in charge of all of the other cadets. This was a brilliant time to be in the CCF, as we would often go shooting on full-bore ranges, and had no fewer than four overnight exercises. These were immense fun for me, as I was always the enemy, being the most experienced cadet. I think the best one we had was when we had four sections, each made of around eighteen cadets. It was three on one, with the best rated cadets in the enemy section. We had reconnaissance work all night, followed by three full fire fights (using blank ammo) at dawn. We then returned to school, to carry out a 'best cadet' competition, with mixed ability teams of four. I had to help organisationally, as power does come with a price, but it was exceptionally rewarding. We also, as a farewell to those leaving, like myself, flew in a Lynx helicopter, and a select few got to fly it. Being head cadet, I was allowed to co-pilot, and the view of the school from above will stay with me forever.

The theatre – what can I say? I lived there for weeks on end this year. When we performed *A Midsummer Night's Dream*, in which I played Puck, myself and the director took turns in providing coffee for morning and evening rehearsals/costume runs/concerned cast visits. It was one of the best plays I have ever acted in, and one of the most enjoyable roles I have ever played – probably because I got to dance around like a fool, and act as silly as I liked – an activity normally confined to the privacy of my house.

The Grecians' Ball was astounding. To see all of my friends in a capacity of actual adults, dressed up and ready to enter the real world outside our sheltered walls, prepared by the school to live life, was a very sobering experience. In amongst the frivolities of our final evening, the eating, drinking, dancing etc., it occurred to all of us that this would be the final time we saw many of our friends, as friendship works differently within CH compared to other schools. The Leaving Service provided me with no small degree of regret to be leaving this wonderful place (in other words, I was one of the first to shed a few tears), but I know that I will keep in touch with as many people as I can.

During the summer, I embarked on a trip with the school to Corsica, in order to climb the highest mountains and swim the deepest canyons there. (We also lazed on the comfiest beaches, and talked to the nicest French women, but that wasn't the point of the trip.) It hit me how large the network of Old Blues is. We had Old Blues who had left the school in 1998, a full eleven years before we had, joining us in the campsite, and the youngest were still in their GE (Greater Erasmus – Year 11 or Upper Fifth), having just passed GCSEs. We had everyone from medical students to actors, quadrilinguists to designers, scientists to Frenchmen in our Old Blue group, and it occurred to me that in every walk of life, there must be at least one Old Blue, prepared to welcome Young Old Blues with open arms. That is the beauty of CH for me – it provides a willingness to accept others through years of boarding, and creates a bond between Old Blues whether they have met or not.

I am so glad to have got to know Dominic and his family over the years. Clearly, he's been very happy and fulfilled at Christ's Hospital, with an equally bright future ahead of him at UCL. It has been a delight to attend the Confirmation of my second Presentee, Charity Griffiths, in the school chapel, and to watch *her* growing up, too. I feel so proud and privileged to be an Old Blue myself, as well as a Donation Governor, and it's good to see Christ's Hospital today caring for girls and boys alike on the same beautiful site.

'Patriotism is not enough: I must have no hatred or bitterness for anyone'. I remember being enormously impressed by these words of Nurse Edith Cavell said on the eve of her execution and inscribed on her statue opposite the National Portrait Gallery in London. She was shot at dawn the following day, 12 October (my birth date, as it happens) 1915 by the Germans for having helped about 200 Allied soldiers escape to the Netherlands. When I saw the huge white statue, and read her words about patriotism, for me she instantly became a heroine: not only had she been a nurse, and helped Allied soldiers, as my mother and Big Susan had done in World War II (she too was a London Hospital nurse), but she was clearly a woman with a conscience, not glorifying in war for its own sake, or hating the Germans just because they happened to be the enemy at the time.

She had spoken the words about patriotism to the Revd Gahan, who had been allowed to see her and give her Holy Communion on the eve of her execution. Her final words to the German pastor, Le Saur were recorded as, 'Ask Mr Gahan to tell my loved ones later on that my soul, as I believe, is safe, and that I am glad to die for my country.'

As a young officer I knew that I should also be glad to die for my country. That was part of the deal as far as I was concerned, if you put on the Queen's uniform and accepted the Queen's Commission: you had to be as brave as your male comrades dying in Northern Ireland at the time, and set an example of courage and service to your own young servicewomen, and after all, we had lost two of them in the shocking Guildford pub bombing, with several others injured. We all lived with the threat, as Service personnel always have done, and I was immensely proud to be part of the British Army with its record of bravery, smartness, teamwork, loyalty and doing your duty, whatever the personal cost. And if I had it relatively easy in the early days of my service in the TA and the regular army, I certainly made up for that during my twenty years in the Army Cadet Force, some of the hardest – and most satisfying – work I've ever done in my life.

As for the *soul* being safe, I know that if I were as faithful as my good evangelical friends in our wonderful parish church, St Mark's, Gabalfa, I ought to have no doubts for myself. I know, however, that I can go along with the beautiful words of the funeral liturgy 'in sure and certain hope of the Resurrection' and pray for the Lord to have mercy on my soul. That in itself brings enormous comfort. The Lord, after all, as we are assured in the Bible, is 'full of compassion and mercy, slow to anger, and of great goodness.' At least He will know that whatever my many shortcomings, I have always loved my God, and when my time comes, I hope that I may have time to say with confidence, 'Into Thy hands, O Lord, I commit my spirit.'

Now with what must surely be not more than a third left of my life on earth, with three beautiful grandchildren, Cora Hope, Ella Munro and Jacob Michael, and even without their grandfather Michael, Mike, the love of my life, I have begun to find real contentment at last. Certainly I have had my battles – which soldier hasn't? – but, like Edith Cavell, I know that it is important not to feel any hatred or bitterness for anyone. Love matters so much more.

Perhaps it's something to do with the beautiful prayer of St Augustine which ends, 'Our heart is restless until it rests in Thee.' Perhaps it is because I'm at last learning what friends, much better Christians than I, have known for years, that although you can perhaps never forget past hurts or injustices, if you can let go now of any resentment caused at the time, a most extraordinary inner peace follows.

Whatever life still has to throw at me, I feel confident that with my church family at St Mark's, my Chaplaincy friends and colleagues at the hospital and my own loving family and wider circle of loyal friends, I can somehow muddle through to the end. Meanwhile, I shall try to go on being as useful as I can, as any good CH girl should.

As for Christ's Hospital, young people like Dominic and Charity are the future now, and in buying this book, you, kind reader, have helped to give other deserving children like them the chance of a Christ's Hospital education. Thank you so much.

Sue Davies-Jenkins.
July 2010

Photographic Index

Index